STRADDLING CLASS IN THE ACADEMY

STRADDLING CLASS IN THE ACADEMY

**26 Stories of Students, Administrators,
and Faculty From Poor and Working-Class
Backgrounds and Their Compelling Lessons for
Higher Education Policy and Practice**

Sonja Ardoin and becky martinez

Foreword by Jamie Washington

STERLING, VIRGINIA

Published by Stylus Publishing, LLC.
22883 Quicksilver Drive
Sterling, Virginia 20166-2019

Library of Congress Cataloging-in-Publication Data
The CIP for this text has been applied for.

13-digit ISBN: 978-1-62036-739-1 (cloth)
13-digit ISBN: 978-1-62036-740-7 (paperback)
13-digit ISBN: 978-1-62036-741-4 (library networkable e-edition)
13-digit ISBN: 978-1-62036-742-1 (consumer e-edition)

Printed in the United States of America

All first editions printed on acid-free paper
that meets the American National Standards Institute
Z39-48 Standard.

Bulk Purchases
Quantity discounts are available for use in workshops and for staff development.
Call 1-800-232-0223

First Edition, 2019

From Sonja

For the poor and working class folks who struggle to access or complete higher education—we're fighting for us. Slowly but surely.

To those (students, administrators, and faculty) from poor and working class backgrounds in the academy—you are not alone. There are more of us here than you might think. If you are able, share your own story.

From becky

Poor and working class folks seeking that degree, keep pushing and pushing and pushing. And know we are in this together— we too will keep pushing.

Family, friends, and colleagues with poor and working class roots now in the academy, your story is profound, necessary, and liberating. Breathe it into all of the spaces that say otherwise. We are resilient, courageous, resourceful, and powerful—shake it up!

CONTENTS

Straddling Class in the Academy

Is it "Forward" or "Foreword"? Or is it spelled "Foreward"? These were the questions in my head after being invited to write the "Foreword" for this book, *Straddling Class in the Academy*. My confusion in the meaning and spelling of this word is an example of why this book is so important. If I were to go to the community in which I grew up and shared that I was writing a foreword for a book, most people would not have any clue what that meant. I have seen and read forewords in my more than 40 years in the academy, but I don't think I really ever knew the purpose, nor did I really pay attention to the spelling. The word *foreword* is, like many other words, part of the language barrier that straddling class invites us into.

The authors speak of the importance of *positionality*. This too is a word that is much more understood in academic spaces. *Positionality, social location*, and *social identities* are all terms that speak to the importance of knowing who you are and how you are positioned in the world in relationship to others. For those of us who are straddling class in the academy, our positionality is reflected in having our early socialization in communities where words like *socialization* and *positionality* were not and still are not used. Language is just one part, but a very important part, of how we begin to understand the important contribution that *Straddling Class in the Academy* will be for our profession.

Because the authors are very clear about how their positionality and that of their contributors is so important. I felt it was important to share a bit about my positionality in this foreword. I began my journey in higher education as a working poor person from an inner-city north Philadelphia community in the late 1970s. This was a largely Black community with most of the community working hourly jobs or being on public assistance. Many of us lived in rented homes or in public housing. I don't know of anyone in my community who had gone to college. There was not a college-prep high school in my community. Of the two high schools in my community, one was vocational tech and the other was our big sports high school. Neither of these places boasted of their graduates getting into colleges in any substantial way unless it was on athletic scholarship.

My mother and I are the only ones in my family to graduate from high school. My siblings, father, and grandparents do not have a high school diploma. I went to undergraduate school with very little information or preparation for the space that I was entering. I want to be clear that I am referring to experience, not capacity to be successful. I did not know what I didn't know, and I was not aware of how much institutions of higher education were not set up for those of us who came from working poor backgrounds. The undergraduate experience provided me a glimpse into a world that was very different than mine. I spent much of my time observing others, largely White others, for cues as to how to behave. Because of my own internalized oppression and fear of looking like I didn't deserve to be in the space, I was not comfortable asking which fork I should use at a dinner or what a bursar's office is. I was not sure why I could not end a sentence with a preposition, since that was the way that everyone ended sentences in my hometown. I had never had fresh broccoli or spinach, and the only places that I had been on a vacation was to my grandparents' house in South Carolina. Thus, a salad bar, spring break trips, and writing differently than I spoke were all real challenges.

While I was able to find community and navigate my way through my four-year undergraduate experience, heading off to graduate school took these dynamics to the next level. My parents had a sense of why an undergraduate degree was important, but graduate school felt like an unnecessary expense. When I left my job to complete a doctorate, my grandfather said to me "You already have more degrees than the president, what you goanna do with another degree?" My family was and still is very proud of what I've accomplished, and I, like many others, live with the concern that more educational attainment will move us further away from our families and communities.

Many of us who are first-generation college students or even first-generation, predominately White institution college graduates straddle class not only in the academy but in our communities and families as well. We are often seen as the "ones who made it." This comes as both a blessing and a curse. The stories shared in this book will illustrate just what I mean. As we move into and through spaces with many of our higher education colleagues, we are expected to know certain things, enjoy or have experienced certain foods, have read certain books, use certain words, or have been to certain places. In addition, there are unnamed values and assumptions that are held about being a so-called educated person. These assumptions and beliefs in a culture that does not talk about class can be exhausting for the straddler.

The authors and contributors provide powerful insights as to why this book matters in the ever-changing landscape of higher education. I believe that readers will find this book affirming, confirming, and illuminating of some experiences they have had in the academy and how this straddling impacts their relationships within their communities and families of origin. As we strive to create campus environments that are more inclusive of diverse backgrounds and experiences, *Straddling Class in the Academy* will offer a window into a subject that is often not engaged. Graduate preparation programs, staff development programs, and more will be able to use this resource to invite folks to reflect on their own experience and engage others in the much-needed conversations to support a welcoming and inclusive environment across class for faculty, staff, and students.

Rev. Dr. Jamie Washington
President, The Washington Consulting Group
President and Cofounder, The Social Justice Training Institute
President, American College Personnel Association
Pastor, Unity Fellowship Church of Baltimore

ACKNOWLEDGMENTS

A book is a collective effort, and we recognize and value the offerings of the many people who helped in turning the idea of this book into a completed publication, one that will hopefully further the conversation about social class identity in higher education.

To John von Knorring and the entire Stylus Publishing team, we are grateful for your willingness to provide space in the higher education literature for the topic of social class identity and the stories of people from poor and working-class backgrounds who study and serve at colleges and universities. We appreciate your belief in us as authors and in the contributing writers who joined us. Thank you for sharing your expertise, which aided us in refining content, developing layout, and promoting the book as well as its purpose of extending the social class identity consciousness in higher education. We are deeply appreciative of our partnership with you.

Contributing writers, this book would have remained an idea had you not said yes. Thank you for being our teachers. You are role modeling bravery, strength, and compassion to communities and individuals you may never have the chance to meet and yet have supported to be better educators, practitioners, and people through your stories. We honor the stories of:

Mamta Motwani Accapadi, Constanza (Connie) A. Cabello, Loren Cannon, Dylan R. Dunn, Daniel Espiritu, Nancy J. Evans, Raul Fernandez, Sara C. Furr, Rudy P. Guevarra Jr., Jacinda M. Félix Haro, Armina Khwaja Macmillan, Timothy (Tim) M. Johnson, Briza K. Juarez, Sally G. Parish, Edward (Eddie) Pickett III, Kevyanna Rawls, Carmen Rivera, Larry D. Roper, Thomas C. Segar, Jeremiah Shinn, Tori Svoboda, Roxanne Villaluz, Brenda Lee Anderson Wadley, and Téa N. Wimer.

From Sonja

Inevitably, when I write about social class, my family and hometown are with me. I always think of my grandparents first because it is their shoulders on which I stand. As farmers, they taught me work ethic, resilience, how to find joy in the everyday, and the importance of seeing the bigger picture. They ingrained the value of education in me, although only my

Mama graduated from high school, and my MawMaw made it her mission for reading to become one of my favorite pastimes. None of them are here to read this, but I know all four of them would be proud because I am living their values, just in a different context. My parents, Evelyn and Steven Ardoin, you have sacrificed for me in so many ways. Know that I recognize your efforts and value your support and ability to keep me in check. And, a huge shout-out to my life partner and new husband, Zeb Jenkins III: You have shown more understanding than I probably deserve. You get me and my tendency to overcommit, and you rallied me through a year that combined this publication, a move, the start of new jobs for both of us, our wedding, and our first few months of marriage. Thank you for being my person.

As I began to explore my own social class identity, I read scholars such as Will Barratt, Georgianna Martin, Krista Soria, William Liu, and Tori Svoboda; thank you to these folks, and anyone else who writes on social class, for letting others learn from you. For Kathy Guthrie, Brian Reece, Vu Tran, Peter Magolda, Rozana Carducci, Shaunna Payne Gold, Darris Means, and Margaret Sallee, I am grateful to you for allowing me to write about social class in your publications. To my NASPA colleagues, particularly those from the Socioeconomic and Class Issues in Higher Education Knowledge Community (shout-out to Clare Cady, Steve Jenks, Dave Nguyen, and Brenda Anderson Wadley) and the Center for First-Generation Student Success (shout-out to Sarah Whitley and Deana Waintraub), I appreciate our shared work on equity in higher education.

To my first supervisor and now great friend, David Pittman, I am forever grateful that you hired me (twice!) and that we share a background that allows us to process social class and higher education together. For the Boston University and Appalachian State University colleagues and graduate students whom I learned with throughout this book project, thank you for questioning, challenging, and encouraging me. To all the folks whom I am able to call friends and colleagues, I value your presence in my life.

And to the key colleague and coconspirator on this project, becky martinez: You often talk about being both gentle and fierce, and I can attest that you live those in a beautiful blend. You do this with your social justice work, including the social class identity projects, as well as with your life, role modeling for others how to walk through the world in a graceful, yet unapologetic way. You have taught me so much, including how to recognize strength and healing in tears, and I am better for every interaction I have with you. I am so grateful for our collaboration on this project and, even more so, for your friendship. Have no doubt—you are making people and the world better.

From becky

My roots ground me to stand and stay strong—thanks Martinez family! Mom and Dad, you two role model humility in ways I am now just beginning to fully understand. Your care, patience, and work ethic help get me through life's madness, including this project. To my sister Drea, thanks for writing snacks and supporting a floor full of books and articles during the final stretch. Although you don't show it, I know you are my biggest cheerleader. My love bug, Jacob, your curious, funny, vibrant energy fills my soul. I've appreciated your daily check-ins of how many more pages I have left to write and giving me candid encouragement to finish. Lastly, Patrick, you are the perfect teacher of navigating life's differences with ease. Your strength, determination, and pure grit, combined with your desire for French-pressed coffee and the need for a second passport, fuel me to further understand the world around me through a different lens.

I am a better version of me with each Social Justice Training Institute (SJTI) I cofacilitate. In this space, I am gifted the opportunity to discover new layers of my story and heal from them. Deep appreciation to Jamie Washington, Kathy Obear, and Vernon Wall for taking yet another chance in creating SJTI 2. Because of it and each of you, I began my relationship with social class and class(ism) in life-changing ways. Deb Griffith and Tori Svoboda, thanks for sharing my light-switch moment back in 2005. You sat with me and my vast pain when I realized I existed in two distinct class worlds while not quite understanding how to reconcile any of it. I am deeply grateful we made it through that day in support of each other and every day since. Shout-out to my bestie, Chris Braustein, who lovingly sits through my rants, tears, and excitement with all things big and small and then takes me out for tacos, frozen yogurt, and laughter. I also want to extend a heartfelt hug to every friend, colleague, and sometimes near stranger who has indulged my question "What's your class story?" Every rich answer helps build my capacity to be gentle and fierce.

Sonja, you take on social class (and life) with power, reverence, and compassion. My friend, your ability to help transform higher education with humility and integrity is refreshing and needed. I vividly remember the conversation that got us here. It went something like, "Sonja, one day I want to write a book from our voices. Those of us from poor and working-class families with degrees working in higher education and yet don't find our stories in it." Your response: "Let's do it. I know a publisher that I think will say yes." This partnership has been nothing short of beautiful; deep appreciation for cocreating it with me. So many thanks for being my mentor in this process; you are a brilliant gift! Keep on keepin' on.

INTRODUCTION

How do you define your social class? Have you reflected on that part of your identity and evaluated why you may associate with a particular social class? What about the students or colleagues with whom you work—do you know how they identify their social class? Have you asked them? Why or why not? hooks (2000) suggests that "class difference and classism are rarely overtly apparent, or they are not acknowledged when present" (p. 5), and Arner (2016) cautions that discussing social class can isolate you from your colleagues; thus, we may not realize the class identities of our colleagues or choose to engage around issues of class in the academy.

So, let's own that social class is commonly taboo in conversation, something that, from an early age, we are actively taught not to discuss (Martin, Williams, & Young, 2018). We act as if it won't exist if we do not mention it. And that is absurd because we are talking about it without really talking about it through coded terminology such as *trashy*, *classy*, and *snobby* (Liu, 2011). The reality is that although social class is a socially constructed phenomenon it influences a large portion of our lived experiences. So, we have to become more comfortable with talking directly about social class. If you have not given it much consideration yet, we invite you to do so now . . . with us. Welcome.

What Is Social Class Identity?

Good question. Social class is something many scholars, educators, policymakers, and pundits fervently debate, with more than 400 different terms being used to refer to *social class* in the literature (Liu, 2011). The clever response to this question is that it is complicated, which is why we get to write a whole book about this dimension of identity; how people experience it; and why it influences how people make it to, through, and within higher education. But that answer won't suffice. We know. So, let's get to it.

Defining and Experiencing Social Class

Everyone wants clear, concise, and often quantifiable definitions for our various dimensions of identity. That really only applies to age, however.

Otherwise, people get to choose how they identify, and often folks identify in ways that do not align with clear, concise definitions that allow for easy data sorting. As McMillan (2017) highlights, "It seems to be that people still approach class . . . wanting something definitive, wanting rigid definitions that don't fit into a new plurality of identities and hybridity which have come to define the 21st century" (p. 90). Although it is common to reduce social class to one of its components—particularly socioeconomic status (SES), occupation, or education level—with the aim of getting to a singular definition or comparable statistic, social class is more than any one of these or even the combination of all three (Garrison & Liu, 2018). Hence, the terms *social class* and *SES* should not be viewed as interchangeable (Liu, 2011), and we need to recognize the "fluid, dynamic, performative, and difficult to define" nature of social class identity (Martin et al., 2018, pp. 10–11). So, let's recognize that *social class* is subjective, and although we cannot provide a precise definition for you, we can offer some descriptions of its broad nature.

Lubrano (2004) describes social class as "the dark matter of the universe—hard to see but nevertheless omnipresent, a basic part of everything" (p. 5) and offers the following characterization of this dimension of identity:

> Class is a script, map, or guide. It tells us how to talk, how to dress, how to hold ourselves, how to eat, and how to socialize. It affects whom we marry; where we live; the friends we choose; the jobs we have; the vacations we [may get to] take; the books we read; the movies we see; the restaurants we pick; how we decide to buy houses, carpets, furniture, and cars; where our kids are educated; what we tell our children at the dinner table; whether we even have a dinner table or a dinnertime. In short, class is nearly everything about you. And it dictates what to expect out of life and what the future should be. (p. 5)

This excerpt shows how social class is everywhere. It influences our lives on a daily basis in small and big ways, causing Garrison and Liu (2018) to frame it as "ubiquitous" (p. 21). Because of this, children begin comprehending social class distinctions by age six through observing materials and behaviors in their everyday environments (Ramsey, 1991).

Barratt (2011) offers that we each have three forms of social class that influence how we experience that identity: (a) our class of origin, which describes our class background from about ages 5 to 16; (b) our current, felt class, which is what we consider our class identity to be at the present moment; and (c) our attributed class, which is what others assume about our class identity. This "tripartite" of class identity can be summarized as "where we came from, what we think of ourselves, and what others think of us" (Barratt, 2011, p. 7).

When these three forms all align, social class may not be at the forefront of our minds because our background, present, and perceived identities all match. When there is contrast among these three forms, social class likely arises in our thoughts, experiences, and primary identifiers. In other words, we probably have more awareness of social class identity and engage in more self-work around it when we experience dissonance among these three forms. This may provide insight into why some folks arrive to college and university campuses with limited consciousness about their social class identity and why others face a challenging transition between their class of origin and the context of higher education.

Experiencing social class contrast can lead people to associate with Lubrano's (2004) concept of *class straddling*. This term describes those from poor or working classes of origin who find themselves in middle or upper class contexts, and it can also reference how people define their current, felt class often because of educational opportunities. The dissonance between their roots and current life circumstances likely results in them having to "straddle two worlds, many of them not feeling at home in either, living in a kind of American limbo" (Lubrano, 2004, p. 2). Yeskel (2014) further illustrates class straddling as "being bicultural with respect to class" (p. 3). Class straddlers do not relinquish their class of origin as they gain additional forms of capital but rather discern which "customs, norms, language, and expectations" (Martin et al., 2018, p. 11) to call on depending on the environment where they find themselves at a given moment.

Recognizing Classism

Each dimension of identity corresponds with an –ism, or a form of bias through stereotypical beliefs about people who are in the oppressed group(s) of that identity. We often engage in –isms to "maintain our psychological consistency" (Garrison & Liu, 2018, p. 22; Liu, 2011) and affirm any privilege and power that come with being in the majority group of that identity. In the case of social class, the –ism is known as classism.

Similar to how we can experience our own social class identity in different ways, we can also participate in classism in different ways. Liu (2011) and Liu, Soleck, Hopps, Dunston, and Pickett (2004) present four forms of classism: (a) downward, (b) upward, (c) lateral, and (d) internalized. Downward classism, the type with which we are likely most familiar, is when someone exhibits prejudice and discrimination against those who are from "lower" social classes than oneself. An example would be someone from the middle class judging a person for not knowing which utensils to use in a large place setting. The opposite is upward classism, which is when someone from a "lower" social class has stereotypical perceptions about folks from a "higher" social class, such as calling people who attended private school "prep school snobs." Lateral classism is when we compare ourselves to others whom we perceive to be in a similar social class to us and try to compete with them (for some mythical prize). Liu and colleagues (2004) and Sonja's dad both call this "keeping up with the Joneses" (p. 109). Last, internalized classism is when someone adopts the stereotypes that society has of one's social class and either performs to those expectations or experiences conflict about diverting from those expectations, or both. Any of these four types of classism can impact one's self-perception, self-confidence, and ability to self-author the social class component of one's identity.

Why Focus on Social Class?

Most important, social class identity has deep meaning for us—as educators, scholars, and people. Social class is often an invisible and inexact dimension of identity that many prefer to ignore, assume, or oversimplify. We want to bring this piece of identity to the forefront, offer its nuances and complexities, tell the stories of people whom others would not assume identify with poor and working-class origins, and compel those in the academy to recognize classism and reimagine higher education to welcome and support those from poor and working-class backgrounds.

We should also mention that we are focusing specifically on the experiences of individuals from poor and working-class backgrounds. We chose this demographic because the world already knows a lot about the middle and upper classes. Our society's upward mobility bias, or the assumption that people should always desire more (Liu, 2011), influences us to perceive these communities as the norm, the good, and the holy grail of making it. We want to provide counternarratives—to give space to the challenges and barriers faced by poor and working-class individuals who access higher education as well as highlight their successes as students, administrators, and faculty; learn from their experiences with class dissonance; and interrogate the academy's attempts to force them to conform. These counternarratives are the "person-level experience [that] allows us to better understand how the individual responds to and incorporates societal-level and structural inequalities, entitlements, and privileges" (Liu, 2011, p. 63). As Waal (2017) asserts, "There are writers and readers in the [poor and] working classes, ready to see their lives depicted in literature, stories that speak of their concerns and lifestyles, written with authenticity" (p. 67).

Accordingly, we have this social class identity focus to honor our backgrounds, increase consciousness, invite storytelling, and champion equity.

Will everyone agree with our focus? No. Are we okay with that? Indeed. Because as Mughal (2017) shares, "I guess now I see my [class identity] presence in certain spaces as a necessary disruption" (p. 77).

The Power of Stories as a Form of Social Justice

There is power in stories, for both the storyteller and reader. A story is able to get to depths lost in a theory or model, it creates connection, it is vulnerable, and it is wise. Bell (2010) writes, "Stories are one of the most powerful and personal ways to learn about the world, passed down from generation to generation through the family and cultural groups to which we belong" (p. 16). History, values, and community are able to live and breathe through stories. The storyteller is able to reflect; feel; learn from; struggle with; and, if necessary, heal from and within his or her story. And with hope, the reader is able to take in another's story to then do the same with his or hers, if even a sliver.

Stories represent the ways in which we make meaning of our world. As life happens around us, we make sense of the messages we receive in both liberating and defeating ways. Cranton's (2006) work on transformative learning highlights how "meaning is seen to exist within ourselves, not in external forms. We develop or construct personal meaning from our experience and validate it through interaction and communication" (p. 23). Parts of our stories give us joy and fulfillment, whereas others are challenging and sometimes too painful for us to want to remember, much less want to share. However, the more we are able to share our stories, there exists the opportunity to make sense of the meaning we make and learn from them.

Although stories hold individuals' contexts and experiences, they are often simultaneously linked to dynamics of privilege and oppression if any form of social identity is involved. As a result, stories "help us connect individual experiences with systemic analysis, allowing us to unpack in ways that are perhaps more accessible than abstract analysis alone" (Bell, 2010, p. 18). Knowledge and learning from the individual level equip us to better understand dynamics within the group and systems in which the individual exists.

Storytelling through an identity lens is a forceful avenue of and toward social justice. Stories can be used as a platform to inform higher education how it maintains social class inequities and what it can do to instead shift toward a more inclusive, socially just campus. We recognize it is a necessary challenging task, regardless of difficulty or timeliness. As we think about social justice, we use the work of Adams, Bell, and Griffin (2007) in that "social justice is both a process and goal" (p. 1). It involves systems thinking and action by members from both privileged and marginalized groups to create a "society in which the distribution of resources is equitable and all members are psychologically safe and secure" (pp. 1–2).

As stated earlier, discussing social class is taboo and yet surrounds us. In her book *Where We Stand: Class Matters*, hooks (2000) writes that class is omnipresent and yet no one wants to talk about it in any meaningful ways other than money. Sure, there are policies to change, but without considering the norms, attitudes, and practices associated with social class, the vision of social justice will fall to the wayside. There is critical learning to be had from those with poor or working-class backgrounds, particularly in the academy because it is founded on and immersed in elitism. Hence, this book. There is collective wisdom, vulnerability, and history embodying the ethos of social justice. It is filled with powerful stories that we hope reach beyond just being stories.

Author Positionalities

Speaking of stories, we want to share pieces of ours. Our identities and stories shape the lens through which we experience and make sense of the world and, hence, the way we approached coauthoring this book. The academic term for this is *positionality*—the realization that who we are as people interplays with how we conduct research and writing as scholar-practitioners (Bourke, 2014; Coghlan & Brydon-Miller, 2014; Denzin, 1986). Positionality is also used in teaching and learning contexts as a form of "acknowledge[ing] the dynamics of power, privilege and difference" that is present between people "to reduce the diffusion of bias" (Relles, 2016, p. 313; see also Creswell, 2013; Martin & Van Gunten, 2002; Milner, 2007). We also believe that if we are asking folks to share their own social class identity stories, then we should be willing to engage as well.

Sonja Ardoin

I identify as a currently able, straight, Catholic, White, Cajun, 36-year-old cisgender woman who straddles social classes. Some of these parts of my identity give me significant power and privilege (e.g., White, straight, able, cisgender), whereas others place me in underserved groups (e.g., woman, class straddler). Although I will primarily share my social class story here, it is key to note that my positionality is not splintered; rather, the lens through which I view the world is formed through the collective of these identities, including my role as an educator who has the opportunity to write about social class identity.

To my recollection, my first memory of social class was through the form of financial capital, which is often how most of us initially recognize social class in our lives. I can clearly recall sitting in a chair in our kitchen for my mom to help me tie my shoes as she began a difficult conversation with me about why it was likely that I would no longer be able to attend my dance and gymnastics class. I was around five years old. She had been laid off from her job, and it was unclear how our family would afford basic necessities much less extras like dance class. I was heartbroken. I loved dance class and my friends there. But I understood from the tears in my mom's eyes, the look on her face, and the tension in the room between her and my dad that this situation would impact us all. Not just that day but for many days and years to come.

The social class moments continued to show up in my life as a kid in a working-class family in a small, rural community where folks seemed to fall into either the "haves," or affluent group, or the "have nots," or poor and working-class group. I often noticed being in the latter group in material ways, such as the bags of donated clothes that showed up at our house from cousins and community members (which I always looked forward to), but I also recognized it in the conversations and behaviors exhibited in our household, such as lessons on how I needed to behave at the houses of affluent families or why it was imperative that I earn good grades in school to have any shot at college. Some of the lessons were positive: teaching me the responsibility and pride of paid work by age 10, illustrating how to be resilient and find new opportunities when it was necessary, and demonstrating how to develop and lean on a community. Some of the lessons were hard: being ostracized from certain community groups or events, facing condescension based on lack of knowledge or material possessions, and worrying about whether I was contributing enough or causing strain on the family.

Social class is present for me through food. Growing up, we primarily ate two kinds of food: (a) items, mostly beef and rice, given to us by our grandparents' farms; and (b) things in cans purchased at the local Piggly Wiggly. I distinctly remember trips to that Piggly Wiggly, where my role was to carry around the calculator and add up the total of the items we were putting into the buggy (i.e., cart). We did this to ensure that there were no surprises when we got to the checkout lane. This practice taught me how to budget and consider taxes. It also makes me highly aware on my trips to the grocery store today. I notice how I no longer have to bring a calculator with me, how I just place items in the buggy with no fear, and how some of those items are fresh and the "real" brand. I was recently back at the local Piggly Wiggly, where I was served another social class consciousness lesson. In looking for granola bars, I realized that, unlike my grocery store in North Carolina, the Piggly

Wiggly only carried a limited selection of options, most of which were the cheaper, less healthy selections. The same was true in the yogurt cooler. Only original Yoplait was available and only four to five flavors. No Greek yogurt, no low fat, no protein. This affirmed for me how the social class of a community influences the food options that impact diet and overall health. And don't get me started on the groundwater that has led to our area being called "Cancer Alley" (Brown & Swanson, 2003).

Social class is highlighted for me through vehicles. Growing up, we owned a number of second-hand cars and trucks. Each one had things that worked and things that didn't, which determined which one we took where and when. The air conditioning was often the first thing to go awry. This was generally okay until the power windows stopped operating. Let me tell you, it is not a fun ride in south Louisiana in the summer with no possibilities for air inside a cooked car. So, when I went car shopping solo for the first time in 2009, I knew it was imperative to do my research and not get taken advantage of by the salesperson because of my gender, age, or social class. I read all the reviews, enlisted the advice of some friends and my dad, and decided to comparison shop between a Toyota Corolla and Ford Focus. I was dead set on my brand-new (not just new to me) car having manual locks and windows to avoid my prior experiences of no access to air and to reduce the overall price by several thousand dollars. That caught the salesperson off guard. In fact, he looked at me warily and stated, "You are way less high maintenance than you look." I wasn't sure if it was a compliment or an insult, but it was probably both, and it served as further proof for me of my class straddler identity. I stood firm on my request, and the salesperson eventually found me a 2009 Toyota Corolla with manual locks and windows. I am still driving this car today.

Social class arises during my travels. As a child, we took one trip a year. We packed our own meals, snacks, and drinks, and we always visited somewhere in driving distance, often the mountains of Arkansas or Tennessee. I loved the adventure! It wasn't until I was 21 that I experienced flight, and I have to credit a student organization for giving me that opportunity. I was a complete mess the first time in the airport, with incorrectly sized toiletries, a too-heavy carry-on duffel that I almost couldn't carry, and countless questions about what was happening with the plane for my seatmate. Now, I travel almost every two weeks, mostly for work, but I am still amazed by air travel—the mechanics, opportunities, interesting people, and relative ease of getting places. I also introduced my parents to flight in their mid-50s, which was a gift for all of us.

Social class shows up for me through education. I attended the local public PK–12 school, where I found and further developed joy in learning.

I didn't realize we did not have the same access to educational resources as many other children until I got to high school. In Louisiana, an opportunity program allowed students to attend public institutions tuition-free if they took specific high school courses and met certain grade point average and ACT requirements. However, my high school did not offer two of the courses on the list: survey of the arts and calculus. The administrators at our school figured out a way to get us the courses through collaborative efforts with a regional university that offered the courses "online" (circa a TV monitor and conference call mechanism in the late 1990s) to all the rural high schools in the state, but we knew we were getting a different version of the courses than more affluent high schools and communities. Nonetheless, the efforts allowed me to qualify for the state's tuition opportunity program, become a first-generation college student, and earn three degrees in education, all from institutions with the word *state* in the name. I still find joy in learning, and I am aware that I occupy both an underrepresented identity as a first-generation college student from a working-class background and a very privileged identity as a faculty member with a PhD. Classism also continues to show up for me in the academy. It is present when I don't know the etiquette rules, when I order a beer and put it in a koozie even though everyone around me has wine in a glass, when degrees from "highly ranked" institutions are given preference, and when my parents worry about looking or sounding "stupid" in front of my colleagues when they visit campus.

I could keep going with each aspect of life and how social class shows up for me in complex and often conflicting ways. As I mentioned previously, I identify as a class straddler. I maintain some of my values, beliefs, behaviors, and worldview from my working-class roots, and I have acquired some forms of capital—financial, cultural, social, educational, occupational, linguistic, and navigational—and tastes that align more with the middle and upper middle classes. For me this means that I have learned how to code switch my word choice and depth of accent based on context, but I maintain the frequent use of my favorite curse word—shit!—to make a point. It is why I still feel like a "fish out of water" at white tablecloth restaurants or "fancy" stores such as Nordstrom, but I see value in working with a personal trainer for physical health and do not fret (too much) when life requires me to purchase a last-minute flight. It means people who do not know my background, including colleagues and students in higher education, are sometimes surprised by my viewpoints, preferences, and triggers. I do not fit into a predetermined social class "box," and this book honors that for me and, hopefully, for others. It also puts me/us in a position to study social class critically, push others to consider how social class shows up in academia and in life, and shed light on some problematic realities that need to be addressed if we seek to further educational equity.

becky martinez

New or preowned certified? Honda or Audi? Finance through a credit union or directly with the dealership? Can I just buy something online to avoid all of the class(ism) stuff that awaits in the negotiation? These daunting questions are on my mind lately as the mechanic recently told me I should consider purchasing a new (to me) car sooner than later. My heart nearly broke with the news because I can't imagine replacing Zeke, my 2002 Honda Accord with more than 275,000 miles that I bought brand new off the lot some years ago. Whenever I share with people my need to buy a new car, they inevitably ask the year and mileage and follow-up with a surprised gasp. In the sphere of car ownership, I guess it's an old car with more miles than most. For me, someone raised in a working-class family, you keep up with the maintenance of your car, and there is no need to buy another unless you have to. I am now at the "have to" buy a car stage, and although I am excited about the inevitable new technology and comfort, I dread a car payment and an increased insurance rate. I have no desire to be in more debt, and yet I need a car to get to work so that I can pay for it—oh, the irony.

This situation and those questions are examples of me straddling two distinct class worlds. One tells me to buy what I need, to be practical, with the other quietly whispering get what you want, you can afford it, you deserve it. Both sides of the coin are valid as I find myself in this conundrum of choice, and yet I feel some kind of way about it. I feel like one choice further connects me to my current social class, with all its markers, and the other choice further separates me from the social class that resides throughout my body. The privilege of choice is also not lost on me. Yes, this class-straddling life is indeed complex and complicated.

I come from a working-class family. They are hardworking, strive to do a good job, do so without complaining, and get up morning after morning to do it again. When referring to family, I include ancestors who taught us living folks about a strong work ethic, to be humble, and to be and do our best. As for my parents, they are some of the simplest people I know, which is a breath of fresh air from my middle-class, educated, often elitist world. They do not ask or seek for more than they need, eat leftovers until finished, combined have fewer shoes than I do, and have instilled in me that if I have money, those around me do too. In my working-class lens, treating others with dignity and respect takes precedence over anything material, a tasty taco truck is a gift, a wrestling tournament or football game over the theater is not even a question, you tell it like it is, and what you see is what you get.

Then there is this other side of the coin, or at least mine. I am three degrees deep and navigate in an entirely different set of rules, norms, and ways of being: a world of rewards points, linen table settings, and disillusion when I say an occasional curse word. I have learned and exist in a different handbook: dress appropriately and speak articulately with only hints of directness so that those around me remain comfortable. The audience determines whether I am sleeved because my love for tattoos is found on my body. Needless to say, the bullshit can be exhausting.

Simultaneously, I appreciate and, sadly, have assimilated into pieces of this other world. Give me a good steakhouse in which I have to separately order a side finished by silky crème brûlée for dessert, and my night is complete. I am grateful for my Southwest rewards privileges of automatic check-in and free Wi-Fi. I have access to language and knowledge that give me amplified voice and power, especially as dr. martinez. I have control of my schedule to run in the morning, take time off to rest, and am paid well to tell the truth.

Most players in my core group are also first-generation college students. We have multiple degrees, work in air-conditioned offices, take vacations that involve planes, and are responsible for making tough work decisions. In our connection of similar social class backgrounds, we discuss navigating class(ism) in the academy—our joys, challenges, and fears. We have learned to be strategic and intentional during meetings, in supervising people, and when interacting with the hierarchy. We have to be smart and informed, yet not too much. We connect with realness in ways that are effortless versus with those raised in a different social class. I can breathe differently with my people.

As a first-generation white-collar professional, I generally understand the terrain of professionalism and the academy. Yes, the term *professionalism* reeks of classism, but that's for a different book. I've learned the dialect, rules, values, and practices of this middle class in the professional, academic world. I know how and when to play nice, that rhetoric is often coded in academic intelligence, and that a lemon drop martini is an acceptable drink to order at a business dinner. I enjoy the comfort of time that exists in this world: time for vacation, time for self-care, time to take long lunch meetings, time to engage in learning, time to think, time to simply be. Yet I am still deeply confused about retirement investing, tax deductions, and the structure of my healthcare plan. I have intense feelings related to class(ism) at most conferences, who gets published in what, and the name dropping involving in either. I think the term *sponsorship* is all kinds of (White) classist indoctrination, but again for another time.

Although complicated, I appreciate my straddling life in social class. I navigate in one handbook that is natural, comfortable, and familiar, and the other, although I am used to it, sometimes confuses, angers, and loses me. Of course it also grants me luxuries and power that I do not take for granted. With my privilege, I have a responsibility to the next generation. They need a better world. I work to not fall into the trap of imposter syndrome, and instead I navigate higher education, and beyond, with skills learned from my working-class roots: resiliency, boldness, integrity, and grit. I am also lucky enough to have people in my life to hold me accountable when I show up as a colluding asshole.

In my existence within two worlds, this book speaks to my soul. It speaks to a narrative that is sometimes scared, embarrassed, or unskilled in how to share. It centers the lives of those of us from poor or working-class backgrounds without needing to apologize for our values, families, communities, and selves. It will hopefully better connect readers to their own social class story and invoke a sense of responsibility to engage social class and class(ism) because it's ever present, in everything.

Over the years and through much self-work, I have found a love for engaging in the identity of social class and class(ism). It is embarrassing and joyous, frustrating and gratifying, painful and liberating. Through this relationship, I've come to embrace and ground myself to exist in the both/and. At this juncture of comfort and tension, I can heal and find my humanity and that of others. To show up differently would fracture my wholeness, and ain't nobody got time for that.

Methodology: Narrative Inquiry

Stories are the "oldest and most natural form of sense making" (Jonassen & Hernandez-Serrano, 2002, p. 66) and aid us in understanding the world and how we experience it (Merriam, 2009). The use of stories, or narratives, is a form of qualitative research. Qualitative methods allow researchers to explore how people construct, interpret, and make meaning of their experiences in context (Creswell, 2013; Hesse-Biber, 2017; Merriam, 2009; Mertens, 2015). Extending the literature on social class identity and higher education, this book utilizes a constructivist, critical paradigm and narrative approach to explore how people from poor and working-class backgrounds experience the academy (Creswell, 2013; Hesse-Biber, 2017; Merriam, 2009). Incorporating a critical lens is key here because it "raises questions about how power relations advance the interests of one group while oppressing those of other groups" (Merriam, 2009, p. 35) and, thus, allows us to not only share the stories and better understand social class identity in higher education but also critique and change the classist nature of the system itself (Patton, 2015).

Narrative

A narrative approach is utilized in this book to focus on the lived experiences of social class identity in the specific setting of higher education (Creswell, 2013; Patton, 2015). This qualitative method is "best for capturing the detailed stories or lived experiences of . . . a small number of individuals" (Creswell, 2013, p. 74) and is focused on using first-person stories as data (Merriam, 2009; Patton, 2015). Twenty-four contributing writers share their stories with us about how growing up poor or working class influenced their time in the academy.

Participants: Story Contributors

We believed it was important to understand how social class is experienced in the academy from a range of perspectives, and we sought to highlight how the influence of social class persists over one's time attending and working in higher education. This is why the contributing writers represent experiences from the viewpoint of undergraduate students, graduate students, multiple levels of administrators, and both nontenured and tenured faculty members. We also believe that social class leads some to depart academia, which is why we invited three individuals who formerly worked in higher education to share their stories as well.

These individuals hold many different identities, naming a range of ways they identify in terms of race, ethnicity, gender, sexuality, age, ability, and religion, among others. However, they all hold similarity in their social class of origin (e.g., poor or working class), and 22 of the 24 folks relate to their first-generation college student status. Although our goal was to offer as wide a range of perspectives as possible, we recognize that 24 stories do not capture all the experiences of people from poor and working-class backgrounds within the academy, and we own the limitation of all campus-based contributors currently being at 4-year institutions. Yet we believe and hope these powerful stories showcase how social class is impacting people's experience in higher education and why we should focus more attention on this dimension of identity. The specific information about coauthor and contributor identities and experiences can be found in Table I.1. You can also find their biographies in the "About the Authors and Contributors" section on page 195.

Analysis

Patton (2015) notes the distinction between stories and narratives as "the stories being the data and the narrative as analysis, which involves interpreting the story, placing it in context, and comparing it with other stories" (p. 128).

TABLE I.1

Coauthor Identities and Experiences

Name	Social Class	Race/ Ethnicity	Gender	Sexuality	Age	Ability	Religion/ Faith	Home State	Current State	Years in Higher Ed.	Highest Degree	Current Institutional Type	Current Functional Area
Sonja Ardoin	Class Straddler	White (Cajun)	Cisgender Woman	Straight	36	Currently Able	Catholic	LA	NC	18	Doctorate	4-Year, Public	Student Affairs Graduate Program, College of Education
becky martinez	Working Class of Origin, Current Middle Class	Mixed/ Biracial (Latina/ Pacific Islander)	Cisgender Woman	Hetero-sexual	45	Non-disabled	Catholic	CA	CA	27	Doctorate	N/A	Consultant

Contributing Writer Identities and Experiences

Name	Social Class	Race/Ethnicity	Gender	Sexuality	Age	Ability	Religion/Faith	Home State	Current State	Years in Higher Ed.	Highest Degree	Current Institutional Type	Current Functional Area
Mamta Motwani Accapadi	Upper Middle Class	Asian/Desi American	Cisgender Woman	Heterosexual	43	Currently Able	Hindu/Sikh	TX	FL	25	Doctorate	4-Year, Private	Division of Student Affairs
Constanza A. Cabello	Middle Class	Latina/Chilean	Cisgender Female	Heterosexual	31	Temporarily Able	Christian	MA	MA	14	Doctorate	4-Year, Private	Diversity & Inclusion: Intercultural Affairs; Institutional Diversity
Loren Cannon	Vulnerable Working Class	White	Trans Man	Queer	54	Not Disabled		CO	CA	12	Doctorate	4-Year, Public	Faculty, Department of Philosophy, College of Arts, Humanities & Social Sciences
Dylan R. Dunn	Transitioning Into the Middle Class	White	Cisgender Male	Heterosexual	24	Able-Bodied		OH	CO	6	Master's	4-Year, Private	Collegiate Recovery
Daniel Espiritu	Working Class	Latinx	Male	Heterosexual	20	Able		CA	CA	20	Current Under-graduate Student	4-Year, Private	

(Continues)

TABLE I.1 *(Continued)*

Name	Social Class	Racial/Ethnicity	Gender	Sexuality	Age	Ability	Religion/Faith	Home State	Current State	Years in Higher Ed.	Highest Degree	Current Institutional Type	Current Functional Area
Nancy J. Evans	Professional Class, Raised Working	White	Woman	Hetero-sexual	70	Wheelchair User	New Thought (Unity)	IA	IA	46	Doctorate	4-Year, Public	School of Education
Raul Fernandez	Middle Class	Latino	Male	Straight	41	Able	Atheist	NY	MA	23	Doctorate	4-Year, Private	Faculty Member in Higher Education, College of Education
Sara C. Furr	Middle Class	Multiracial Asian American	Woman	Hetero-sexual	38	Temporarily Able Bodied and Minded	Catholic	NC	IL	20	Doctorate	4-Year, Private	Graduate School Enrollment Management and Student Affairs
Rudy P. Guevarra Jr.	From Working Class to Middle Class	Mexipino (Mexican and Filipino)	Male	Hetero-sexual	46		Spiritual	CA	AZ	12	Doctorate	4-Year, Public	Faculty Member, School of Social Transformation
Jacinda M. Félix Haro	Working Class	Afro-Latinx/Nuyorican	Female	Hetero-sexual	43	Unseen Disabilities	Catholic	NY	MA	25	Master's	4-Year, Private	Dean of Student Office, Student Affairs

Name	Social Class	Race/Ethnicity	Gender	Sexuality	Age	Ability	Religious/Faith	Home State	Current State	Years in Higher Ed.	Highest Degree	Current Institutional Type	Current Functional Area
Timothy M. Johnson	Lower Middle Class	African American	Male	Heterosexual	27	Able	Christian	MD	NC	7	Master's	4-Year, Private	Student Leadership and Engagement; Division of Student Affairs
Briza K. Juarez	Working Class	Chicana	Female	Heterosexual	36	Able	Mostly Christian	CA	CA	15	Bachelor's	No Longer Working in Higher Ed.	Student Affairs
Armina Khwaja Macmillan	Middle/Upper Middle Class	Brown/POC/Pakistani American	Female/Woman	Heterosexual	29	Physically Able	Ismaili Muslim	GA	WA	11	Master's	4-Year, Private, Religious	Student Conduct
Sally G. Parish	Class Straddler	Caucasian	Female	Heterosexual	35	Temporarily Able		TN	TN	17	Master's	4-Year, Public	Student Leadership and Involvement
Edward Pickett III	Working Class Raised, Current Middle Class	African-American (also Filipino and Mexican)	Male	Straight	32	Able		CA	CA	13	Master's	PK–12	College Counseling
Kevyanna Rawls	Working Class	Black	Female		20	Able	Christian	AR	TN	3	Current Undergraduate Student	4-Year, Public	

(Continues)

TABLE I.1 (Continued)

Name	Social Class	Race/Ethnicity	Gender	Sexuality	Age	Ability	Religion/Faith	Home State	Current State	Years in Higher Ed.	Highest Degree	Current Institutional Type	Current Functional Area
Carmen Rivera	Middle Class	Chicana/Latina	Cisgender Woman	Queer	42	Non-disabled	No Affiliation	NM	CO	24	Master's	4-Year, Public	Organizational Dev for the Division of Student Affairs
Larry D. Roper	Middle Class	African-American	Male	Heterosexual	65	Temporarily Able	Unitarian Universalist	OR	OR	47	Doctorate	4-Year, Public	College of Liberal Arts
Thomas C. Segar	Working Class	Black/African American	Cisgender Male	Straight	45	Artificial Joint Recipient	Christian Non-denominational	MD	MD	28	Doctorate	4-Year, Public	Division of Student Affairs
Jeremiah Shinn	Professional	White	Male	Heterosexual	41	Able		AR	ID	23	Doctorate	4-Year, Public	Division of Student Affairs and Enrollment Management
Tori Svoboda	Working Class Roots Straddling Professional Class Now	White- also Native, raised as White	Cisgender Woman	Bisexual (Though Benefit From Hetero. Privilege Married to Cisgender Man)	48	Neuro-Diverse (Depression, Dyslexia, Narcolepsy)	Agnostic	WI	WI	30	Doctorate	4-Year, Public	Student Affairs/Higher Education Graduate Program

Name	Social Class	Race/Ethnicity	Gender	Sexuality	Age	Ability	Religion/Faith	Home State	Current State	Years in Higher Ed.	Highest Degree	Current Institutional Type	Current Functional Area
Roxanne Villaluz	Working Class	Pacific Islander/ Ilokanx	Gender-Queer	Queer	43	Persistent Deppressive Disorder	Pantheist	CA, VA, & TX	CA	11	Master's	N/A	Worker-Owned Cooperative Bakery and Pizzeria
Brenda Lee Anderson Wadley	Working Poor Upbringing; Currently Lower Middle Class	African American /Black	Female	Straight	26	Able	Follower of Christ	TN	AZ	8	Master's	4-Year, Public	Higher Education Case Management
Téa N. Wimer	Working Class/ Poor	White	Woman	Bisexual	21	Learning Disability: ADHD		NJ	NJ	3	Current Undergraduate Student	4-Year, Private	

Notes 1. All respondents identify as first-generation college students except Mamta Motwani Accapadi and Roxanne Villaluz.

2. Other salient identities provided include: becky martinez, "Aunt; Farmer/ Migrant Worker; Ancestry"; Mamta Motwani Accapadi, "Mother"; Constanza A. Cabello, "Immigrant, non-US born"; Nancy J. Evans, "Married"; Rudy P. Guevarra Jr., "Chicano, Latinx, Pinoy, Pacific Islander, Mixed Race"; Jacinda M. Félix Haro, "Mother"; Briza K. Juarez, "Mother"; Sally G. Parish, "Mother; Wife; Scholar-Practitioner; Raised in a single-parent home"; Carmen Rivera, "Parent"; Thomas C. Segar, "Race-Ethnicity-Gender-Size"; Tori Svoboda, "Adoptee"; Roxanne Villaluz, "Committed Nonmonogamist"; Brenda Lee Anderson Wadley, "Former Foster Care."

This book includes the direct stories written by the contributors as the raw data because we wanted to honor their lived experiences in their own words. We then construct our narrative, thematic analysis (Creswell, 2013; Patton, 2015; Polkinghorne, 1995) to "probe for the meaning of words, phrases, and larger units of discourse" (Creswell, p. 75; see Gee, 1991) and "the importance and influence of [social class identity] in the participant's life" (Merriam, 2009, p. 33). We do this in two ways: (a) chapter themes, which speak to the influence of social class by positionality within the academy (e.g., student, administrator, faculty); and (b) overall themes, which provide insight into the overarching premise of how individuals from poor and working-class backgrounds experience the academy. This dual-analysis approach allows us to capture "separate voices to reveal diversity of perspective of an issue [social class]" (Mertens, 2015, p. 441) as well as a collective voice to speak to the broader classism present in higher education.

Overview of This Book

Now that we have piqued your interest about social class in the academy, we want to share what the rest of the book will offer you. Chapter 1 provides a brief review of the literature on social class in higher education and several theoretical models as a base from which to understand the stories shared in this book. We hope this information will also help frame your understanding of how social class identity might be experienced by people from poor and working-class backgrounds on your own campus. Chapters 2 through 9, the bulk of the book, focus on the narratives of the contributing writers. Each chapter offers literature on the specific population (e.g., undergraduate students through tenured faculty), three stories from contributing writers in that population, and a narrative analysis of the three stories to showcase the themes within their experiences. Chapter 10 presents an overall thematic analysis of the 24 narratives to highlight the similarities and differences between their lived experiences of being poor or working class in the academy. This leads into a conversation about intersectionality of identity, including how social class is influenced by one's other dimensions of identity (e.g., race, gender, ability). Finally, in Chapter 11, we share strategies for how institutions of higher education can raise class consciousness and reduce classism to be more inclusive of students, administrators, and faculty from poor and working-class backgrounds.

I

SOCIAL CLASS IN THE ACADEMY

Education, including higher education, can be experienced as a "harsh version of basic training . . . about class, class conflict, and differing class values," which can result in "class shame and embarrassment" (Collins, Ladd, Seider, & Yeskel, 2014, p. 56). Higher education in the United States was created to instill particular, social class–based values and behaviors into privileged, wealthy, and aristocratic White men to prepare them to lead their families, churches, and communities (Hurst, 2012; Rudolph, 1990). It began with Harvard in 1636, and it was not until Joliet Junior College opened in 1901 that we began to truly consider expanding access to other social classes. It should be noted, however, that we only offered a two-year option to keep the "unprepared" out of the elite University of Chicago, so it was not an attempt of inclusion but, rather, an act of persistent exclusion of women, people of color, people with disabilities, certain religions, and the poor and working classes. Even today when more students from poor and working-class backgrounds are entering the academy, the higher education system is still encouraging and replicating de facto segregation among social classes, with preference being given to the middle and upper classes, who typically view college as a "rite of passage" (Thomas & Bell, 2008, p. 273).

According to hooks (2014), "Nowhere is there more intense silence about the reality of [social] class differences than in educational settings" (p. 144). This situation is ironic because higher education is framed as the engine of social mobility, or the way in which people from poor and working-class backgrounds can capitalize on their supposed individual merit to ascend to the middle and upper classes (Elkins & Hanke, 2018). A degree is a presumed golden ticket to more opportunities, prestigious employment, and a "better" life (Ardoin, 2018a; Lathe, 2018), but it also frequently comes with the expectation of leaving one's prior social class worldview behind to fit in with the middle and upper classes (Borrego, 2008; Reay, 2005).

Hurst (2012) acknowledges that the presence of poor and working-class folks in academia is consistently "more of the exception than the rule" (p. 24), whereas Stich and Freie (2016) note, "The working classes arguably remain devalued and pathologized within our contemporary [higher education] context" (p. 9). Even when poor and working-class individuals gain access to the academy, there are challenges with navigating the system (Ardoin, 2018a; Soria, 2016) and an expectation to assimilate to the middle- and upper class milieu. Additionally, many policies, practices, and cultures in higher education reproduce the status quo, contribute to class stratification, and exhibit classism (Soria, 2015). As Ardoin (2019) mentions, "The system was, and is, set up to sustain the broader social constructs of class stratification—championing the rich to get richer, not only in finances but also in culture and connections" (p. 204). This is further supported by Locke and Trolian (2018), who believe that higher education institutions have merely shifted from overt to implicit class-based customs and biases. Thus, it should not surprise any of us that it will take significant time and effort to undo and reimagine the dynamic we have created in the academy.

How Social Class Influences Higher Education Experiences

Simply put, social class influences most higher education experiences. It shapes which institutions we pursue and choose (Ardoin, 2019) and then permeates the classrooms, laboratories, residence halls, dining facilities, student centers, student organizations, faculty and administrative offices, fund–raising efforts, and alumni associations on the campus (see Barratt, 2011; Martin, 2015; Soria, 2015). Understandably, you may be wondering how many individuals from poor and working-class backgrounds find themselves at a college or university. We wish we could tell you, and we know other scholars feel the same. Remember how we talked about social class being ignored? That challenge applies to not only general conversation but also official data collection. Federal agencies and educational institutions and organizations do not track students, administrators, or faculty based on social class identity (Hurst, 2012; Thomas & Bell, 2008). This finding is not shocking because social class can be subjective and difficult to quantify, but it is troubling. It leaves us to rely on elements such as free or reduced lunch programs in the PK–12 sector and Pell Grants in the higher education realm. Although these measures do offer a starting place, we want to point out that these types of data are flawed. They hinge on people correctly applying for these services and grants, discount those who are ineligible due to citizenship status, and overlook anyone who might be on the "bubble," meaning their eligibility ebbs and flows with each year. But if you want two statistics to work from, Hurst (2012) cites 3% as the number of people from the poor and working class who will attain a college degree in their lifetime, and Locke and Trolian (2018) share that "more than half of all students in U.S. K–12 public schools are currently classified as low-income" (p. 72). Thus, if we want to increase the former statistic and be prepared to welcome students from the latter statistic, then we need to be ready to do some work and be advocates for change.

Students

As educators, we believe in and enjoy extolling the benefits of higher educa-tion—and there are many, particularly for poor and working-class students. However, do we ever consider what this opportunity might also be costing students both literally, in terms of tuition, fees, and room and board, and figuratively, in terms of their social class identity and connection to their backgrounds? Literature (e.g., Hurst, 2012; Lubrano, 2004; Soria, 2015; Warnock, 2016) references the processes of self-censoring; feelings of guilt, betrayal, and shame; and the sense of loss related to the tension between stu-dents' backgrounds and their experiences in the academy.

Hurst (2012) notes that "students are aware of this chasm the very first time they return home, be it for Thanksgiving, Winter Break, or the very first weekend of college" (p. 112), and the gap widens with each year in the acad-emy. Although some may describe this as a natural growth process, Lubrano (2004) warns that "we speak grandly of this metamorphosis, never stopping to consider that for many class travelers with passports stamped for new terri-tory, the trip is nothing less than a bridge burning" (p. 48). Many people also assume that students should forgo their roots and assimilate to the middle- and upper-class frames of the academy; this can result in microaggressions toward students who retain their poor or working-class values, behaviors, and preferences (Garrison & Liu, 2018). Some students may experience both shame about their backgrounds and guilt about their current situation (e.g., that they "got out" when others didn't). Liu (2011) points out that this shame is a form of internalized classism and can arise for a student when

> revealing or discussing a past or current situation (i.e., that they grew up poor or work at a fast food restaurant) that is not necessarily congruent with the way they are presenting themselves (i.e., a typical college student) may cause them to feel vulnerable and not congruent with the social class group to which they belong. (p. 211)

This is just the beginning. Students from poor and working-class backgrounds also have to navigate the assumptions made about their academic preparation and their desire to engage in the cocurricular opportunities on campus.

Stich (2012) argues that "knowledge . . . much like the social system itself, is differentiated and classed" (p. 49). Where and how someone is formally educated and if he or she is prepared for higher education are connected to social class (Thomas & Bell, 2008), not to mention the academy's preference for particular kinds of PK–12 schools, teachers, and counselors, often those who have expectations, information, and resources to support college-going (Ardoin, 2018a; McDonough, 1997). What types of institutions are more open to students from poor and working-class backgrounds? Often they are funneled into community colleges, four-year regional public institutions, and online institutions (Archer, 2003; Ardoin, 2018b; Stich, 2012; Thomas & Bell, 2008). How do we perceive those who need remedial coursework? Do we tilt toward the individualized view that they are not as capable or do we acknowledge the systemic perspective and consider the education they could access?

Even when access challenges are not at play, class shows up in what students choose to study. Our fervor for certain types of learning and knowledge can create social class splits among academic areas of study (i.e., majors and minors), with students from poor and working-class backgrounds favoring more practical fields such as nursing, education, or business that align directly with employment pathways and students from the middle and upper classes pursuing liberal arts foci that allow them to sample from a new array of topics with limited concern about postdegree job prospects (Ardoin, in press). What about individual course content and instruction? Do students ever read about social class in their courses? If so, do they see their own class identity represented? Do they know any fellow students or faculty members who share their social class background?

The academic curriculum can also value types of verbal and nonverbal language that often contradict poor and working-class students' forms of communication (Lathe, 2018). Elkins and Hanke (2018), citing White and Ali-Khan (2013), note that how a student communicates, in both verbal and written forms, can determine how he or she is viewed by peers, faculty, and administrators. One's fluency in Standard English, word choices, tone, and comprehension of academic terminology and rules can strongly influence others' perception of intelligence and the desire to listen to and include that person in academic pursuits.

On top of all this are issues of time. Course offerings and sequencing present barriers for some poor and working-class students who hold part- or full-time employment or have caregiving responsibilities for children or other family members. If we only offer courses between 9 a.m. and 3 p.m. or only once per year, then we may be inadvertently creating challenges for students to stay on track academically. Time further impacts students' ability to engage in study habits, perform group work, and utilize faculty office hours, not to mention get involved in cocurricular activities (Ardoin, 2018b; Locke & Trolian, 2018).

The reluctance or inability for some poor and working-class students to be the "superinvolved" student archetype aligns with the upward mobility bias mentioned in the introduction. This bias may lead educators to believe that all students should desire to do more and be more. As Liu (2011) notes, we can often perceive "these individuals who do not want extra responsibility or do not strive for more . . . [as] not 'fully self-actualizing' or optimizing their potential" (p. 214). We can also misread this as students not being aware of opportunities or motivated to engage in their campus experience, when in reality they may be choosing the one or two experiences they feel are most beneficial or we do not comprehend what their time and life circumstances allow (or don't). Martin's (2015) findings support this; her research highlights how students from poor and working-class backgrounds often feel overextended from the combination of academic requirements and jobs they need to remain enrolled, thus limiting their capacity, interest, and/or engagement in cocurricular aspects of higher education.

In either space—curricular or cocurricular—students from poor and working-class backgrounds may find themselves code-switching their communication, purchasing certain material goods, and engaging in behaviors to hide their social class of origin (Elkins & Hanke, 2018). This may be rooted in their concern about not being "right" for higher education; as Locke and Trolian (2018) explain:

> Classist microaggressions might manifest themselves in [students] not wearing the "right" clothes, not attending the "right" events, not having the "right" letters of recommendation, not having the "right" terms of language, not having parents or family members with the "right" jobs or connections, or not being able to take advantage of an internship. (p. 69)

So, when you meet students from poor and working-class backgrounds on your campus, recognize that "these students are the ones who are disrupting the normative expectations from the data which suggest that their intergenerational inheritance is to remain poor" (Garrison & Liu, 2018, p. 19).

Faculty and Administrators

For those from poor and working-class backgrounds who remain in the academy postgraduation as faculty members and/or administrators, social class remains influential. Hurst and Nenga (2016) point out how those employed by colleges and universities conduct their work within environments "surrounded by and immersed in social class . . . but we are not always cognizant of the ways social class shapes our language, our bodies, our behaviors, our norms, and our actions" (p. 6). hooks (2000) illustrated this sentiment:

> I, like most of my working class peers, was not prepared to face the class hierarchies present in academia . . . when class was mentioned at the school . . . negative stereotypes about poor and working class people were the only perspectives evoked. (p. 42)

Whether it is the ever-present question of "Where did you go to college?" that elicits assumptions of attributed class (Barratt, 2011), a hiring practice of only considering applicants from "peer-plus" institutions to boost rankings (Ardoin & martinez, 2018; Fuller, 2012; Warnock, 2016), or not talking "proper" enough to fit in with your colleagues (Streib, 2016), it is clear that social class is ever present in the academy regardless of one's role on the campus.

Approximately 25% of faculty members in higher education have poor or working-class roots (Arner, 2016). To our knowledge, there is no equivalent statistic for administrators, but organizations such as the Working Class Studies Association and NASPA's Socioeconomic and Class Issues Knowledge Community, with an intragroup for Professionals from the Poor and Working Class, represent the need of administrators from poor and working classes to connect with others who share that identity. This tells us that there is some representation of different social classes within the academy. We often do not recognize who these folks are on campus, however, because some faculty and administrators attempt to assimilate to their campus's middle- or upper class expectations for fear of being labeled as "whining, having a chip on the shoulder, or claiming victimhood . . . or undermining credibility" for discussing their social class background (Arner, 2016, p. 57). This is counterintuitive to celebrating diversity of identity on campus and inhibits poor and working-class students from connecting with faculty and administrators who could serve as role models (Warnock, 2016).

There is also distinction among where and how these individuals from poor and working-class backgrounds are employed; Archer (2016) shares that many of these folks are filtered to two-year and less selective campuses, often based on the level of prestige of the institutions from which they earned their degrees, and are more likely to be in part-time positions. Further, tactics used to advance one's higher education career through the constructs of professionalism (Ardoin & martinez, 2018) and "self-promotion, self-assurance, and visibility—are veritably antithetical to the values of humility and invisibility taught in working class families" (Soria, 2016, p. 132). Much of this is intertwined with the political climate of higher education. Rothe (2006) discusses the "political gamesmanship . . . of academic ethos, virtues, and practices" (p. 57) that is foreign to those from poor and working-class backgrounds. For example, these faculty and administrators can be viewed as too passionate, direct, or uncouth when they lean on their natural tendency to "tell it like it is," which "collides with the rhetoric and diplomacy in the academy" (Wilson, 2006, p. 160). In short, there are a multitude of contradictions between how faculty and administrators from poor and working-class backgrounds might prefer to show up and how the academy expects them to look, speak, and behave (Rothe, 2006).

Lathe (2018) calls out the paradox of the social mobility rhetoric of higher education falling flat for faculty and administrators from poor and working-class backgrounds, stating, "The supposed emancipation and transformation via attainment of higher education was not necessarily the reality for [these] individuals" (p. 24). Instances of class hostility can incite imposter syndrome among faculty and administrators from poor and working-class backgrounds, provoke feelings of needing to prove themselves through heavier workloads or "passing" behavior (Lathe, 2018), and raise questions about continuing their employment in the academy.

Theoretical Models and Concepts

Although our minds often imagine money when we hear the term *social class*, this dimension of identity is much broader than one's financial situation. Social class includes one's attitudes, experiences, knowledge, resources, and opportunities. To frame this broader picture, we provide a brief overview of four theoretical models or concepts: (a) Bourdieu's concepts of cultural and social capital; (b) Yosso's (2005) community cultural wealth model; (c) Liu, and colleagues' (2004) social class worldview model; and (d) Hurst's (2010) social class concepts.

Bourdieu's Cultural and Social Capital

Bourdieu recognized that educational systems favor those with privileged identities whose knowledge and behaviors are perceived as highly valuable and who have tools to navigate the systems, creating a social reproduction cycle, and he offered development of cultural and social capital as a means to interrupt this cycle (Mullen, 2010; Soria, 2015). Bourdieu (1977, 1984) defines *cultural capital* as the knowledge, language, and culture that privileged families transmit to their children (Archer, 2003; MacLeod, 2009; McDonough, 1997). The acquisition of cultural capital begins at home and involves cultural reproduction (Barratt, 2011; MacLeod, 2009; Schwalbe et al., 2000), which embraces the culture and practices of the dominant group as proper and normative while coercing marginalized populations to "accept [their] place within existing hierarchies of status, power, and wealth" (Schwalbe et al., 2000, p. 429). So, although everyone possesses his or her own versions of cultural capital, educational institutions—including colleges and universities—tend to place the highest value on the cultural capital of the White, middle- and upper classes who have collegiate experience (McDonough, 1997; Schwalbe et al., 2000; Soria, 2015).

Cultural capital is further explained through the concept of habitus. *Habitus* is a deeply internalized, common set of viewpoints and experiences that individuals attain from their immediate environment (Bourdieu, 1977, 1984; McDonough, 1997). Habitus materializes as individuals' aspirations, perceptions, thoughts, feelings, expectations, practices, actions, and appreciations—an enduring sense of "one's place" in the world (Bourdieu, 1977; MacLeod, 2009; Mullen, 2010; Soria, 2015; Stuber, 2011).

Social capital describes the actual and potential benefits of individual relationships and memberships in groups or communities (Bourdieu, 1986). It is the collective value of everyone you know. These connections can be self-sought but are mostly inherited, "guaranteed by the application of a common name (the name of a family, class, or tribe or of a school, party, etc.)," and "maintained and reinforced, in exchanges" (Bourdieu, 1986, p. 21). Social capital provides access to opportunity and power through the direct and indirect connections to others; this often manifests in the form of introductions, information, and favors, including nepotism. It pairs with cultural capital in that those with similar types of cultural capital often seek to be in relationships with each other, hence tying social capital to cultural capital.

Community Cultural Wealth Model

Yosso's (2005) community cultural wealth model focuses on "the array of cultural knowledge, skills, abilities and contacts possessed by socially marginalized groups that often go unrecognized and unacknowledged" (p. 69). The model expands on Bourdieu's (1986) concept of cultural capital into six forms of capital: (a) aspirational, (b) familial, (c) linguistic, (d) navigational, (e) resistant, and (f) social (Yosso, 2005). Aspirational capital is about future-focus and resiliency. Familial capital focuses on connections to one's family and community through kinship and culture. Linguistic capital is the ability to communicate in more than one language or dialect. Navigational capital "acknowledges individual agency within institutional constraints" (Yosso, 2005, p. 80). Resistant capital is the recognition of inequity and the drive to challenge it. Social capital is an individual's network of resources and the use of those resources to assist others. Although the model was originally created for racial and ethnic identities, it has since been applied to other dimensions, including class identity.

Social Class Worldview Model

Liu and colleagues' (2004) social class worldview model (SCWM) provides a framework incorporating individuals' perceptions and experiences of social class through the capital accumulation paradigm, which includes three types of capital—(a) social, (b) human, and (c) cultural—and five interrelated domains: (a) consciousness, attitudes, and salience; (b) referent groups; (c) property relationships; (d) lifestyle; and (e) behaviors. These domains capture self and others' awareness, emotions, and significance about social class identity and systems; the people who influence one's social class worldview, including group of origin, peer group, and group of aspiration; one's material possessions and presentation of social class; how one spends one's time and resources (e.g., cultural capital); and how one acts, or an "observable manifestation of a social class worldview" (p. 106). Liu and colleagues offer this combination of capitals within these domains as a "lens through which people perceive their world" (p. 107).

The SCWM demonstrates the complex layers that one has to explore and recognize to gain a deeper understanding of social class identity. It also provides student affairs educators with an outline from which to assess office- and campus-level policies, practices, and culture and to build support structures for students from poor and working-class identities. For example, if a student's referent group of origin belittles higher education, they may be weary of returning to campus for the second year. If a student hears of all the glamorous locales where others spend spring break or summer while they work at a local restaurant, their sense of belonging on campus may wane because of the lifestyle differences between them and their referent peer group.

Social Class Concepts

Hurst's (2010) work on social class compliments the aforementioned scholars' work by providing framing for the different ways in which social class manifests and shifts as a dimension of one's identity. Her work on social class mobility and straddling highlights how poor and working-class people who attend college make "crucial decisions about their political class allegiances and identities as part of the process of 'becoming educated'" (Hurst, 2010, p. 4). Specifically, she found that individuals from poor and working-class backgrounds generally identified in one of three ways: as loyalists, renegades, or double agents (Hurst, 2010). Loyalists reject being associated with the middle class, despite their new education level, and maintained association with the family and home communities. Often loyalists see life as us versus them, with us being poor and working-class folks whose forms of capital are not recognized by them, meaning those of the middle and upper classes. Renegades are the opposite; they reject their poor or working class identity in favor of association with and acclimation to the middle class. It is common for renegades to hide their background or harbor some negative feelings about it. Double agents are the hybrid group; they tend to ebb and flow among the social classes, with an ability to shift among the languages, behavior, and customs of each community or context. Hurst's (2010) three responses to social class identity association highlight how individuals react differently to "the classifying process of educational achievement" (p. 6) while also making the crucial distinction between class position and class identity. In short, this means that although someone's position among the social classes may shift, likely financially or educationally, that person may still think, act, and feel like a member of the poor or working class and identify that way.

Summary

This chapter provides a brief review of the literature on social class in higher education and several theoretical models to form a base from which to understand the stories shared in this book. Recognizing that higher education was set up to be classist from its origins helps us conceive why individuals from poor and working-class backgrounds face barriers in accessing and feeling welcome in the academy. Understanding that everyone possesses forms of capital and a unique social class worldview allows us to reframe a deficit mind-set into an asset-based framework and asks us to consider why we, as the academy, only value certain, privileged forms of capital. Finally, recognizing our upward mobility bias helps us understand the different responses people have to the class mobility narrative, and the nuances between class position and class identity inform us that not all people who arrive at our institutions—as students, administrators, or faculty—want to conform to the academy's elitism or classism. We hope this information will also build on your consciousness of how social class identity might be experienced by people from poor and working-class backgrounds on your own campus. In the following chapters, the contributing writers offer their lived experiences as people from the poor and working classes in the academy as examples of how social class can and does show up in higher education.

2

THE UNDERGRADUATE
STUDENT PERSPECTIVE

Narratives by Daniel Espiritu, Kevyanna Rawls, and Téa N. Wimer

We do not make it easy for undergraduate students from poor or working-class backgrounds to access and succeed in the academy, as chapter 1 highlights. We can further understand how social class shows up for undergraduate students through the stories of three current undergraduate students: (a) Daniel Espiritu from Chapman University in California, (b) Kevyanna Rawls from the University of Memphis in Tennessee, and (c) Téa N. Wimer from Princeton University in New Jersey. Their stories show us how, across institutional type and location, undergraduate students from poor or working-class backgrounds are present in the academy and are prevailing despite the barriers we have created for them.

Daniel Espiritu's Story

Developing a Sense of Social Class Identity

Growing up, I viewed my identity as a first-generation Mexican American as the primary factor of my positionality. My parents were both immigrants, and after my dad was deported, my mom was left to raise my brother and I with the help of her Spanish-speaking parents in Orange County, California. If my hometown is known for anything, it's the high cost of living. We were fortunate enough to find an apartment in a complex in a peaceful area where our income is taken into consideration and where the rent is significantly lower than that of the rest of the surrounding community. Things were going fine for us until the financial crash of 2008. This was when I began to understand that my position as a member of the working class affected me more than any other part of my identity.

I was 10 years old when my grandpa had to leave his job as a salesman at Nissan. People simply didn't have enough financial security to buy cars anymore. My grandpa struggled to find work before obtaining a part-time position at a fast-food chain restaurant named El Pollo Loco. At this point, my mom, the only other working person in our family, had to take a larger portion of the financial responsibility. Our standard of living didn't necessarily decrease to the point where we were living in poverty, but we did have to make cut backs. We switched to generic brands, cut our cable, cut back on energy consumption, and began to shop for clothes at thrift shops and discount stores, just to name a few.

At one point, my grandpa invested some of the money he could save into purchasing the parts necessary for the assembly of water filters. However, with a lack of education in entrepreneurship and no means of calculating the legal risks of running a water filtration business, he failed to get his business off the ground. The supplies still sit in our garage today. My grandpa was eventually able to pursue full-time work again and was fortunate to find positions in office settings. However, he still earns a minimum wage. With the rising cost of living in Orange County, my family never truly recovered from the recession.

My family is a working-class family. Although we do not necessarily find ourselves breaking our backs to put food on the table, we don't have the same flexibility as others. Having a working-class identity means having every one of our financial decisions questioned by people who do not understand our financial situation. It means being constantly told we should stop trying to derive any pleasure from our lives and simply focus on maintaining our physical selves at the expense of cultivating our mental, spiritual, and intellectual selves. Through our labor, we make a high quality of life possible for those with the most privilege in our society, yet those same people blame our struggles on our laziness and irresponsibility. When we are seen toting our material treasures with pride, people think we are lying about the obstacles we face. What they don't see is that my grandpa had to declare bankruptcy after being served a lawsuit for the time he spun his car out on a freeway ramp on a rainy day. They don't see my mom working twice as many hours as they work just to help put me through college. They don't see me staying up into the early hours of the morning doing homework after a long shift. Being working class means being misunderstood.

Social Class in Higher Education

To discuss the role of social class in higher education, the role of social class in PK–12 education must be understood. Public schools that serve working-class students fail to bring about the opportunity for class mobility. They merely further the conditions that lead to the social reproduction of the working class. The elite-class school demands students develop the critical thinking and reasoning skills necessary to lead a society, whereas the working-class institution is satisfied with the working-class student knowing better than to take what doesn't belong to him or her. There seems to be a consensus among teachers and administrators at these schools that as long as students can sit quietly without disrupting others for the length of the class, and as long as an acceptable number of students pass any required standardized tests, they have done their jobs properly. Correspondingly, any student from a working-class school who manages to make it into the university, despite having to work twice as hard for half the results, now bears the burden of having to compete with students who have spent their whole lives preparing to excel at an institution that demands deep thinking.

Challenges in Higher Education as a Working-Class Student
Despite having passed several honors and Advanced Placement (AP) courses in high school, the transition to the university has been one of the most challenging times of my life. I began to understand just how influential campus culture is in educational settings. At my high school, most students were satisfied with earning the minimum 2.0 grade point average required to play sports. In reality, none of us knew why we were even required to be in school. Our teachers, so concerned with teaching us to behave, get all our work done on time, and pass statewide exams, never got around to inspiring the intellectual curiosity that distinguishes a student from a scholar seeking enlightenment.

Suddenly as a student at a university, I found myself struggling to keep up with the speed and intensity of my classes. I initially attributed this to the horror stories I had heard about the difficulties of college. However, I soon came to realize I was having more trouble than my peers. One example of this came during my second semester when I took Introduction to International Relations. At first the complexity of the assigned readings and concepts that came with them went over my head, and I struggled to grasp key concepts in the course. Most of this was because I simply couldn't keep up with the reading. The texts were far lengthier and more intense (in terms of academic language) than I had ever been exposed to. It wasn't until I began to personally investigate different reading comprehension strategies online and ask several clarifying questions during class that I began to do well. Oddly enough, I began to realize that I was passionate about the subject and how close I came to giving up just because it was difficult.

Adjusting to a campus culture dominated by affluent students is also difficult. Public PK–12 schools are localized in my state, meaning we all came from similar backgrounds. I was socialized among working-class students, and, to be frank, we all grew quite resentful of those who had more than us. Although I did make a determined effort to rid myself of these prejudices, I found that students from affluent backgrounds stood strong with their belief that people like me are freeloaders who should work harder. What many people close to me fail to understand is that navigating campus culture wasn't only about my ability to make friends and be sociable. It has a direct effect on my experience in the classroom. The views and perspectives I share during class discussion have been shaped by the experiences and hardships that I faced during my upbringing and that I continue to face. It is easy for students and faculty alike to dismiss these views as outrageous or unrealistic if they haven't come from a background like mine. When a "constructive dialogue" ensues in these cases, it is discouraging to watch as my peers make bold claims about "those people" in the working class and watch the instructor do nothing to ensure the conversation is realistically applicable to our world. In these cases, the working-class student loses an opportunity and the rest of the class misses out on the opportunity to thoroughly understand an issue they are, or should be, trying to investigate. When my perspective is toned down or blocked out, my peers risk walking away knowing nothing more than new ways to express what they already believe.

Making Higher Learning Work Better for the Working Class
Accessibility to institutions of higher learning is one of the most important challenges that universities must face. The cost of education continues to reach new heights each year, effectively making it difficult for working-class students to earn a degree and become educated citizens. Sending a student to a university is a high-risk commitment for a working-class family. I was fortunate enough to earn a large scholarship, but it didn't exactly cover all my costs. Like most other students at my university, I had to accept loans to pay for school. However, unlike many other students, there is a pressing urgency to be able to pay these off as soon as I graduate because I cannot guarantee that I will be able to financially rely on my family. In fact, they may soon rely on me. As tuition rises each year, we find ourselves borrowing more money and working more hours just to cover our costs. This puts a strain on my ability to be a fully committed student.

The good news is that there is a greater institutional effort to address this problem. The federal government currently offers grants, affordable loans, and work-study programs to low-income students. California, where I live, offers its own grant that can, in some cases, have a value twice as high as the federal Pell Grant. Universities and university systems also take steps to address this issue. The California State (Cal State) University system offers some of the lowest tuition rates in the country to in-state students. San Diego State University, with a total undergraduate enrollment of 29,853 students, charged $7,460 in tuition and fees for the 2017–2018 academic year (*U.S. News & World Report,* 2017a). The University of California (UC) system is a highly renowned research university system that doesn't charge much more than the Cal State system for in-state students. UC Berkeley and UCLA charge $14,098 and $13,256 in tuition and fees, respectively, for the 2017–2018 academic school year (*U.S. News & World Report,* 2017b, 2017c). Furthermore, students in the UC System who earn less than $80,000 per year have found themselves not having to pay a dollar out of pocket in system-wide tuition fees through the UC Blue and Gold Opportunity Plan (University of California Admissions, 2017). Even private institutions are setting up programs to grant need- and merit-based financial aid to large sums of students.

This transformation in how working-class students pay for college is much needed, but it doesn't fully address the problems we face. Institutions of higher learning need to create a campus culture that is inclusive to students of all backgrounds, with an emphasis on social class as a priority. As I previously stated, one of the most difficult parts of my life was the transition from my working-class high school to the university. The quality of education before going to university puts working-class students at a major disadvantage when placed in a college classroom. Many of us find ourselves feeling that we are not good enough to be where we are because we haven't had enough experience in critically thinking about complex topics or in critically analyzing the content discussed or assigned in class. Just like any other case of social difference where privilege plays a large role in the development of entire communities, we find ourselves working twice as hard to earn half as much.

Let me be clear that acknowledgment of this problem in the academy does not mean the academy should make education easier for working-class students. On the contrary, institutions of higher learning should encourage students from working-class backgrounds to investigate any shortcomings they might be experiencing in their studies and challenge them to voluntarily work harder with support from the institution. Educators may interpret that in any way, as long as the goal is to help working-class students be as successful as they want to be. Some methods to accomplish this goal could include free tutoring, critical reading and writing workshops where attendance is incentivized, and the addition of for-credit courses meant to help students develop critical thinking skills and examine their positionality in the academy and society.

I personally believe education is a pathway to success as well as the manifestation of humanity's attempt to understand our world. However, my experiences show that educational institutions are yet to become places where all voices are equally welcomed and understood. Education is a tool that is yet to be fully utilized by the working class, and arming us with it would open up the possibility of class mobility as well as bring about new voices in the echo chamber that is the academy. The innovative ideas and practices the academy is currently missing out on have the potential to alter the way we understand the world.

Kevyanna Rawls's Story

"I'm going to go to college for free," I would say eagerly to everyone who asked about my plans for college. And each time they would respond the same way: "How?"

This was one of the hardest questions I would have to answer. As I was growing up, my parents always told my brother and me that we needed to go to college, and if we did not go to college, we needed to go to a trade school. Although they both attended college, neither of my parents graduated with a college degree. Because of that, neither of my parents genuinely knew how college worked and neither did I.

In my household, my parents never discussed financial issues around us or alluded to a need of any sort. Because of this, I have never had a clear understanding of what social class we were in or what role that played in our lives. As a child, I can recall living with both sets of my grandparents and spending a lot of time with them without my parents present. Although I was never clear on where my parents were, as I grew older, I simply assumed they were working. With my dad being a self-employed musician and my mom a claims specialist, money was tight sometimes, but they always managed to make ends meet. My brother and I never had to worry about not having clothes or shoes for school, and that was typically all that mattered to us at the time.

Because we attended a school where uniforms were not necessary, one could tell the background of most children at our school by the way they dressed. Located in one of the wealthiest parts of central Arkansas, our elementary school was full of students whose parents were doctors, lawyers, stay-at-home parents, business owners, and state officials. Most of the children lived near the school and in the surrounding areas; however, that was not the case for me and my brother. Growing up, we lived in one of the more impoverished neighborhoods about 30 minutes away from the school. When we first began attending the school, my parents would have to make the drive to the other side of town to secure the best education for us. At the time, my brother and I thought it was cool to be some of the few kids whose parents could drop them off at school every day. It was not until we got older that we realized the strain driving us to school put on our parents. With my mother working in the downtown area and my brother and I going to school about 20 minutes from downtown, the need to constantly refill the gas tank put restrictions on where we could go and eat that week. Because of this, my mother took it into her own hands to demand a bus drive to where we lived. Although she ultimately won this case, the reality of our family not having an unlimited amount of funds available made us realize the unfair access to opportunity other children at our school had.

The different experiences I endured during my elementary school days did not necessarily raise awareness about my family's social class; however, they planted a seed that I have seen blossom over the last decade. Since that first incident of identifying privilege, I have been more exposed to the financial condition of my family. The older I got, the more my parents would tell my brother and me about what we could and could not afford to do. This became more prevalent as we entered our high school days and carried on into our college lives.

Upon applying to college, I heard the stories of how college students only ate ramen noodles and cereal because they could not afford to pay for school and live a financially stable life. Although I knew my parents would support me if I could not afford something, I made a promise to myself to not plague them with my financial problems. Approximately one year before I began college, my brother departed for a college in southeast Arkansas. During this time, I was a senior in high school and had seen my parents struggle to pay for his schooling, provide for themselves, and make sure I had everything I needed for my senior year. Although I was working, I knew I would have to save my money and apply for as many scholarships as possible to ensure my parents would not have to do the same for me. The summer before attending college, I worked more than 50 hours a week making minimum wage; despite this, my parents stood firm in their idea of me not working during my first year of college. Although we had numerous arguments about it, I ended up not working and used all of the money I had saved over the summer to support myself during the academic year; however, paying tuition was a burden in itself.

"I Want to Go to College for Free"

Initially, I thought I had achieved this goal by getting my out-of-state tuition covered and being awarded the Dean's Scholarship; however, I was disappointed to find out that this was not the case. With the scholarships I had, I would still owe the university about $4,000 per semester. To counter this, my mother had to take out a Parent PLUS Loan. Although this was not my personal preference, my mother accepted this loan for my first 2 years of college, totaling approximately $18,000 in debt, to pay for my education. Although this amount is substantially lower than the loans many other students will have to take out, learning that I could not get enough money to cover my education, despite the information on my Free Application for Federal Student Aid (FAFSA), took me by surprise. At this time, I learned what it meant to be stuck in the middle.

What I mean by being stuck in the middle is the idea that with the amount of money I made combined with what my parents made, we did not make enough money for us to pay for my schooling out of pocket, but we made too much money to receive large contributions toward my tuition from Pell Grants, unsubsidized loans, or subsidized loans. Ultimately, the argument was that my family's income looked substantial on paper; however, there was not a way to factor in other basic needs that decreased the value of my parents' salary. By excluding the costs of medical bills, car notes, rent, utilities, and other emergencies, people in the middle are expected to be able to afford paying several thousand dollars to attend a university while also engaging in other activities on campus and still survive.

Over the past two years, I have been identified as someone who comes from a family with money. Initially, I attributed this to the fact that not many people knew anything about my background and where I came from. Most of the information people knew about me came from the way I presented myself to them and the idea that I was financially supporting myself. This idea gained support from some of my peers at the beginning of my sophomore year when I returned to school with a new car. Because I had never explained my work habits and the way I was able to survive the school year without working, the people around me assumed that my parents must give me money and provide me with all of the things that I need. People perceived that I was among the upper class and born with a "silver spoon" in my mouth. Unfortunately, I do not identify with this perception. When asked, I identify as a part of the modern-day working class. By working class, I simply mean my family and I all work one or more jobs to support ourselves and contribute to the family's overall financial situation. Although I do possess valuable objects, all of these things were gained at an expensive cost to me or my parents, whether that means I work two jobs all summer or during the school year or my parents work overtime to make ends meet—working is all we know.

Before coming to college, I had little awareness of the significant role one's social status plays in one's life and mental stability. With the help of those around me and my exposure to people from different backgrounds, I have had the opportunity to learn a lot more. Over the past few years, I have made numerous friends who admit to coming from wealthier families or depend on their parents for their day-to-day necessities. Typically, I would argue that this fact is not significant; however, I learned it does have a meaningful impact on how people perceive themselves and their family. During my early years of college, I recall being ashamed of where I came from, ashamed that I could not call my family every week and request money, and ashamed that I had to work harder to make grades because I could not afford to fail because I needed a college degree to pay for the cost of attending college. The psychological implications of coming from low or middle-income homes on one's ability to perform in school while integrating into a community of individuals who have more access to financial freedom and stability can be intimidating and unappealing.

It has been discussed and agreed that college is expensive, but what exactly does this mean to students at colleges across the country today? What I know is, many high school students across the country have the potential and skills necessary to attend college but cannot afford going into higher education. I know many students currently enrolled in colleges across the country have to sacrifice their basic needs to pay for college. I know students struggle to pay bills, feed themselves and their families, and work countless hours to get an education. I know some students cannot afford textbooks and are penalized for it with failing grades. I know some students have to work to survive, so they cannot get involved in school, and they are at a disadvantage when they apply for scholarships, graduate schools, and positions within their designated career. I know that a disconnect exists between administrators discussing college affordability and the students whom this affects. Although I am privileged enough to not have to deal with many of these problems, I believe these same issues look different for every student.

For me, navigating through my undergraduate career has been a rollercoaster. As a student leader on campus, I have the opportunity to represent students at administrative meetings and when talking to faculty. Because I am speaking for an entire population, I have found myself trying to learn what issues students face and what they believe needs to be done. Through my research and conversations with various individuals, I see social class present in every aspect of higher education. Although higher education is broad and encompasses a variety of people, the impact of social class is most evident in student involvement and on-campus leadership opportunities. Student leadership and involvement roles are glorified on college campuses, yet we ignore all of the factors that prevent people from getting involved. The idea is that if students get involved on campus, they are leaders and capable of being successful members of a larger community. The issue arises when students cannot get involved because of their commitments to their families and work obligations. To be a student leader, one must have a degree of freedom, whether that is financial or time. Although some student leaders are able to balance these things, other students cannot even if they want to participate. It can also be a harder task for this population of students to identify a group of people to support them in their student involvement. Most student leaders gain support through fraternity and sorority life, but many students cannot afford to participate in this costly investment. When I initially arrived on campus, I had to eliminate organizations I was interested in because I could not afford them. Although not all of them were prestigious, I recall missing out on the opportunity to join honor societies that would have allowed me to network with people from all over the country. The limiting of students' access to organizations, networking opportunities, and events because of money is one of the most flawed aspects of student life. Although admissions processes, surviving outside of school, and maintaining good grades are important, the feeling of being included and part of a larger community is just as important.

Téa N. Wimer's Story

Over the course of my career at Princeton University, I've asked myself questions upon questions. I have searched for definitions and understandings of my situation, for the way that other students and faculty treat me, and the way my family related to me, too. I've struggled to be a student alongside being a human and daughter and sister and friend and partner and mentor and all the other roles I play in my life. I might settle on a holistic picture of myself one day and then find that picture shattered months or even a week later. For me, being poor at an Ivy League school has been a constant redefining of the self and the way I relate to others around me. My time here has been a time of discomfort and of finding myself at odds with many pieces of my life, especially that of social class, and then growing to like that discomfort in many ways. In writing this, I hope to flesh out some of the most tangible roles and identities I've played that have drawn me closer to my social class status.

Learning what my difference was as a peer came from the very first day I arrived on campus. My move-in was permeated by dreadful anxiety rather than the joyful anxiety of my roommate and her mother. My roommate was a legacy admission and an athlete, with parents who met at Princeton. While they obsessed lovingly over every detail of her side of the room, my mother and brother brought my things into the room as if they were participating in a death march. They dropped my things anywhere, and after my bed was made and boxes of clothes were stacked near the closet, they were quick to leave from the shining radiance of my roommate and her mother.

They came and had lunch with me before they left, back toward Southern Illinois, and they didn't quite know what to think or do—they stared at anything but at me: the fancy cheese ravioli and glistening grapes among the various other brunch foods, the thick napkins emblazoned with the Princeton shield, the other students who chattered among themselves (as many of them, I quickly noticed, were already friends from either private schools or high school summer opportunities or wherever else higher class students met each other) while their parents did the same. All three of us were in uncharted territory, but I never stopped to think that it wasn't just me who was experiencing college from a first-generation lens; it was my entire immediate family.

Even so, my difference as a peer became even clearer later on. With the risk of possibly contributing to the fetishization and romanticizing of low-income people (e.g., See how hardy they are! See how much they love to work! What a quaint life they lead!), I think that being of a "scrappy" background made me prepared for the curve balls that come with growing into an adult, whereas many of my peers struggled more than I did with the transition.

For example, a friend's parents made her pay her own phone bill when she started university. This already was surprising to me—my family had been asking me to help pay bills since I had started working at a local fast-food place the day I turned 16, and I had taken care of myself financially from the day I turned 18. My roommate struggled, and when her first bill was due for her phone, she didn't know what to do. I watched her grow more and more distraught as the minutes went by. She contemplated calling her parents or perhaps just not paying the bill at all and waiting until she had the money. For me, the answer became crystal clear within minutes—I advised her to sell some of the clothes she didn't wear much anymore and to put that money toward her phone bill.

This has happened so many times over the course of my time here. Many students don't know how to pay their bills online or how to balance a checkbook. This ignorance extends beyond the financial sphere, too; students don't know how to cook or care for themselves in many basic ways. Their learning is a natural part of growing up, and I don't mean at all to discount those students for learning as they should. What I do mean is to highlight how many of my other low-income friends and peers and I already have these skills because of the degree of independence being raised in a low-income household asks of a child. My mother worked three or four different jobs at a time. Some nights she wouldn't come home until much, much later than our bedtimes. I appointed myself as her helper. I cooked and cleaned, looking to make her experience easier. I learned these things far earlier in life than more fortunate people, and at double speed, too. Being poor meant there was no safety net below us; we made the situation work or we didn't and we faced the worst. Now it's my job to teach my peers, and although I'd like to say that I take this responsibility in stride, I don't always. Sometimes it strikes me as so unfair.

When you're low income in the academy, even at Princeton (which boasts an unparalleled financial aid program), it is expected that you will work at least a few hours a week. The financial aid package holds a stipulation for those who need aid: you will work a federal work-study job as part of the package. It will always be odd to me that high-caliber universities bring in poor students in droves, thinking that this is the end of the challenge. The point has always been to "level the playing field," to give less fortunate students the same opportunities as more fortunate students. So why are low-income students expected to devote 10 hours per week of their already highly compromised schedule to working jobs that other students will not? This will always ensure that more fortunate students maintain higher levels of access—without needing to work, they can navigate a professor's office hours more readily, and they might also have more hours to study or devote to more nurturing extracurricular activities.

Although all of these realizations came to me when I was working in the dining hall the spring of my first year here, I never expected to fall into the comfort of being a student worker. For a year I washed dishes with a disgusting yellow apron tied around my waist and comically large gloves on my hands, with a black cap obscuring most of the candy pink hair I wore stubbornly. I was furious at the world, and I couldn't believe I was being made to work there when other students could see me—but all of the other library and assistant jobs on campus had been taken so I had no other options.

Fast-forward a month, and I couldn't wait to go to work, to be with the professional staff and to banter with them, yelling friendly challenges across the tight kitchen space. They all treated me like their child. They cared for me and offered to cover for me so that I could study (I never took them up on this). I would practice my beginner French with one of the head cooks and the person in charge of the salad bar; I might talk about the musical and cultural legacy of Prince with the man in charge of the grill and then go to the man in charge of the pizza bar and talk about his old sports bar. I felt more at home and comfortable there with them than I had in the previous entire semester at Princeton.

I've tried understanding how this happened, and all I can think of is that my first job on campus reinforced my low-income status, making it clear for others to see. Class is an invisible section of identity, and it doesn't operate in the same way that identities such as race and sexual orientation might operate, in that we usually have tangible ways to observe those identities. It has always been difficult to observe class or build community among lower class statuses. It is even more difficult when, all of a sudden, the cool trend among youth is to look like you have been struggling—to identify with the "poor struggle," even if parents paid for the apartment. All of this is to say that perhaps this job gave me a chance to relish my low-income identity without exactly having to shout from the rooftops. I was around other low-income people (more on that in a bit), and I was working tirelessly to make money. I had tried other tactics to differentiate myself from others—dying my hair, getting tattoos, or refusing to participate in the most "Princeton" parts of Princeton—but none of them really performed the difference that this job did.

However, working in the dining hall also complicated my understanding of my class. It made me question whether I could claim that piece of my identity completely anymore. The workers I mentioned before most often had not been to college; they came from surrounding cities in New Jersey—Hamilton or Trenton but never Princeton because most can't afford to live here. Even being around them highlighted my own quickly accumulating privilege—I didn't fit in a space that I would have a year before.

I "ascended" during my sophomore year to working in the Gender and Sexuality Studies office because I had met the program manager my freshman year when she was conducting her dissertation research on first-generation and low-income students. We connected. I networked. This is what being invited into privilege does: It spawns and generates more privilege, creating pathways for better futures.

I am a bisexual female. This is how I identify myself to my family. Learning what it means to be "queer" has been a recent realization for me, something that I am struggling to come to terms with even as I type. The stereotype around being queer is that it's an identity for those of a higher class status. I keep wondering why this is the case. Why aren't people like my mother or the ones I grew up with not allowed access to being queer or to the notion of exploring gender and sexual orientation? Furthermore, why is it that the people who love me most in the world cannot interface with me when I talk about queerness, about why queer sexual education matters, or even use the term *queer*? My grandmother still winces when I use the word to talk about myself.

I realize now there are two notions of queerness: one of being gay, and one of being queer in terms of one's politics and attitude toward the world.

This is why we see things like gay Republicans—because, although radical politics and queerness have been linked for decades as queerness becomes more socially acceptable, it becomes less radical and more pliant to other types of political leanings. In my hometown, it was more or less acceptable in a public sense to be gay but not necessarily queer. This dichotomy shows up in my conversations with the people I love. They ask, "Why do you have to *act* that way? Why does everything have to be a fight for your life? Why is everything such a big deal?" This has led me to understand being queer as being explicitly politically left of center and viewing one's (a)sexuality and gender as inextricably a part of oneself. This has also allowed me to understand why my family can understand that I like women but cannot understand why I talk about queerness.

Of course, social class is not just a financial issue; it is also about access to knowledge. Access to knowledge doesn't always correlate with class, but the two are unavoidably connected. There are times, such as in my current situation, where the two are different. Although I am poor, I am surrounded by and have access to a vast wealth of knowledge on what it means to be queer, whereas the people I mentioned earlier do not have access to that knowledge. Within the academy, we pretend that educating people is a burden we shouldn't have to bear, when in reality it is. We are gatekeepers of knowledge, and we decide who gets access to that knowledge.

Being low income in the academy has challenged my identities and the way I view myself. It has made me question whether I truly get to consider myself as *low income* or if I even want to use the term. This is also partly why I have turned to using *poor. Low income* carries a sanitary feel and allows those who employ it from the outside to maintain a certain distance from the real issues that being low income means; it allows people outside of the identity to make presumptions about me.

Calling myself poor both surprises the people I talk to on a daily basis and makes them acknowledge me—as if they cannot believe I would dare to describe myself in such a way. Therefore, they listen because I must have something important to say. I also use it because I want to believe it brings me closer to who I was before I came to Princeton, begging to be noticed by the world, begging for the world to care about me.

Narrative Analysis

The stories of Daniel, Kevyanna, and Téa exemplify what the literature tells us about the experiences of students from poor and working-class backgrounds in higher education while also adding nuance and humanness to that literature by showcasing how even when students share a dimension of identity, it may manifest differently in each individual. Collectively, these students name both the complexity of defining one's social class and how it weaves with the other dimensions of their identities, with Daniel mentioning race/ethnicity and Téa discussing sexuality. They talk about how their social class identities are invisible, unspoken, and misunderstood and the isolation they can feel in higher education based on a campus culture that plays to middle- and upper class ways of being. Kevyanna and Téa discuss how they manage straddling social classes among their peers and work-study coworkers and why they choose to identify with one social class term over another (*modern-day working class* and *poor*, respectively) and what those terms mean for them. This confirms the subjective nature of social class and the need to ask students how they identify.

The students share the financial pressures they have experienced throughout their lives and into their college experiences and how money can inhibit access and opportunity, particularly with the rising costs of tuition, fees, and other associated expenses. Téa points out that colleges and universities should not stop the equity work at access but consider how to support students while they are on campus. Daniel speaks candidly about challenges he has faced in the classroom, having to teach himself how to read and think critically and encountering resistance from others when he tries to share his experiences during classroom discussions. Kevyanna mentions the obstacles (e.g., costs, time) that poor and working-class students face when trying to engage in the cocurricular and the compromises that result (e.g., less social capital), and she describes how class markers such as clothing are noticed on campus.

Classism also shows up in their stories in various forms. Daniel mentions his feelings of resentment toward more affluent students as a nod toward upward classism and his peers' views of poor and working-class folks as free-loaders, an example of downward classism. Kevyanna describes the lateral classism of her peers misidentifying her as having a silver spoon because of some material goods she acquired. It is clear from the students' stories that social class is salient in their higher education journeys and they experience classism in the academy.

3

THE GRADUATE
STUDENT PERSPECTIVE

Narratives by Constanza A. Cabello, Dylan R. Dunn,
and Carmen Rivera

G raduate school is hard work. Add to it the dynamics of class amid
those from poor or working-class backgrounds, and navigating the
academy becomes even harder. Managing coursework, work, life,
and a more elusive, elitist class culture than the undergraduate experience
is all part of the package with, again, little direction or conversation in the
process. Figuring out where each piece of life fits to complete the degree is
like an academic puzzle. Constanza (Connie) A. Cabello, a doctoral student
at Northeastern University, Dylan R. Dunn, a master's student at Colorado
State University, and Carmen Rivera, a doctoral student at Colorado State
University, share with us the complexity of existing as students in the academy while being part of its administration. Their shared call to engage social
class in higher education in hopes of better supporting the next generation of
educators is a lesson for all of us.

Constanza A. Cabello's Story

When it comes to my social class identity, I've come to one conclusion: It's
complicated. I didn't really think about my social class until I entered higher
education and actually had to start paying for school. As a current doctoral
student, my awareness about social class continues to be heightened. Perhaps
it's because I've reflected more, or maybe it's just because life is getting more
expensive (note: adulting is hard). In any case, I hope my narrative can shed
light on the ways in which social class impacts the holistic educational experience from pre–K through terminal degree attainment.

To understand a little bit about my relationship with social class, you need to know about my parents and how I grew up. My father is a strategic person who always has some master plan brewing. He thrives in the hustle. My pops loves a good challenge, and the mundane is unsettling to him. He has acquired an absurd amount of knowledge from education, life experience, and YouTube. He is a fixer who doesn't want to know the backstory; he just wants to resolve the problem to reduce any level of stress one is experiencing. My mom is skilled at a lot of random things. She is a quick learner and also likes a good challenge. She is silly, talkative, and hospitable, and she wants everyone around her to be happy.

My parents met in the 1980s in Chile and got engaged five months later. They move fast. Shortly after, my brother was born, and then 11 and a half months later I was born. Again, they move fast. As a baby, my brother had asthma and breathing complications. My parents knew they needed to get quality health care for him to have a chance at a normal life, and unfortunately, that care wasn't available in Chile. My father had family in Boston and heard about the world-renowned Boston Children's Hospital. So, in his typical fashion, he saw the problem, saw a solution, and went for it. That is how we landed in the United States in 1987.

In general, my parents had good lives growing up in Chile. My father's family was well off, and the children attended prestigious private schools. My mother's father owned a stationery store, and she too attended private schools. My father started university but never finished. My mother made it through high school by the skin of her teeth. Despite their different educational journeys, they both had great careers in Chile. My dad was an accountant, and my mom was a librarian.

Moving to the United States to get my brother health care was an act of necessity, not comfort. Pops knew a little English from school and had some family in the United States. My mom, in contrast, knew no English and was pretty unfamiliar with the United States. The truth is my parents had no intention of staying in the United States after my brother got the care he needed. Why would they, really? They could go back to the comforts of a familiar language, community, food, and so on. But my father noticed the higher education opportunities in the United States, specifically in Boston. My parents decided that they wanted their kids to go to school here, so we stayed.

Growing up in the United States, my family was working class. My parents both started out as janitors. They worked everywhere: offices, schools, department stores, and so on. I fondly remember playing in a barber school while my dad cleaned it. I enjoyed playing with the doll hair (aka: mannequins), pretending to be a teacher in the classroom, and helping my dad clean so that he would give me a dollar to get candy from the vending machine (a noteworthy life skill). My parents worked a lot, and maybe that's why I never remember being working class. My mom recently reminded me that we had virtually no furniture in our first apartment in Jamaica Plain (Boston). I don't remember this at all—maybe because I don't want to or maybe it didn't matter to me at the time. We always had what we needed for school, we played sports, and we were well dressed (except for bed; I had my brother's hand-me-down pajamas in an assortment of Ninja Turtle and World Wrestling Entertainment characters). As a kid, I didn't worry about money, generational wealth, or saving. I don't think most kids do.

When it was time to start school, we moved outside of Boston to a town that was diverse in many ways. My community had many different races, religions, and social classes. By the time I entered middle school, I felt middle class. This was probably because my father received a promotion and significant pay bump at his cleaning company and was now an operations manager. My mom also went from being the custodian at Filene's Basement to a store associate. I had my health, family, and "things" (e.g., brand-name clothes and a Nokia cell phone), so I was doing pretty well compared with many.

Then it came time to apply for college. Now remember, this is a major reason that we stayed in the United States. My college selection process went like this: (a) What schools near me go far in March Madness? and (b) Which schools does my guidance counselor think I can get into? My parents did their best to counsel us on admissions, but they didn't have much context, which is often the classic first-generation college student experience. Their primary concern was that we went to a good school that wasn't going to put us in debt forever. My brother went to the closest business school to study accountancy (following in my dad's footsteps). I was aware it was extremely expensive. I figured that because I had no clue what I wanted to study, I was better off picking a more affordable public institution. The University of Connecticut (UConn) was a sports dynasty, far enough from home where I felt somewhat independent, and gave me a scholarship. So, I went to UConn.

I quickly realized being a broke college student was defined differently. There was not being able to eat, and there was not having enough money to go on spring break vacations. Everyone thought they were broke based on their friend group. I got my first credit card when I was in college. I remember my parents signing for it with me, and they reminded me daily it was to be used only for emergencies. The few times I used the card, I produced a brief for my purchase, the rationale, and the repayment plan and sent it to my mother via text. She would always respond with, "Okay, that's fine." Today my mother calls me cheap, to which I remind her that she instilled this "for emergencies only" mentality in me! I also had a work-study job that was a saving grace in many ways. In the midst of having two kids in college, my dad had an idea: quit his job to start his own company. This plan was terrifying, but I always knew he would be successful. I worked enough to pay for most of my extras (true extras such as socializing, guac on my burrito, and the million sorority T-shirts). I always had what I needed and more. I worried about the loans I was accruing, but I figured if my dad wasn't freaking out yet, then I wouldn't either. Plus, in comparison with my brother's debt, I wasn't doing too badly.

After UConn, I attended Central Connecticut State University to get my master's. It was clear that graduate school was not an option unless it was free. At this point, I understood how much debt I was in because Sallie Mae was ruthless. I applied to one school and one internship that would cover tuition and provide a stipend. I was accepted and went about my life.

Now, I'm a nerd. After being out of graduate school for four years, I started to feel the desire to go back. I never thought I would pursue a doctorate. Frankly, I didn't know many people who had a terminal degree, especially people like me: a first-generation college student from an immigrant family. I had great mentors who made me realize it was actually attainable. So, I went for it. I thought about all of the typical program selection debates: EdD versus PhD, online versus in person, higher education versus other concentrations, and so on. In the end, I realized I needed a program I could finish and pay for. Everything else was flexible.

I was most stressed out about the financial piece of starting a program. Some people told me to consider a full-time PhD program, but the thought of not working a traditional full-time job was not something I could comprehend. I had worked since high school, and I couldn't rationalize how I would not have a salary at this point in my life (see Destiny's Child's song "Bills, Bills, Bills"). I also didn't know enough about how people finance terminal degrees to even consider the options. I had to keep working full–time.

I applied to one program: the Northeastern University Doctorate of Education. I was accepted and didn't tell anyone until I knew I could actually go. I made a budget, looked at my expenses, and realized coming up with more than $10,000 a year to pay for school was going to be impossible. My work benefits didn't cover tuition remission for Northeastern, and there was no way I was going to take out another loan. I refused to put everything on a credit card, and my "for emergencies only" mentality made it more difficult to make doctoral studies a reality.

My parents taught me that, in life, you must make sacrifices for what you really want. When I looked at my budget, I figured out that the only way I could come up with money was to eliminate some of my expenses. I humbly asked my parents whether I could move back in with them, and they welcomed me. I realize how blessed/privileged I am to have had that option. I also wasn't partnered and had no dependents. Although the last thing I wanted to do as a 20-something-year-old was to move into my parents' basement, I knew it was the only way to make this work. I admit, at first, I was horrified. I didn't tell many colleagues I was moving home because I was embarrassed I needed to live at home to pay for school.

Once I was in my doctoral program, I quickly began to see social class show up in different ways. When you enter a program, people ask you why you are doing it or what your aspirations are when you finish. One consideration was the fact that I literally could count the number of Latinas with doctorates I knew on one hand, but I definitely didn't know any Chileans or immigrants. I want to change that narrative. My parents drilled into my head that education was the key to success. They worked so hard to change their social class over the years, and they believed education would provide even more opportunities for my brother and me. Education equaled career opportunities, career opportunities equaled financial stability, and financial stability was a force in creating healthy and happy lives. It makes me uncomfortable to admit that I believe money is a factor in happiness. But the truth, for me anyway, is that in our current political, social, and educational landscapes, people with money have less stress (from the outside looking in anyway). I wish it were different. I am working to dismantle systems of oppression that historically create a culture of haves and have-nots.

I remember attending my first doctoral program concentration meeting. We broke into small groups and were asked to share why we wanted to be doctors. I'll never forget an older male telling me how he already had a doctorate and was doing this one "for fun." I'm pretty sure my mouth dropped, not because I was impressed but because the privilege oozed out of his mouth with no hesitation. Once I composed myself, I realized I needed to get away from the judgments I had about different motivations to be in the space. I also learned that my motivation was being judged by others. To this day, I profess that those who have doctorates are not necessarily the smartest people in the world. However, they are often folks like me who have smarts and discipline in addition to privilege and access.

Beyond tuition and motivation, social class shows up in other places in doctoral programs. There are the expenses: laptop, books, software, transcriptions, and so on. I figured if I had the cash, I would be okay. However, as I learned during my undergraduate experience, while money can get you material things, the most important thing it can buy you is social capital. Someone once told me that getting a doctorate should be easy for me because I'm smart. Easy? I am not convinced doctoral programs are easy for anyone, but I do think some people have the capital to navigate doctoral studies more

easily because of social class. For example, did you have dictionaries or ency-
clopedias in your house growing up? Did you attend private school? Have
you always had your basic life needs met (e.g., food, housing) so you could
actually focus while at school? Did you have access to people with knowledge
about the U.S. higher education system or who had terminal degrees? Can
you speak academia? These are just a few of the ways in which social class
impacts the educational experience, and it shows up no matter what level of
education one is pursuing. I left with the question, "For whom is education
easy or at least easier?"

People now see me as a middle-class woman who has degrees, owns a
nice car, and enjoys good health and wonderful vacations. Honestly, this is
how I see myself, too. I know there are assumptions about who I am and
how I've grown up. I am sure people think I've had it easy. I actually think I
have had it easier than many. I regret nothing about my social class journey
because it has made me who I am. As my father recently put it, "In reality, we
have always been rich; for the most part we have good health, we work hard,
and we try to do the right things for others." He is right.

It's my hope that through our collective story sharing, we can change the
narrative about social class in the academy. Often people will call education
the great equalizer in society. The great equalizer is a metaphor for access to
education, yet access isn't enough. What happens when people make it into
the pearly gates of higher education? We must have more dialogue on the
ways in which social class permeates education at all levels—from pre–K
through terminal degree attainment.

Dylan R. Dunn's Story: Skipping Class: The Experience of a Graduate Student From the Working Class

I was approaching the end of a graduate program interview where I was asked
about my journey into student affairs. I spoke about my siblings in recovery
from heroin addiction and alcoholism, how overwhelming it was to fly for
the first time to get to the interview, and the internal role conflict of wanting
to advance in an educational system that I still knew little about. I knew I
had been inspired and empowered by professionals whom I could never truly
pay back, yet I felt a deep calling to pay it all forward. I was confused as tears
formed in the eyes of the panel of interviewers. They explained that my voice
and my story of a lower class upbringing were needed in higher education
and student affairs. I wasn't sure whether to feel awkward, misunderstood, or
humbled because my experiences were normal in my eyes—they were part of
the life story with which I was most familiar and comfortable.

A similar experience occurred a year and a half later at the same institution during a preliminary review of the culminating project for my master's program. The committee of higher education professionals began to push me to believe my point of view was legitimate and important in this field of work. They recognized in my writing that I was hesitant to consider myself and my stories as important or critical to the academic or practitioner sides of student affairs. They had noticed a struggle that I had suppressed: the struggle I continuously felt regarding the lack of recognition of social class as a legitimate or urgent topic of conversation in higher education. I was reminded of the times that faculty members had commented on my papers with statements such as, "Wow, that must have been hard" or "You must struggle with the fact that things like that happened around you growing up." Meanwhile, my internal response was always, "Actually, that's kind of just how life works."

This story shares my perspective as a graduate student in student affairs from the lower class. I explain the internal struggles I have felt, the power I have found, and the role of higher education as I see it in my experiences. My hope is that you leave this chapter not with answers but wanting to ask large-scale questions about how we can better serve students at all levels from backgrounds that may be similar to, or even vastly different from, mine, but with one thing in common: a profound impact on their life from growing up in or experiencing lower class life.

While beginning my graduate program more than a year ago, I remember seeing that we had a class session dedicated to social class theory. I waited patiently for more than half of the semester. About two weeks before that session, I had a mid semester check-in with the instructor. We spoke about my background, my progress in the course, my professional passions, and how it all came together to formulate my plans for the future. I spoke about my incredibly White hometown and its two universities that no one could afford to attend. I struggled aloud to make sense of my feelings of personal responsibility to return home to help young adults like myself growing up. At the same time, I considered the personal pain that comes from returning to my hometown and being reminded of just how much it is not home for me anymore.

Two weeks later, I walked into Student Development Theory looking forward to a rigorous discussion of the social class identity development theories. Instead, I got: "There really aren't available theories on social class identity development. Here are some articles and approaches that we believe apply to the role of social class in higher education." We quickly spoke about Yosso's (2005) cultural wealth model and Bourdieu's social reproduction thesis (Tzanakis, 2011). In short, students from the working and lower classes enter our educational system without access to the types of social capital valued by the middle and upper classes, which serve as the foundation of our educational system, and therefore are made to either adapt and change or fail. Meanwhile, our marginalized students—particularly students of color— bring with them various other types of cultural capital that are valuable and can be drawn on for student success within more inclusive pedagogy.

As the lecture continued, I sat back in my chair in a sudden existential crisis. The material presented to me regarding social class made me feel like my work and the work I was doing with students was simply a long and painful audition for the middle class for myself and my students. Yet I was an agent of that. I was a gatekeeper with shiny leather boots and a collared shirt. Although I had been told during my interview that the voice of the working class was important and needed in student affairs, that notion now felt absurd.

Although each university has its own nuanced approach to supporting students from limited-income backgrounds, one thing remains consistent from my perspective: the feeling of dismissal surrounding social class identity in ways as blatant as lacking literature to the glorification of the financial struggles that "everyone" faces during the college years—a culture of jokes about mac and cheese and ramen for dinner each night. As a graduate student looking to pursue a career in student affairs, I have heard countless presumptuous comments to the tune of, "Well, I'm sure you didn't go into student affairs for the money!" This conversation starter, intending to ask why I am going into student affairs, quickly silences the reality that what I earn as a graduate student exceeds the wages of my siblings with children in their single-income households back home.

However, while writing the previous paragraph, I felt the dissonance that my experience creates. I am currently a graduate student with a well-paying assistantship in a state farther away from home than most of my family has ever been. I have spent much of my life running from my social class identity and the experiences that were facilitated largely because of my family's lower class status. However, the more involved I become with higher education—my ticket away from small-town Ohio—the more salient I find my lower class experiences to who I really am and how I approach my work. The more I engage with the culture of higher education, the more I identify with the experiences of my life before college. I now have the positional power and privilege to deeply and boldly support students from lower class backgrounds, yet I am also comfortably seated financially within the middle class. Where I now have the tools, education, and dissonance to begin to understand my social class identity, I am also slowly becoming more financially distanced from that identity. In what feels like the opening and closing of a door at the same time, I find both empowerment to share my life experiences and a deep conflict between pride and guilt because of my current lifestyle.

As a graduate student from the lower class who is now financially independent and stable, I find that my lower class identity is still relevant to my experience because it has provided me with skills and talents that won't go away, even as my class status seems to evolve. The same skills that helped me persist as an undergraduate student are now tools helping me earn my master's degree and develop students—skills such as resilience and complex critical thinking that came, in part, from seeing siblings commit crimes to feed their substance use and learning to love them anyway. My approach grounded in candor and storytelling was developed as I held on to every word during hard-hitting holiday conversations in our smoke-filled living room—where curse words were used with artistic precision and affect. These same skills and approach helped me begin to come to terms with the complexity of White poverty but not feel daunted by the amount of self-work necessary to approach the nuances of simultaneous privilege and struggle. I use this same approach to help students in conduct hearings to feel supported, cared for, but also personally accountable for their actions and making the most of the amazing opportunity of a higher education. For me, this magic of social class identity, the incredible variety of skills and experiences, is lost with an approach that seems to begin with financial aid and end with the hope that students find, and know enough to seek out, support and involvement to help them persist despite whatever they left back home.

I believe that higher education and student affairs can do more to better serve lower class students, and I believe all students by honoring social class as a valid identity and important experience through storytelling. Especially in conversations about power and privilege, when we do not fully recognize social class as an identity with great impact, we can quickly reinforce bias and systems of oppression. However, through intersectional storytelling and showing compassion with ourselves through being honest with our own stories, we can encourage many students to both integrate the pieces of their identity and refuse to simplify or conflate identities for others. If we can notice the importance of acknowledging the complexity that social class presents and the impact of its intersections with dominant and marginalized identities, we can begin to dismantle struggles within identity groups that can, in part, be rooted in access and financial privilege.

With lower class identity being commonly coded with shame, worthlessness, and laziness throughout my experience growing up, it is important to assist students in the identity development of understanding the ways in which social class has led them to contribute to social injustice as well as developing tools that can be positively used for the success of themselves and others. I have clear memories of entering conversations about inequalities as a first-year student where a professional explained many of my identities as having power and privilege. Sitting in that residence hall lobby, I thought to myself

> Come to my hometown and tell me about the privilege of Whiteness with the front page of the newspaper in front of you talking about the heroin epidemic, chronic unemployment, and the utter lack of hope. Come sit at our Thanksgiving table and tell everyone they have privilege. Let's see how that conversation goes.

I could have, as I believe that many students do, left that conversation and never turned back or reconsidered my privileges and the incredible insight that can come from interrogating the intersection of Whiteness and poverty. I could have dismissed the jargon and held even more tightly to the story I had been told growing up—the subtle and not-so-subtle bigotry and White supremacist beliefs and actions. I believe that when we fail to properly recognize and research the complexity of social class identity and implicitly deny its importance, we run the risk of dismissing many of our students from conversations about social justice, especially by failing to meet students where they are in their development. I believe we shut the door on compassion and connection for students whose social class identity is especially salient. As a result, here I am as a graduate student, still deeply struggling with my own social class identity in a system in which I'm not sure I truly belong, navigating how to best use my experiences to empower students like me to tell their story and find support in making sense of it all.

Carmen Rivera's Story: If Only We Could Have Filled Bank Accounts With Cultural Wealth

Growing up, my mom constantly told me things such as, "We may not have much, *mija*, but you must always take pride in who you are and what you do have" or "It's not what you have but who you are that matters." I come from generations of northern New Mexicans who were and are proud of our heritage and have built a legacy of being supremely resourceful. My dad and grampo taught us to save every usable nail or piece of wire because "they come in handy and you can use them again." I was taught in overt and covert ways that wealth was much more than the money we had. We had very little of that. We valued more than money. We valued time. We valued family. We valued the earth. We valued friends. When you had these, not having money didn't seem as bad. This context continues to inform how I see myself in terms of social class and how I place value on money.

I didn't know what working poor was as a kid; I didn't know that's what we were. Many of my neighbors, my schoolmates, and the families with whom we spent time came from a similar financial background. I went to an elementary school that I would now assume got subsidies to serve the large number of poor kids who attended. We got things such as dental care, free/reduced lunch and breakfast, and vision checks. It wasn't until I got to junior high that I started to see material differences between my peers and me. I was placed in the "enriched" track of classes. I was one of the few Brown kids, and for the first time I felt like I had "less than." My peers started asking me about the brand of my clothing or sneakers. I had never been asked those things. When I brought those questions home, my mom deflected. By the time I got to high school, I was focused on getting a job of my own so that I could afford to buy the clothes and shoes my friends had. I accomplished that, and I was also then helping my family with supplemental income. I started seeing the strategic maneuvering of making the gut-wrenching decisions of which bills to pay that month. My mom had previously guarded me from that. I started seeing things differently.

I enrolled in Upward Bound in my sophomore year of high school. My mom said I had to when she learned about the opportunity. She was in the program when she was in high school. It is a federal TRiO program that focuses on helping first-generation/low-income high school students get into college. I knew I wanted that. I wanted to go to college. My family wanted me to go to college. I went to the six-week summer program, and for the first time, I felt like college was a real possibility. I had no clue how I was going to pay for it. My parents told me I had to get scholarships. I would be the first in my family to do it, so I needed to listen to my teachers and advisers. They had that kind of faith in my educators. Thankfully, those folks saw potential in me to guide me. I was a lucky one in that way, and not all of my friends had that same luck. My confirmation teacher at church took me on a college visit out of state, and I felt a spark that I was afraid to acknowledge. I wanted to leave home to go to college. I was so worried about what it would cost my family, and yet I was so drawn to the independence and adventure that I perceived going to the university an hour away as too much of a compromise.

When I got accepted to a university that also happened to be 500 miles away, I was proud, excited, and torn. I wanted to go so desperately, yet I worried about what it meant for my mom, for my family. I was the oldest kid. I had worked to help out since I was 15 years old. It would be a sacrifice for my whole family for me to go and realize this dream. Although I was admitted, I didn't get enough scholarship money, and it meant that I had to go to the school an hour away. I was devastated. I tried to be excited because I would be going there with my friends and I could still live an hour away. Although she didn't like to see me disappointed, my mom was relieved. I would still be going to college, but I would remain close to home.

Then the letter came. I got a scholarship that would make it possible for me to attend the university in Colorado. I was so happy I could have burst. Yet I was also holding the gravity of what this meant for my family. The scholarship didn't cover all my costs, so I was still going to have to take out student loans. My parents didn't love that idea. I called the financial aid office, and they said that I could take a parent loan. That wasn't an actual possibility. My parents did not earn enough money or have enough credit to qualify for a parent loan. I had to take out a loan from a bank that first year to cover the remaining costs.

I convinced my mom that it would be okay for me to go, and I promised to return home to New Mexico on graduation. She wanted me to be happy and to go to college, so she agreed, despite her fears. We weren't able to afford to go to orientation during the summer, so I had to attend the last session right before school started. I had a tough first year. I got a job right when I arrived. I saw my peers getting financial help from their families. My mom would send me care packages with socks, food, and sweets to share with my roommate. I loved getting those boxes. I got a calling card to be able to call home on Sundays. I struggled to know how to manage my money. The subsequent years, I got student loans and borrowed more than I needed to subsidize my work. I would get refund checks and think it was the best payday ever. It helped me do things and buy things that made me feel like I was like everyone else. My loans even helped me study abroad. I was doing things I never could have dreamed up. I felt like I was changing my fate.

Coming Full Circle

My first job out of college was in many ways a dream job for any person who was a Hispanic studies and Spanish double major. I was working with youth to help them get to college. The stars aligned, and I landed a job working for an Upward Bound program. Although it was a great opportunity for me, it meant that I would have to delay my return home to my family. I was going to be helping students who were just like me. What I didn't plan for was my low salary. I thought that by going to college, I would have secured a better financial future for myself. That future couldn't come soon enough. Although I absolutely loved my job, I was struggling to make ends meet every month. I had to start paying back my student loans. I had rent, a car payment, a phone bill, insurance, food, and every other cost it takes to maintain life as a 22-year-old single person. The real world was proving to be harder than college in many ways.

I got my benefits package from my institution within the first month of getting hired. It might as well have been in another language. I had to pick a health insurance plan. What? I had to pick a retirement plan. What? Also, pick a life insurance plan. What? I had not one idea about how to make those decisions. I was overwhelmed and didn't know where to turn. These tasks seemed like something I needed to take a class on to understand. I hadn't grown up talking about insurance or retirement plans. In fact, I remember the stress it would cause if we had to go to the doctor because of the unplanned expense it represented. We didn't go to the doctor regularly. My parents didn't have a pension or retirement plan. I made choices on educated guesses. I rationalized that I was going to have to work forever, so my retirement wouldn't matter that much. Although I would like to say I have grown and learned more in this regard, I still find myself struggling with knowing how to make financial decisions all these years later.

Social class continued to show up for me in unexpected ways as a professional. I had my first professional development opportunity to attend a national professional association conference. I had no idea what that meant. I was excited but had a ton of questions and was worried I wouldn't be able to go because I couldn't afford it. What do I wear? What do I have to pay for? How many roommates can I bunk with to make it more affordable? Luckily, I had colleagues and supervisors who shared many of my identities, and they addressed these concerns before I even had to ask. This was one of the many benefits of working for an organization that centered on experiences of low-income folks. It also showed up in the way I developed programs. I was always looking for the most affordable way to do something. If we took our students on trips, we were packing lunches and trying to get as many things as possible for free. Those skills of resourcefulness and creativity were helpful in this context. Also, because I was working with low-income students, I saw so much of my experience in their lives: Families who wanted to provide for their kids but were struggling to do so. I was able to help in some ways, and in others I still didn't know what to do. As I continued to grow as a professional, I reflected on my own experiences of my social class and how they socialized me and remained a constant issue for me to navigate in my life.

Now You Think You're All Good

One of the most significant by-products of my continued journey in higher education is the distance that I feel from my family. When I earned my bachelor's degree, everyone was so happy and proud. I had carved a new path. At that point, I thought that was it. Then I learned about advanced graduate degrees, and I wanted that, too! So, when I told my family I applied and was accepted into a master's degree program, they were happy but unsure of what it meant. Honestly, I wasn't entirely sure either. On one visit home, I was talking to a cousin and an aunt of mine, and they asked me about how school was going. They couldn't figure out why I was still in school after already graduating. They asked me, "What, now you think you're all good?" I know they were giving me a hard time and teasing me and it wasn't malicious. However, it did strike a nerve. As I continued my education, it made me more and more different than my family. With each visit home, I was reminded that while I will always be from there, I'm not the same as when I left. Some of that is great in that one of the main objectives of education is to grow. However, it makes me feel out of place sometimes.

In many ways, deciding to pursue a doctoral degree was rooted in my desire to continue to make my family proud and to use the resources afforded to me to represent my family and my people in higher education. I can take nine credits per year as a study privilege at the institution where I work. That was one of the factors that I considered when applying for my program, despite being able to afford to pay now. I am entirely focused on making sure that I know what classes I have to take and in what order so that I don't pay for a single credit that I don't need to graduate. I've also learned that my social class experiences, as my other social identities, have influenced the type of researcher and scholar that I am. I feel compelled to make a difference, to make things more equitable for people with my voice and platform as a researcher. Now that I'm nearing the end of my doctoral studies, I'm still feeling the dissonance of creating distance. In fact, in my preliminary exam defense, I was asked about the process of earning my degree, and I couldn't respond without getting emotional. I don't know how to reconcile that, and yet I am proud of what I am doing and my family is proud too.

More Money, Same Frame

When I talk about social class and growing up poor, I usually land in a place of pride. I feel like I am my family's dream realized. I find community with folks who had a similar upbringing. Inevitably, we talk about government cheese, being latchkey kids, and having to figure out how to fit in. We breeze past feelings of shame and rush to get to the pride we have in having come from there. I continue to make money mistakes despite being middle class now and living in a dual-income family. I both worry about not having money and spend it when I have it because I want to live a life that is not always constrained by the worry of not having enough. We are able to make ends meet and still have money for leisure. Yet I still have anxiety about retirement, insurance, and savings. I save plastic containers and use towels until they are frayed on the ends. At the same time, I pay for conveniences such as Prime memberships and know about earning points for flying and staying in hotels. I navigate in a middle-class world from a poor kid's lens. I don't know how to build wealth or how to teach my sons about money. I paradoxically feel secure about where I have landed as well as unsure about what do with it all and how to prepare for the future.

Narrative Analysis

The writers discuss skills they learned throughout their social class of origin, which they use to navigate life. From resourcefulness to resilience to hard work, these skills, whether required or role modeled by family, are a part of their story to persist through their degrees, work space, and life in general. In Connie's pursuit of her master's and doctoral degrees, she talks about lessons learned from the hustle of her dad and the hard work of her mom, and Dylan finds his resilience and critical thinking skills useful in dealing with life situations.

In their class shift, there is a sense of pride and responsibility to pay it forward. Dylan discusses his feelings of needing to go back home to help those who grew up similarly to him. Through her roles as a researcher and a scholar, Carmen shares feeling "compelled to make a difference, to make things more equitable for people with my voice and platform as a researcher" (p. 61, this volume). They all have a consciousness that their education, resulting in privilege, extends beyond their individual self, and they all have a desire to give back to the community. In this desire, there is also a shared tension of feeling out of place with where they grew up. There is a consciousness that they are no longer the same as when they left (for college) or hold a sense of pain in their return home.

As the contributors share their racial identities, there is a difference in the ways in which they discuss class in relation to their families. Carmen and Connie, both identifying as some form of Brown, discuss that their families regarded wealth beyond money. It is about hard work, being healthy, and valuing aspects such as family, friends, time, and the earth. In contrast, Dylan, identifying as White, minimally mentions class in relation to his family and does so in terms of job pay and poverty.

There are also different themes found across each of their stories. Within Connie's narrative, there is a debt-related theme. She shares the ways in which she has tried to avoid debt, from working during her master's and doctoral degrees to having a "for emergencies policy" mentality for credit cards, instilled by her mom at an early age. The thread woven into Dylan's story is about wanting to use his positional power to empower students who come from a similar social class background. He discusses his use of story-telling to better understand his own class story as it intersects with his other identities and, in doing so, he can model for others to do the same. From her involvement as a student and professional with Upward Bound to her anxiety around insurance and retirement, Carmen's story is woven with the theme of navigating systems—both understanding and not understanding the systems within the academic setting. Luckily, with this skill of navigation, she is able to be a doctoral student on her institution's dime while working full-time. She, like Connie, uses her skills for the hustle to support students and her own livelihood while staying true to her values.

In the obtainment of degrees, there is a shared understanding from each writer of the privilege in doing so. They recognize the impact their social class background has had on their ability to navigate the academy and the respon-sibility to elevate social class within their sphere of influences and communi-ties, both on campus and in their personal lives.

4

THE EARLY CAREER ADMINISTRATOR PERSPECTIVE

Narratives by Armina Khwaja Macmillan, Timothy M. Johnson, and Brenda Lee Anderson Wadley

Entering a career field can be a daunting process, particularly when you already know from prior contextual experiences that the environment, in this case the academy, has historically marginalized one or more of your identities. Regardless of whether you begin an administrative career in higher education at age 22 or 52, you will likely experience a negotiation process to figure out who you need or want to be as an administrator and how that may align or conflict with who the academy will allow you to be. This dance of sorts is described by three early professionals: (a) Armina Khwaja Macmillan from Seattle University in Washington, (b) Timothy M. Johnson from Guilford College in North Carolina, and (c) Brenda Lee Anderson Wadley from the University of Arizona. Their stories inform us how early career professionals experience the beginning of their higher education careers and continue their journeys in understanding their social class identity.

Armina Khwaja Macmillan's Story: How I Passed My Social Class

Most of my life has been spent in relation to navigating social class and mobilizing my advancement through it. Similar to many other immigrant parents, mine consistently recited that my future was not to involve serving customers from behind the counter of a convenience store; they would constantly reiterate that I deserved a better living. I often did not understand what that meant. Regardless of what our household income stated (the good times and the not-so-good times), on the outside looking in, everything appeared as it should. I guess one could call it "class passing" because outward presentation, perception, and image were upheld. I vividly remember one of my sixth-grade teachers handing my mom a brochure about cotillion and etiquette courses; I have no recollection of the price tag, but I remember being excited to learn proper manners and understand where my classmates spent their weekends. I learned to carry myself appropriately through networking dinners, pageants, and interviews. Yet difference still existed when friends traveled across the country or world by plane, and I only first stepped onto a jet in my mid teens.

The only route to social class mobilization of which I was aware was education; in my family, education was and continues to be a top priority. The irony is that in order to not only receive an education but also retain and persist through educational institutions, one needs money, but the whole reason you're getting an education is to one day earn money. I am a proud product of public education, but even public schools have their costs: honor society dues, cross-country uniforms, and evening hours when I could not work my part-time job because I had a choir concert. I felt incredibly grateful if my mom came to one of my concerts because I knew she left work early, did not even get a chance to change out of her uniform, yet she was still willing to be there to help make the iconic choir punch.

I know there are people in the world who believe that joining clubs and having extracurricular activities is not essential to growth in college. I wholeheartedly disagree; involvement begets feelings of community, connection, and belonging. Research will certainly prove that, and my own personal experience holds true to Astin's (2001), Lambert's (2004), and others' findings. I would not have gained study groups, friendships, time management skills, or leadership potential without these activities. I joined a National Panhellenic Conference sorority in college but had to wait until my second year to complete the recruitment process because of finances. My family and I had a decent arrangement: If I could maintain the Georgia Helping Outstanding Pupils Educationally (HOPE) Scholarship throughout college, my parents (and my fluctuating Pell eligibility) would pay for room and board, and I would pay for my membership dues. Prior to this arrangement, some wonderful folks at my religious home sent me to Boston to tour colleges, and I begged my parents to let me go. I convinced myself that I would and could go to college in New England, only to face the reality that out-of-state education was not a feasible option. I truly loved that trip and experience to learn about higher education, but now I can see that my parents were most likely protecting me from getting my hopes up too high. I only applied to three schools because college admissions costs set the tone early:

two in state and my one out-of-state dream school. I would end up attending Georgia Tech on the Georgia HOPE Scholarship, which honestly placed me in the best financial and emotional situation.

Although the Georgia HOPE Scholarship has profoundly impacted my life, it certainly is not perfect. The program was the nation's first statewide merit-based scholarship program and has increased access to postsecondary institutions for students who belong to marginalized populations by decreasing the costs of college education. That said, just because HOPE scholarship students have access to affordable education, it does not mean they are set up to succeed throughout college and eventually graduate. Of course the scholarship money helped, but the biggest factor of my college career that made me feel connected to undergraduate education was my involvement in sorority life and new student orientation. These pockets of campus gave me unique friendships, professional opportunities, academic assistance, and a place to call home. Even better, two of my positions on campus also offered stipends based on performance. I commit a lot of myself to succeeding, and I was devastated when the students we served voted to revisit the stipends our executive board was receiving. I had quit my part-time job off campus to balance my commitments, and I feared that future students would not be given the resources needed to be as connected and successful as I felt.

When making the decision to go into student affairs and higher education, there was no shortage of people doubting my decision: "Why would you go to a top-ranked undergraduate institution and then choose to go work in education?" If I'm being honest, I still get asked that question and roll my eyes every time. The only people in my life to whom I truly had a hard time explaining my decision were my parents. This was partly because, as a first-generation college student, I often avoided explaining higher education concepts, and partly because the salary or prestige of being a college administrator is not what they had planned for my future. For me, my school selection came down to a unique personal decision: to move away from home and my comfort zone. I still hold that my biggest accomplishment in life thus far has been my time in graduate school largely because of the personal transition and growth I experienced during those two years.

I moved from Georgia to Texas; then Texas to Massachusetts; and, most recently, Massachusetts to Washington. During each search, I was set on accepting a position outside of residence life. In fact, for each move, I applied to only one residence life position among several other opportunities. Each time I have been offered and accepted the residence life position. There are many reasons I have chosen residence life: city living, supervision of staff, proximity to my partner, breadth of responsibility, graduate school tuition remission, and so on. Although I have often downplayed these benefits, the biggest reasons are the free room (and sometimes meal plan), the graduate school tuition benefits (I was conditioned to avoid any and all debt, so this was a golden ticket), and the ease of moving across the country. When you do not need to search for an apartment or transport furniture, things become a lot easier and cheaper. Starting a new job is stressful enough when filling out a W-4, figuring out insurance, sorting through benefits, and navigating a new campus culture, not to mention that human resources paperwork and benefits are that much more difficult without the know-how and navigational capital (Yosso, 2005).

Let's be frank: Entry-level student affairs salaries are not generally high, especially when most individuals in the field have postgraduate degrees. I think a lot about our graduate students and the weight we place on them, especially without being aware of its implications. I'm guilty of this, too: promoting full-time, two-year master's programs coupled with part-time employment; the necessity of attending expensive conferences; setting expectations for attire in the workplace; and reprimanding for not communicating within the hierarchy properly. Most of these hold true for new and mid level professionals, too. The worst part, in my opinion, is that we recruit many individuals from low-income and underrepresented communities into the field, setting the tone that it is an inclusive place. It is the same area that tried to help you succeed as an undergraduate student, so of course it'll be just as wonderful when you join as a graduate student and/or professional. How often do we validate and affirm the concerns of our staff? How often do we set up an environment where they feel comfortable expressing concerns and asking questions about attire and event attendance? When we say we are having a departmental social, are our staff hearing,

> We are hosting a back-to-school event off campus, and the department has bought 2 appetizer plates for 20 staff members. We know that will not be enough food for everyone, but hopefully you can enjoy water for free. Oh, and if you do not come, it will reflect poorly on your commitment to the team.

That holds true for me, too. One of the main reasons that I wanted to work in higher education was to help build inclusive communities, specifically for students with marginalized identities. I would not come to realize until working professionally that there is a lot of work to do around inclusion among faculty and staff. Although it is hypocritical and frustrating, it makes sense. We work within a system that promotes hierarchy and yet sets a tone that talking about social class and capital is taboo. Most faculty and staff on campuses have earned graduate school degrees, which equate to earned social and cultural capital (Yosso, 2005). I would argue that we could divide faculty and staff into two groups. The first would be those who started from a privileged social class and, thus, had little difficulty navigating systems of education and maintain a social class identity from youth. The second would be those who started from a marginalized social class identity, who have through fortunate means navigated systems of education, and have mobilized upward from their youth. The unfortunate reality is that, within this second group, some are responsible for projecting their upward mobility onto students, assuming their individual success means it could be just as feasible for students, too. That concept sounds scarily close to hazing if you ask me.

Most days, I feel full of purpose working in higher education. Other days, I wonder how my values allow me to continue forward in an inaccessible and oppressive culture. Every day, I am reminded that the work I do, no matter how small, contributes to the larger goal of belonging and inclusion. The amount of trauma that our students, faculty, and staff are experiencing in today's climate makes inclusion more essential. When an undocumented student shares with me that they cannot come to a shift, I have the power to say, "Yes, and we'll make sure you can make up those hours elsewhere." When a graduate student cannot fly back on New Year's Day for move-in because flights are too expensive, how can I balance coverage while also holding financial burden? When our office is requiring an all-day training, I should seek funds to provide lunch. Let me assist in coordinating flights and hotel rooms for conferences so that we can then preserve funds and maximize university attendance.

I wish I had the power to grant all supervisors the empathy and courage required to act. I truly believe that small actions, no matter where you fall on an organizational chart, can truly make a difference in the satisfaction and retention of our students and staff members. It can be easy to say, "I don't have control over that" or "That's too hard." I want us to be unafraid to be uncomfortable by talking about social class and to know that social class includes money but is much more than only that. I do not want a student to fear losing compensation or scholarships, nor do I want staff members to feel reprimanded for actualizing forms of self-care and self-preservation. We do have control over that. It is hard, complex, and uncomfortable for people to not only recognize difference in others but also embrace and appreciate those differences as we begin to realize our own narrative has limited our perspectives. Creating an environment where our colleagues and students are encouraged to bring their whole authentic selves requires an open mind, empathy, and role modeling. However, being vulnerable is crucial if we want to eliminate barriers and truly help others succeed and belong.

Timothy (Tim) M. Johnson's Story: The Mattress in the Living Room

On January 2, 1991, Patricia Johnson brought her first-born child into the world on what used to be just her birthday. I, Timothy Michael Johnson, now share the greatest day in the world with my mother. We moved to Davidson, North Carolina when I was around age five, and all we had were a few bags of clothes, some pots and pans, a box spring, and a mattress. I remember my mother making that box spring and mattress so much more exciting than it really was. She would tell me we were having a sleepover and created a fort that I could play inside to hide the fact that we could not afford more furniture. I told myself that when I was my mother's age, I would be able to fill the living room with a couch, a table, and a TV. It was important to me to fill a space that once contained nothing more than a box spring and a mattress.

Where we lived up until about the third grade would be considered the slums or low-income housing. In the small town of Davidson, North Carolina, this was the only apartment complex, and it was filled with at least 85% to 90% people of color, more specifically those who identified as Black. Luckily, the elementary school I attended was well resourced. At school, I had access to healthy meal options, manicured playgrounds, two teachers in each classroom, proper physical education equipment, all the books you could ever read, and even the Internet. When I returned home from school, my neighborhood had one slide, an outdated basketball court, and spotty grass, and no one I knew had access to the Internet or a computer. I lived in a single-parent home, with a mother who worked close to 10 hours a day and still found time to raise me. To paint an even more vivid picture, I was the only person of color in my classes until the second grade and the only Black student until the fourth grade.

The turning point of my early academic career was when my third-grade teachers told my mother I had attention-deficit/hyperactivity disorder because I asked too many questions, finished work at the same pace as my White counterparts (which she saw as problematic), and always inquired about what activity was coming next. My mother was not pleased and asked my other teachers if they thought the same thing. She was curious to know what the teachers thought about the other students—White students—in class. Let's just say I was the only student she had strong concerns about. I see this happen to a lot to students of color in predominantly White spaces at a young age. This can be damaging to the mind of tomorrow's leaders when we continue to let people like this into the world of education. Moving forward, my mother had me transfer schools to the west side of town during my fourth-grade year because she felt it was time for me to have a more Black experience.

The next three schools I attended, from fourth grade through senior year of high school, were predominantly Black, but the ratio of people of color to White students was about 60/40. I struggled with my Black identity because of my early experiences of race and the fact that I was not accepted by the Black community until sophomore year of high school. This had a lot to do with my speech, my clothing, and my inability to relate with Black culture outside of TV shows such as *Family Matters, Martin, Good Times,* and *College Hill.* By the time I reached high school, my mom had married my dad (stepfather), my younger brother was born, and we moved to the suburbs. We had moved up in social class.

Grass in the Backyard

We finally had a backyard to call our own, grass we could cut and care for, and a neighborhood that had access to a pool, tennis courts, bike trails, and so much more. My parents had reached points in their careers that allowed them to be flexible and have a sense of understanding of who I was as their child. This meant Dad could attend sporting events on a consistent basis, Mom did not have to work overtime (unless she wanted extra money), and I could play with my younger sibling in a safe environment. This is where I began to identify all of the social class tiers and where my family fell among them. In my vague understanding at that time, it appeared to me that we were now working middle-class citizens. It seems as though my parents had consistent income, we ate great all the time, my wardrobe had more designer items, and I was allowed to drive the car. Granted, my dad still served in an on-call rotation for his job; however, it was shorter than it once was because of his promotion to maintenance property manager. My mother was now working part-time and had begun her own dessert catering and party designer business. My family appeared more comfortable financially, able to take risks in business startups, and shift some work from full-time to part-time.

High school was a time where I explored my Blackness, built authentic relationships with people, and made my stride to become the first person in my family to attend college. Knowing that I would be the first to attend in my family, scholarships were essential to my success and stride toward college. When I began to look at options, the closest I got to campus tours were the virtual visits on my computer. I was never part of the equivalent of a boys and girls club that took students on college tours. My high school never presented an opportunity for students to visit institutions, nor did my parents think to take tours as they thought it was a part of my high school counselor's role to provide guidance through the admissions process and recommend schools for me. Let's just say I had one hell of a high school counselor. Ms. Jones is who I wish every student could have as a high school counselor. She was my introduction to options outside of the predominantly White institutions, she understood I was struggling with my Black identity, and she pitched the idea of attending a historically Black college or university.

I choose to name this chapter of my life "the grass in the backyard." For the first time in my family's life, we owned something and we had control over the space. All my life, I was sharing a common space and was constantly being told what I could and could not do. The grass in the backyard is also a metaphor of my high school career. I was able to take ownership of my journey, discovering who I was and what I could be. My resources seemed to have doubled with people who had fantastic knowledge about the world around me. I also felt like I did not have to share with anyone. These people were always there, ready to listen, challenge, and support me if this meant my potential would reap results.

Upon graduation from high school, I attended the illustrious North Carolina Central University (NCCU) in Durham, North Carolina. I would be going with more than $10,000 in scholarships, high academic honors, and college credit. For a kid from Baltimore County, this was more than a dream come true. This was a chance to finish something that was started many generations ago. Now the road was not easy: I struggled with obstacles such as financial aid and the cost of a meal plan, and until I realized the bookstore was not the only option, I tended to overpay for course texts. I also realized that just because there is more grass in my backyard didn't always mean I had the tools to deal with it.

I was prideful, hardheaded, and ill informed in my first year and a half of college. I mean I was as stubborn as they come and then add some "slap yo mama seasoning" on top of that. I wish someone had told me that asking questions was okay and that I did not have to feel the need to figure things out on my own. Being a first-generation college student, I find this expectation that everyone who enters the ivory walls of a college campus should know how to "do college" baffling. I remember attempting to join a program that was designed for first-generation college men or those who needed a mentor and being told that I was overqualified for the program. To use the words of my current students: "How sway?" In all seriousness, that moment of being denied did nothing but reinforce my stance of not asking for help and figuring it out on my own. It was not until I landed my second job on campus that all of this would be challenged and I would meet my first college mentor: Christopher L. Medley.

I began working as Christopher's office assistant within the department of residential life. My first day on the job, he made me return to my room and change clothes because sweatpants and a hoodie at 8:30 a.m. was not acceptable in the office. This is only a small moment in one of the many lessons I learned and continue to learn from this great man. Without the transformative experience of working in his office, I do not think the idea of becoming a higher education professional would have ever arisen. I would go on to work in conference and guest service at NCCU, where I found hidden talents for risk management and customer service. Here I met Jeremy Faulk, the guy who challenged me the most throughout my college career.

Think of the hardest coach you have ever played for or a teacher who always called on you to answer questions in class. This was and still is Jeremy. I believe that to thrive in this field having a mentor to guide you through this journey is super important. Jeremy pushed me outside of my comfort zone, brought about talents I never knew existed within me, and presented opportunities that I would have never come across on my own. The opportunities I was able to partake in have been some of the most fulfilling moments in my early higher education career.

Ultimately, this led me to what I consider is my deepest passion within higher education: student activities. I was able to intern with our campus activities board and put on large-scale programming with the wonderful Melanie Bullock. In my last semester of college, I was afforded the opportunity to work alongside Melanie, whom I consider a legend in the student activities realm of higher education. The level of thoughtfulness and creativity she brought to our campus was truly amazing. I am blessed to have been taken under her wing as a protégé. I also let her and another amazing human being, Whitney Watkin, down when I decided not to submit the five graduate school applications we completed over my last semester because I did not believe I was competitive enough for graduate school, so I made the decision not to apply. Instead, I would graduate from NCCU, move back home to my parents' house, and work at the YMCA as an after-school teacher and lead summer camp counselor.

An Office Full of Windows

I did end up in graduate school later to pursue a master's degree in higher education, and, upon graduating from the University of North Carolina at Wilmington, I accepted my first professional role at Guilford College. I would be the assistant director of student leadership and engagement. My primary responsibilities would include advising the campus activities board, the campus information desk, intramural sports, and the office interns. This is when I began to recognize that my own life—separate from my parents—was becoming part of the middle class. Despite the limited amount of privilege I had as a child, I had pursued opportunities and gained some advantage over the years. From my perspective as a new professional, the understanding of socioeconomic status is known and understood by other professional staff members. Many of us are not always compensated for the work we do, and many times we go over and above to make the most of our students' experience. Yet students tend to see just the end product and think we have it made or seem to think I am on the higher end of the middle-class socioeconomic spectrum.

I tend to spend a lot of my own money on students and their needs, most often pertaining to their health and school materials. For many, I have helped purchase books, meals, gas for transportation, and perform other small acts of kindness that help my students in the long run. Although this comes at some expense to my own well-being, I recognize I can help, and, because of my privilege, I have access to many resources that may be helpful. Another way that my social class identity shows up in my workplace are the different levels on which I am able to relate to my students and their backgrounds. Being able to share my experiences and how those have shaped me into the person I am today typically gives hope to the students or people who may have a similar identity or characteristic. It can provide them with someone to process with and discuss how to take challenging experiences and use them to their advantage.

As you might note, there is a trend within this story. Each section has a metaphor that is connected to my life story and helps to paint the picture of my social class climb. My last slogan is that I work in an "office full of windows," which is true. If you were to enter my office space, you would see I am surrounded by windows in every direction. This is a metaphor for the lives of most new professionals. Your work performance can be seen by everyone, and you can see everyone looking at you and even hear some of the comments about your job performance. On the other side of this, as a new professional, I am able to view my workplace with an open mind and explore the views from a new perspective.

Brenda Lee Anderson Wadley's Story: An Ode to Growing Up Poor and What It Teaches You

Growing up poor teaches you many things. Some lessons are common sense, whereas others are part of the daily struggle to remain resilient and determined, which are two elements of my innermost being. Despite being born and raised in adversity, resilience flows inside my veins. Between smiles and moments of achievement lies a constant internal battle between pride and the shame over my past struggles. I am constantly humbled by my personal journey through the academy, particularly how I have used it to disrupt generational trends of poverty in my life. I hope that my personal story of how I have continued to navigate social class within the academy will inspire other practitioners within the field.

Social Class Background

I have multiple intersecting identities, but my worldview is shaped largely by my social class. Honestly, I think I knew I was poor before I knew I was Black. From a very young age, I perceived that my circumstances were somehow different from those of others I'd met. For example, the "first of tha month" (a popular rap song by Bone Thugs-n-Harmony) wasn't only a song my siblings and I knew the words to, it was our reality as we waited for the first-of-the-month check to arrive in our parents' mailbox. At the beginning of the month, food was plentiful, but as the month progressed, food grew scarcer, and my parents' faces grew more worried about how we'd survive until the next check. It's a wonder that we survived that way for so long, and my siblings and I often joked that our lives reflected a sad Lifetime Network movie whereby the person overcomes so many different types of extenuating circumstances that one has to question, "Is this even real life?"

I am the daughter of two poorly educated individuals. Continuous employment was often disrupted by their frequent arrests for lower level crimes such as driving with a suspended license. These crimes often trap poor Blacks into making one difficult choice after the next. Obviously, you can't make money if you're in jail, and it's hard to pay the fees to regain your right to drive if you don't have money. It's even harder to maintain a job if it doesn't pay a living wage, and you are largely dependent on governmental benefits such as food assistance, Head Start programs, and subsidized health care. It's all part of a vicious cycle.

This cycle is something I constantly push back against, knowing that it is intended to perpetuate endless struggles resulting in systemic poverty for many poor and working-class individuals. Although I have climbed and continue to climb the socioeconomic ladder as an early career professional, I am reminded of the harmfulness of this cycle to the most vulnerable poor and working-class individuals and families. As a child, I witnessed firsthand how systems that were intended to empower individuals actually disadvantaged them. I remember attending food stamp benefit verification meetings with my mother, and two things were clear during these meetings: (a) my mother had to miss work if she wanted to continue to receive food benefits because the meetings were only held during the workday, and (b) my father never attended these meetings. For my mother, as well as many other individuals, it was a choice between attending work and attending your reverification meeting. Attending these meetings could take away from monetary income that could be earned at work. During these visits to the Department of Family and Job Services, I always noticed how there was a large number of women and children but rarely any men. It was not until later in my life that I realized my mother had to navigate a system that offered more benefits to alleviate poverty if families were headed by a single parent, inadvertently (or purposely) discouraging family formation. These harmful policies helped to perpetuate persistent stereotypes about Black fathers being absent from their children's lives.

I was born and raised in Toledo, Ohio, and grew up on the south side of the city. I have immense pride in the state of Ohio and the city of Toledo. It was rare in my upbringing for individuals to successfully leave the south side of Toledo and prosper elsewhere. When I was younger, my friends would plan to meet up after school for a free dinner at the local church, with the catch being that we had to sit through the whole sermon before they would serve us dinner. Similarly, the local church ran an after-school program, and even though you didn't feel like going, you went because you knew anything was better than being home. I identify as a critical Christian, meaning I can recognize God and still be weary of how power and oppression show up in the kingdom of God. However, it took me years to unlearn things I accepted as absolute truth from the church, one being the belief and support of prosperity gospel. Prosperity gospel is the idea that an individual's health and wealth are connected to the will of God. This means that if you are wealthy or poor, you are that way because it is the will of God. As a young child, that equated to the idea that me and my family were poor and struggling because we were living in sin. So, if I asked for forgiveness, prayed, and did not sin, God would reward us with financial freedom and long, healthy lives.

For many years, I was unable to recognize oppression for what it is: fear and bondage. I spent countless hours repenting for my sins and the sins of my parents and family members. When I challenged a church leader that maybe I was poor because my parents lacked access to jobs and opportunities, I was told I was being radical. I was told that being a supporter of democratic ideology and being a follower of Christ were mutually exclusive. In my experience, supporting ideology connected to the prosperity gospel was toxic and damaging. As a critical Christian, I don't believe it is the will of God for people to suffer. I think people suffer because they lack access to basic human needs such as health care, education, jobs, and other opportunities.

I believe growing up poor was even harder because of the harsh realities of substance abuse. The impact of substance abuse resulted in growing up constantly wondering if your parent(s) had paid the bills or used the money intended for bills to feed their substance use needs. I had many days filled with utility disconnection and eviction notices, coming home to no lights or heat. I remember having to hide my birthday or paycheck money because it was entirely possible to wake up the next day and it not be there. Even the family televisions were not safe. I could come home on any given day to find them missing because my parents had pawned appliances for money. I remember waking up to my parents saying, "We are leaving to go make money, you and your siblings need to look out for each other." Because my parents did not have jobs, making money meant scrapping for metal, donating plasma, or my father picking up odd jobs as a plumber.

I have continued to disrupt generational trends of poverty in my life with my education. As a child, when my surrounding circumstances were full of chaos, it was easy for me to get lost in the pages of books. Throughout my educational journey and as I better understood my social class identity, education became a direct path toward upward mobility. However, my desire for an education didn't shield me from the harsh realities of how my education would alienate me from my family members. In my family's eyes, I was now part of a more dominant and foreign culture. I believe this is a common experience among first-generation college students, and learning how to bridge that gap between new educational horizons and family dynamics is an ongoing struggle.

Social Class in the Academy

As educators, we need significantly more attention directed toward the influence of social class on the experiences of marginalized groups in the academy. By *academy*, I mean institutions of higher learning as experienced by students, practitioners, and faculty members. In my view, the academy does a disservice to aspiring and current professionals around issues related to social class, and the scholarly literature on this identity is limited. Considerably more time and energy are focused on identity development as it relates to race, gender, sexuality, and other social locations, but we spend limited, if any, time on social class identity development. This lack of critical consciousness does harm to the individuals the academy hopes to empower through its work because practitioners are left without an explicit knowledge base on how to navigate interlocking socioeconomic and political structures. Our common lexicon for socioeconomic status includes words such as *FAFSA, financial aid, Pell-eligible*, and *first-generation college student*. However important these terms are, they do not challenge practitioners to dig deeper and develop critical consciousness around what multilevel support looks like for marginalized individuals.

Yet another barrier related to my social class that I continue to navigate within the academy is imposter syndrome. Imposter syndrome is twofold in my own experiences and manifests as "keeping up with the Joneses" and "What life would be like if . . . ?" I was convinced after my time as an undergraduate and graduate student that I was moving on up in the world. I was idealistic in thinking that with a little bit of education and a dream, nothing could stop me. However, when I was faced with the looming and daunting tasks of job searching, even the "most prepared" practitioners in the field struggle, and I was no exception. It is imperative that members of the academy (broadly defined) are cognizant of misrepresenting the experience of finding a job. The narrative that everyone will find the perfect job with great benefits and live happily ever after is certainly a myth. This narrative neglects a relevant truth that many practitioners may have to make imperfect choices that weigh available positions against the right "fit" for their multiple intersecting identities and needs. Individuals within the field with lower socioeconomic backgrounds may face additional stressors around the job market, including taking a job poorly aligned with who they are but one that provides financial security and having family-related financial responsibilities that impact their ability to move to other geographic areas for more promising job prospects.

As a relatively new professional, my upbringing in a lower socioeconomic status family is still a large part of who I am. After I accepted my first professional position, it was quickly evident that onboarding and getting off the ground would be challenges. Even tasks such as selecting benefits (a new experience for me) made me nervous. After receiving my first paycheck, I remember calling my husband to confirm with him over and over again that my check looked correct. This was not because I had a large income but because such a significant portion of my wages went to employee-related contributions and health care. Even in a moment of happiness, a sense of overwhelming worry filled my heart. Would I ever be able to pay back my student loans living off the income I was bringing in? Would I ever be able to provide for a family? Would I ever own a home?

Although I would now identify as lower middle class, I would also acknowledge that I have gained significant cultural capital. However, buried beneath my pride for having overcome so much to ascend to a solid, stable, and challenging academic position, I continue to struggle with shame for what I don't know and what I haven't yet accomplished. Despite evidence in my life to the contrary, those fears of returning to poverty are still real. As an act of continual self-care, I'm constantly assessing my internal dialogue regarding what is a real fear and what may never be a reality for me again. Although I'm critical of what we as members of the academy have yet to do to better support students and the workforce, I'm also hopeful and grateful for the ability to travel to places through my work that I never imagined, to have the ability to invest in my personal goals, and, most important, to share and utilize my own story to demystify the academy and encourage the next individual with aspirations for this career path.

Narrative Analysis

Armina, Tim, and Brenda provide us with three distinct experiences of beginning one's administrative career in the academy. All identifying as people of color, they mention how the combination of racial, ethnic, and social class identities intertwines in their lives and the messages they received both explicitly and implicitly from society, religious institutions, and their families about social class.

Although each individual faced different challenges in their pursuit of higher education, they all speak to the complexity of being poor and working class folks trying to operate in middle- and upper class spaces. Armina mentions her desire to attend an institution in New England for her undergraduate work and the reality of her need to stay in state for tuition remission. Tim talks about the scholarships he had to pursue to gain access to higher education and the lessons he had to learn about asking others for help. Brenda describes the systemic issues in public assistance and how she used education to disrupt the cycle of poverty in her family. Armina and Tim also suggest that their cocurricular engagement in student groups and campus employment aided them in being successful as undergraduate students and in pursuing careers in higher education. All three of them speak about fighting imposter syndrome and the criticality of having people to support them through their pursuit of higher education.

They go on to explain how earning bachelor's and master's degrees helped them build more financial, cultural, and social capital, which led to some class mobility, at least in the economic realm. However, they describe moments where their original forms of capital or background continue to show up. Tim shares that he initially did not apply for graduate school, even after completing the applications, because he did not believe people from his background could be competitive enough. Armina admits to accepting residence life positions because they provided room and board benefits that appealed to her class background, and she describes trying to understand the cluster that is human resources policies and benefits. Brenda mentions forms of lateral classism, using the exact same phrasing as Liu (2011) about "keeping up with the Joneses," and encourages educators to share the sometimes harsh realities of job searching in higher education or any field, really.

These early career administrators also highlight three commonalities in the beginnings of their careers in the academy: (a) low salaries, (b) being socialized into the profession, and (c) the desire to pay it forward. The first, although debatable, and certainly relative, speaks to the reality that higher education administrators can face lower salaries than their counterparts with graduate degrees in other fields and is tied to the financial capital that early career administrators can access. The pieces on socialization and professionalism are rife with classism; it is the field's attempt to indoctrinate people into the academy's middle- and upper class milieu. Although informing folks of the cultural and social expectations of a profession can be helpful, it becomes suspect when we expect people to assimilate to ways of being, or at least presenting, that are contrary to who they are. Armina, Tim, and Brenda all offer ways that they now use their knowledge and experiences to aid others (students, administrators, and faculty) in navigating higher education, and they challenge us to consider how we can think and act in ways that create more social class equity in the academy.

5

THE MID CAREER
ADMINISTRATOR
PERSPECTIVE

Narratives by Sara C. Furr, Jacinda M. Félix Haro, and Sally G. Parish

M id career administrators find themselves at the crossroads, with some power and authority yet not enough for division-wide decisions. It's neither good nor bad; it just is. This place in between is familiar to mid career professionals from poor and working-class roots and their lived experience in the academy: a place of somewhere in the middle requiring the skill to exist within both ambiguity and certainty. Not always having a clear direction or answer on how to best navigate parts of life yet moving forward with, mostly, success. Effectively navigating the complexity is shared in the stories from Sara C. Furr at University of Chicago, Jacinda M. Félix Haro at Massachusetts College of Pharmacy and Health Sciences, and Sally G. Parish at University of Memphis. Their stories help us better understand the tension in living somewhere in the middle regardless of degrees, paycheck, or positionality.

Sara C. Furr's Story

Growing up, I never thought about social class; heck, I didn't even really think about money. Not because we had much but because we all seemed the same. Growing up on a military base overseas had a leveling factor. There were different housing sections for officers and enlisted personnel, but the differences seemed minimal. Every once in a while, you'd go to someone's house and they would have fancy furniture. This usually meant the family had shipped their furniture from the United States. It was more of a novelty because it was rare, and most of us had the same furniture. That's the best way to describe my experience growing up.

Everything was the same. We all had access to the same things on the base. Even if there were two elementary schools available, the only difference between the two is what side of the base they were on, and everyone just went to the school closest to where they lived. It was all very practical. After school we'd hang out at the youth center or maybe you'd have dance lessons or played an instrument. But it was all available; you just had to sign up. Certainly, you might have to purchase an instrument or costumes for a dance recital, but it was all very accessible. Our schools were the same, the hospitals were the same, and we shopped at the same stores. Because all of our basic needs were taken care of, my parents did not fight about money.

That all changed when my dad retired and we moved back to the United States. We moved to a small, rural town in North Carolina. That was the first time I realized we were much more low income/working class than I ever knew. Being in the military, especially growing up overseas, distorts your view of social class because everything is the same or at least seems the same, especially as a kid.

When I reflect on social class, I realize the development of my critical consciousness around class is marked by a series of firsts. The first time I went to public school. The first time I had to accompany my mom to a bank, hospital, or any other social service. Applying for college, scholarships, my first job. Moving into my first apartment and being terrified I wouldn't have money to pay rent. I didn't know how to do any of these things. And my mom didn't know. And my sisters didn't know. All the things we didn't know became an indicator of our/my social class.

More Than Money

Most days I have to remind myself that social class is more than money because that is often where the conversation starts and stops in higher education. We might talk more thoroughly about social class when it comes to our *students nuancing* food insecurity, homelessness, access to health care, and so on. Among student affairs professionals, I experience an assumed sameness as I did in the military. When I lived on campus and thus had my housing costs and meal plan to cover basics, there was an assumed sameness. We all had similar apartments, furnishings, and benefits. We may even have had the same salary, but social class is more than that, and we don't talk about it. I remember the first time someone gave me the advice to pay myself rent while I lived on campus. At first, I thought this was absurd. First of all, I was making $27,000 a year, and although that was a dramatic increase from the $8,000 annual stipend I received when I was in graduate school, I was still living paycheck to paycheck. Where was I going to find money to pay myself rent?

My coworkers would go on vacation to places all over the world, and I realized, for me, vacation just meant I didn't go to work. If I did travel, I was probably just going to see my mom, from whom I always lived within driving distance. As I got older, vacation started to mean traveling to places where my friends lived because the only additional cost was getting there. I was in my 30s when I actually started planning vacations. Although I had an increased consciousness of what that meant (more than just days off from work), I still had minimal knowledge of how to do it. Worse than that, I realized how my notions of vacation were in contradiction with my family's. They didn't always understand why I was vacationing. There were times when my mom cautioned me about taking too much time off because they (my employer) might fire me. It was a new notion to have a job that accumulated a benefit of vacation time.

In higher education and student affairs, I have seen more conversations and conference presentations about salary, but they are few and far between, and we rarely go beyond that. In my experience, there has been increasing awareness of first-generation college students and what that means without explicitly tying that identity to social class. I know there are distinctions among all of these things, but I often wonder what stops us from talking more deeply about class. I know shame, fear, and guilt have made it difficult to talk about my own experiences and understandings. I found it easier to give tips around salary negotiation and even shared my starting salary when I first moved to Chicago, and yet I'm still sensitive when people respond with, "How did you ever live on that salary?" Here I thought I'd done fairly well.

The Continued Struggle

The truth is I never wanted for anything. When my dad was in the military, my mom often worked two or three jobs at a time. My mom and dad both came from low-income, single-parent households and never wanted us to feel the effects of their struggle. Still, as I went through high school, I knew I was on my own to figure out how to get to and through college. My mom would always tell me, "You'll figure it out." She's always been my biggest cheerleader. Even knowing that, I recall a time I lashed out at my mom when I felt challenged in my class identity. I was in graduate school, and she had stopped by on her way to visit my sister. She was trying to tell me something I needed to do with my finances, and I got frustrated so I responded, "I know, Mom, I have a degree." I regretted it immediately, but I couldn't take away the harm I had caused.

This is my continued struggle. No, I'm not lashing out at people when given advice or when I feel targeted, but I do feel like a fraud. I am firmly upper middle class. I have climbed the ladder and currently have a role where I have decision-making power. I live in a condo I purchased four years ago. My income allows me to plan trips and live the life I want to live. On an everyday basis, I don't have to worry about having a meal or buying something I like on a whim. I can help my nephew fill out the Free Application for Financial Student Aid (FAFSA) and college applications and also explain it to my sister. These days if I don't know something, I probably know someone who does. My circle of friends and colleagues resembles me or at least that's what I assume unless I learn otherwise.

A Changed Identity

With all of this, I still struggle with my working-class sensibilities. I have rarely had only one job. Since finishing graduate school, I've always done something on the side, from working at a clothing store to teaching group fitness classes. It has taken many years for me to figure out how to reconcile my social class identity with my various family members. It's not about my income bracket because my sisters certainly surpass me there. It's about being the only one with an advanced degree. It's about being in, and sometimes living and breathing, the academy. As we have all grown older, my sisters have told me, "We don't talk about serious things around you because you're going to get defensive or challenge us or teach us." I have only learned some of this more recently, and I have to fight the urge to get defensive. (The irony is not lost on me.) This may seem small, but I wonder, if I'm not able to connect and be in community across difference with my family, how can I do so outside my family?

Social Class and Social Justice

Two things come up for me when I think about social class in higher education within the context of my social ideology or critical pedagogy. The first is the inclination to avoid conversations about social class, outside of trusted friends and colleagues, because of the dominance I hold in this identity. The second is the always perilous position that I exist as a staff person doing social change work within institutions not built for change. The first is very straightforward, and I have no deep insight to offer but believe it's a major barrier for me. Somewhere in all my marginalized identities protesting, advocating, and working for social change, I internalized a message that to be valuable and valid as a social justice educator, I should not be concerned with my own income, power, and so on. Somewhere I decided that to be in service to others, I certainly had better not go on vacations, have disposable income, or generally benefit from capitalism.

The second issue of being employed by institutions not built for many of my identities and not designed to change is not one with which I always struggled. I have always known that as a staff person there were limited to no protections for me and my job. Early in my career, I felt less threatened because I had limited familial and financial responsibilities. Although the idea of being fired is not desirable, I always knew I could live with my mom or sisters. I've always known I could make money in some way even if it wasn't in my career field. There is a lot of privilege in knowing that, regardless of other identities, I know a lot about the world of work. Regardless of desirability, I can figure it out and manage. As I have gotten older and progressed in my career, my concerns are the same yet different. I have to be much more thoughtful with my challenges to the institution. Although I know I can still maneuver the world of work and find ways to make money, the risk seems greater these days. Simultaneously, it feels classist to just assume I can always get a job at Target or Old Navy or some sales or food service position. My own internalized dominance around class is much harder to confront.

Educational Status and Social Class

For me, these identities are related—they inform one another for all of us in academia. It is much more socially acceptable to proudly claim dominance in our educational status versus our social class. In almost any environment I am in, I am congratulated when I say I have a PhD in higher education. However, I rarely share I finally have a six-figure salary (just barely), I pay to have someone clean my home once a month, or I even bought a new jacket. Side note: I once lied to my supervisor when he commented on my jacket. The conversation went like this:

> Supervisor: Nice jacket, is that new?
> Me: No, I've had it.
> Supervisor: Oh, I guess it's my first time seeing you wear it. It looks great!

That was the end of the conversation. I couldn't believe I lied about something so meaningless, and I wondered why I had done it. I still wonder why I felt shame about spending money on a $30 jacket but never hesitated to share I was in a PhD program. And no, my institution did not provide any financial assistance for the degree.

Over the past few years, I have grown more and more comfortable sharing my class story, but I still have a lot of work to do to confront my internal dominance around class. I believe that it actually keeps us from having deeper conversations around social class in the academy. I worry that we believe social class is earned, like our educational status, without interrogating the systems or structures that allowed us to access a different social class identity. We harbor classist ideals while also advocating and striving for social change. It can be both. We don't have to arrive. Personal reflection can be the start of the journey.

Jacinda M. Félix Haro's Story

My dad and I walked into the candy store as we often did so he could buy his newspaper. I always liked asking him for candy, and he would always oblige, getting me gum, a lollipop, or some other sweet. Today was different. I said to myself, "Jacinda, do not ask Daddy for candy. He is on strike again and money is tight." I was probably 10. While we waited in line to pay for the paper, I saw a new candy I had not seen before. It was bubble gum in a tube! Like toothpaste! I was amazed and wanted it. I forgot my talk with myself and asked my dad for this candy. And he bought it. It was 25 cents. That was more than 30 years ago, and I remember it like it was yesterday. I had a lot of guilt for asking for that candy, which is clear because I can tell this story today like it just happened.

Growing up, I did not think of us as having less. We did okay. I went to Catholic school, and we had everything we needed and a lot of what we wanted. We lived in a working-class community with people of similar backgrounds. My friends' parents were a lot like my parents. They had not gone to college, but they worked hard to provide more than decent lives for their kids. Most homes had two parents working, and many of us were people of color. We lived in apartments in high-rise buildings, and as kids we took public transportation or walked everywhere. It was an extremely diverse community, and in the Bronx, New York, there was not a lack of people of color with whom we could bond. I grew up feeling validated, worthy, and grateful for the life I had. I recognized, however, that although we were normal, normalcy came with the knowledge that we were not the sports car driving, popped collar polo and Ray-Ban shade-wearing White kids of every John Hughes movie. If the 1980s were known for anything, they were known for their excess. And excess is something working-class people in the Bronx did not have on most days.

What we did not have in trust funds, we made up for in love, support, and resiliency. Thanks to the words of Duckworth and Quinn (2009) and others, our profession has taken to this idea of resiliency and grit as tools for surviving college and life. Although that may be true, people of color and working-class folks have been gritty for a long time. We are not the people whose parent called the admission counselor at Yale or whose uncle knew the hiring manager at PricewaterhouseCoopers. We did not vacation in Europe or "summer" in Newport. We spent weekends camping; taking road trips; barbecuing in the park with music blasting; and, if we were lucky, driving to Florida to visit friends or relatives who moved from the Bronx for a "better life." Our families and friends' families supported us, watched after us, and would even scold us if we got out of line. If it truly takes a village, then our village was filled with neighbors from 33 floors, relatives from down the block, friends' parents, bus drivers, security guards, the elders, the lady at the deli, and religious and community leaders. We had a network—a network of people who understood us, knew where we were coming from, and loved us. When you think about this, it is no wonder marginalized students (students of color, first-generation students, students from low- or working-class socioeconomic status [SES]) struggle in college. Where are our people in this new environment?

To critique my experience as a mid to upper level professional in student affairs from a working-class background and as a female Nuyorican, first-generation college student, I have to begin at the college choice process. When I was a kid, my mother went to Lehman College to complete a certificate program. This was the closest I ever got to college. My brother did go to college, although he did not persist. I had to learn about college from brochures, college fairs at my high school, and the few older relatives or friends who went to college. There were no college road trips and certainly no overnight stays to get the "full college experience." I do recall visiting some schools, but they were all in New York City and had to be accessible via public transportation because we did not have a car. In many ways, I was lucky because I went to a college preparatory high school. College was nonnegotiable in my family. The expectations of my family and high school were that people would go to college. That was a lovely sentiment, but with hundreds of students and not enough counselors, there was not a lot of time dedicated to each student to explain the process or discuss colleges. My future lay with my mother and me researching everything we could about college and the college admissions process.

Even in a private school in New York, college counselors could not see the potential in their working-class students of color. I had people in my life unequivocally tell my friends not to apply to certain colleges—colleges that they ultimately would apply to, attend, and from which they would graduate. It is almost like saying, how dare these kids think they will get into these schools? I even had one friend who was told to not even bother with college.

What makes a high school counselor so uninformed and uncaring? I never had a counselor tell me that I should not apply, but I also was not applying to any elite institutions.

Over the years, I have wondered whether I should have applied to more elite schools. I was not allowed to apply to colleges out of state, and the majority of my college applications were to state schools. I recall my mother not wanting me to go away to college; she preferred I commute. For some of my older relatives, it would be unheard of to leave home to live in a residence hall. Although my mother wanted me to stay home, she did not stop me from applying to colleges that required me to live in residence. I think about what I know now versus what I knew then. If I had only known that you should apply to a school even if you think you cannot afford it, that colleges in different states can be just as affordable as ones in your home state, who knows where I would have landed?

I have no regrets about attending a state institution for my undergraduate degree. I made lifelong friends and gained valuable experiences. Also, I graduated debt free because there was more money for school in the 1990s. I went to a state school; my mother planned and saved to pay for my school. My master's degree was also free so I graduated with little debt from loans. However, this did not mean I was debt free. Before I went to graduate school, I was unemployed for a year. Although I had a supportive family, I was already an adult living on my own, and I had to figure out how to live that year on unemployment benefits. Afterward, I went to graduate school for two years; when I graduated, I found my first job in student affairs. I learned quickly that student affairs work, especially when you are just starting out, pays pretty poorly. Considering I had debt to pay off and was now living and working in New Jersey, it felt overwhelming and impossible to get ahead. I had a master's degree, I was almost 30, and I had to get a second job as a hostess in a restaurant just to live.

I have often said that student affairs work is for the privileged. Who else could afford to work long hours for low salaries, all while paying off debt from their education? I recall a time at a former institution when a leader in our division wanted to know why we were buying dinner for people who stayed late. I never thought this could be an issue. I think our field is the only field that expects you to work late, well past your 35 to 40 hours, and still buy your own dinner. Yes, people can bring items from home, but we really cannot afford a meal once in a while for people who are putting in long hours for low wages? I quickly learned student affairs work is elite work. To get ahead in this field, you need to put in extra hours at work as well as in professional organizations. I think about the friends I know in other fields. They may go to a conference and be involved in a professional organization, but their job opportunities are not hinged on their involvement. My accountant friends do not have to shell out thousands of dollars a year to attend a conference so they can get another job someday. I have been active in professional organizations for my entire higher education career. I greatly value these organizations, but the truth is, if I did not get funding for professional development, I could not afford to go to most conferences. In fact, in our profession, not only do we pay to go to conferences for professional development, we pay to go to conferences to get a job.

When I say to get a job, I do not mean in a few years someone will remember you and offer you a job; rather, I mean there are actually people recruiting for positions at these conferences. There is time dedicated before the conference for people to interview and "wow" an employer in hopes of getting an on-campus interview. For someone like me, who was raised in a working-class environment and chose a profession that initially pays low, it would be hard to imagine having money for a plane ticket, hotel, conference registration, food, and so on for a few days to find work. Even if your institution pays for you to attend a conference, many times these funds are limited, so a person who chooses to attend the recruitment portion of the conference may not attend the full conference. In that way, the candidate is missing out yet again because he or she would not be able to attend receptions, networking opportunities, or valuable sessions where he or she could learn best practices.

I often think about how professionals in these national organizations keep asking me and other folks from underrepresented communities how we can increase diversity in not only these professional organizations but in our field overall. My answer has always been, "Make them more affordable." How can we expect folks from marginalized identities to step into these intimidating spaces—spaces we were not taught to navigate, especially when we cannot afford to be here? Yes, just because you are from a traditionally underrepresented group does not mean you cannot afford a conference. However, even if we can afford it, so many of our people cannot; therefore, we are left alone once again trying to navigate intimidating spaces, spaces where we feel we do not belong.

That sense of not belonging carries through to my professional life. At work I am one of only a few people of color. This is the same story at every institution I have worked. I also recognize that my working-class roots may not always jibe with others from more elite backgrounds. I like hip-hop, I swear, and I code-switch. For me, making it to a senior associate dean of students role meant I had to learn how to dress; how to wear makeup (properly); how to speak in different ways; and, of course, which fork to use at dinner. I basically prepared myself for this my whole life. I would ask friends, observe others, and listen to older, "fancier" people whom I assumed knew more than me at least in this aspect of society. I remember times in college or in my early career when I was shamed for not dressing or expressing myself properly. I remember feeling guilty for not knowing better. I grew up in a working-class environment, but my mother worked in downtown Manhattan and always had to dress the part. I used to love her stylish work clothes. I think I conflated fancy clothes with any clothes that were not jeans and sneakers. I did not realize all fancy clothes are not proper for all events.

I promised I would do for others what was once done for me. When I mentor a young person from a working-class background, sometimes I feel a sense of guilt over telling them what drink is better to order and what outfit is more professional, knowing that all of these rules are part of the White male upper class system that created the rules in the first place. I tend to struggle with the aspects of my job that require people to conform to this particular set of professional standards. I also struggle with not telling them these facts. I know how easily working-class people are judged by those in power who look to them as less than just because they do not know all the rules. My job as a person who has made it quite far in her student affairs career is to mentor not only students but also new professionals who are still figuring out how to navigate this environment—an environment that may be grossly unfamiliar.

I also promised myself that when I got to a position of power and influence in my career, I would consider class issues. It amazes me how people still do not understand that some students cannot afford books or food, let alone tuition. If they cannot understand the issues faced by students, then they certainly will not understand issues faced by professionals in our own field who may also be struggling with food or housing insecurity. Trips to coffee shops and lunches at nice restaurants are some ways in which we exclude lower and working-class colleagues. You cannot afford lunch, so you do not go, and when you do not go, you do not network. I recall at a previous institution our leader sent an e-mail to the entire division not asking but telling us we needed to donate to a scholarship fund. I remember complaining, "I am sure most people want to donate to this, but we cannot assume everyone has the means in which to do so. It would have been better to ask them or strongly suggest they donate instead of outright demanding it." I could not understand why my colleagues did not get how these issues affect our staff. It does not end there.

When you reach a certain level in this career, you are expected to give money back to the institution. I think about how difficult that must be for a working-class person. Some folks may be taking care of their own family as well as extended families. They may be sending money to their parents, putting a cousin through college, or lending money to their uncle. For folks who come from these lower SES backgrounds, just because you may make a big salary one day does not mean you had a nest egg to begin with, and it does not mean you have not been helping others along the way. I wonder, when my time comes will I be able to donate in a way that is deemed worthy to my board of directors and president?

Sally G. Parish's Story: The Area Between Privilege and Poverty

I drive a car my father built. When it rains outside, it rains in my car. Puddles of water fill the floorboards and sometimes short out the electrical circuit, making it impossible to use the interior lights or automatic locks. The leak in the roof has been there for three years. I am now at a place in my life where I can afford to have it fixed, but I know the real fix lies in replacing the car. I can't bring myself to do it. This car is the first thing I have ever owned that was truly my own. I bought it on the day I graduated from college at The University of Memphis—the first in my family to achieve such a feat (college and the brand-new car). My father and grandfather helped me pick it out, and they both gave 30 years each to the company that manufactured it. Blue-collar work at General Motors is what relocated my family from Flint, Michigan to a small, rural, middle Tennessee town where your social class defined you from the earliest of ages. You were from either old money or no money. As the daughter of a single, divorced, alcoholic dad, we were the latter.

We were poor, but we weren't in poverty. I had enough, but I had to be strategic about what I had. We were as working class as they came. My dad was a union man and worked on the line at the Saturn plant. He left for work before I even woke up most days, and at the age of eight, I started waking myself up with an alarm and getting myself dressed, fed, and on the bus by 7:15 a.m. to begin my school day. In later years, I would hoard my lunch money to buy feminine products. I learned how to cook at a very early age and was doing my own laundry before most kids had transitioned out of their training wheels. I grew up in a home with no computer and no Internet. To this day, that home is still without both. Extracurricular activities were not always an option for me because I did not have a parent who could pick me up after school for meetings, practices, and so on. So instead, I read. I read anything I could get my hands on, which later turned into my first job at our public library—a gateway to a better life.

We may not have had the most, but I had enough. I did not have clothes from the Gap or the Limited (high fashion in the 1990s), but I rocked some pretty sweet sale items from the local Walmart. The mid- to late 1990s thrift store trend probably saved my high school years because it then became cool to buy second hand clothes, when in reality that was the only way I could afford a dress to go to the prom. To this day, I cannot pay full price for an article of clothing, and I still get anxiety when I set foot in a mall. I remember all too well the shopping trips of my preteen years when I foolishly lifted nail polish as a measure of bravado intended to distract from the fact that I truly had no money of my own to make an actual purchase.

I have spent the past 30 years living somewhere between privileged and in poverty. As most working-class folks know, the pendulum often swings one way or the other depending on the current circumstance. In college I flew mostly under the radar with my working-class identity, self-opting out of opportunities that came at a higher cost and waiting tables to cover the costs that seemed surmountable. I was and am ever aware of the lack of a financial safety net in my life. I knew then and know now that I do not come from a family that can cover me should the financial bottom fall out. All expenses and debts from the age of 18 forward are my own. As a college student, that meant navigating rent, meals, sorority dues, gas money, and so on. As a young professional, that meant navigating student loan debt, conference registrations, job-searching expenses, and so on. Today, it means managing a mortgage, continued student loan debt, and expenses for two small children. Although I have more today than I have ever had, I am still lost somewhere in the area of privileged and poverty.

I am privileged for so many reasons: a great job (with a title that makes it sound like I do something really important), an amazing partner, two beautiful children, a stable and sufficient salary, health care, a roof over my head, and a leaky car to get me around. I am a White, straight, cisgender woman pursuing a doctorate, and I acknowledge the inherent privilege laden in those identities, yet I still cannot admit to now earning a wage that technically makes me part of the upper middle class. I still take Tupperware to events because I cannot bear to see the excess food go to waste, recalling nights of my childhood that included a fried chicken TV dinner as the special of the day, courtesy of the $1 bin at the local Save-A-Lot, eaten alone while my father was tossing a few back after a long day's work.

My entire life I have been stuck in the in-between: not privileged and not in poverty. I could pass as either as needed, and some of the most salient parts of my identity come as a result of my working-class experiences. Some of the most painful ones do as well, many of which come from never feeling privileged or poor enough to claim either.

Countless aspects of the higher education experience are still rooted in a philosophy that a life learning and leading in academia is only for the privileged few. I have found myself at countless professional dinners, conferences, conventions, and so on where I quickly knew I did not fit in. I have had to turn down interviews because I could not front the airfare. I have awkwardly sat through overly fancy dinners with donors feeling nothing but shame for the country club experience I was being afforded. I have worn secondhand suits to The Placement Exchange. I have used the wrong fork. I have eaten the wrong roll. I have packed my lunch every day. I have paid rent late because my checking account was depleted while awaiting a $1,000 reimbursement check from the university for a program I advised ("Why didn't you pay with your credit card?" I hear you ask. "Because I had to spend seven years rebuilding my credit from a charged-off card in college").

Over the years, colleagues and students would often provide a chuckle or warm smile from across a clothed table and say, "Oh, Sally. . . . I love that you are such a mess!" or "You are so awkward," as though those terms of endearment somehow made me feel more comfortable as a stranger in their strange land. Not privileged like them but somehow not poor enough either. I was given a seat at the table (hooray, right?), I just didn't know which fork to use.

I have ridden in students' cars that cost more than my annual salary. I have taught a student whose first job straight out of their undergraduate experience offered a starting salary that was double the highest household income my family ever made. I have paid six-figure invoices out of my departmental budget that would make my father's head spin, and I still download coupons to my Kroger card every Saturday morning. The complexities of this identity are not lost on me. I am a working-class woman, serving upper class students, taking home a middle-class paycheck.

I have been asked from time to time by students like me who have been told to just "fake it 'til you make it" if I have ever experienced imposter syndrome, or a feeling that I would be found out somewhere along the way— that I didn't really belong, know the lingo, get the references, and so on. The answer is absolutely yes. But the times when I have truly felt like an imposter have not been within higher education, where I really was and still am an outsider. My true feelings of imposter syndrome came from the visits home, which have sadly dwindled over the years. The visits back to the working-class home that raised me—where I was worried I would be figured out by those I left behind. Did I seem too intelligent, evolved, uppity, or out of touch with reality to my dad? Would he judge me for the experiences I have sought to grow and learn and earn? Was my career too big, my dreams too large, to fit in that cabin on Bradshaw Creek Road without sucking all the air out of the room? And, what the hell does an associate dean do anyway? I try to grow and rise to the occasion in professional settings, and I find myself trying to shrink into the dustiest corners of the house that was once home. It is exhausting, this place between privileged and poverty.

Institutions of higher education boast broadly of programs and services to support first-generation college students like myself, and financial aid and TRiO programs often triage the immediate financial necessity of our working-class students, but higher education institutions are still falling short. Working-class students are still struggling to find their way; they are often as lost as I am in the area between privileged and impoverished. Throwing more programs, conferences, retreats, workshops, and so on at this group is often the proposed solution, but the reality is that these students aren't coming. They aren't coming because they, like me, are at work. Tinto, Astin, Pascarella, Terenzini, Kuh, Pike, and Schlossberg, I hear you. We know participation in programs such as alternative break trips, extended orientation camps, and the fraternity and sorority community are all practices that lead to an increased sense of belonging on campus. We know students should live on campus their first year. We know students should get involved in their first 6 weeks. Yet what about the financial barriers to accessing each of these programs? Working-class students see the dollar signs associated with these experiences and, if they are like me, shut down. So maybe a handful of schools offer a handful of students a scholarship to participate; can you also reimburse me for the $350 I am out because I gave up my shifts waiting tables this weekend to go sing camp songs in the woods? Doubtful. I don't have all the answers, but I do know we cannot keep promoting the same programs and services to this group of students and blame them when they don't show up. Maslow knows what I am talking about. We have some basic human needs to take care of first.

Every day I show up somewhere in the middle—in the middle of privileged and poverty, in the middle of the organizational chart—and I try to advocate for this often forgotten group of college students and professionals. I try to lead up to the folks with six-figure salaries with deference and respect and lead for and to my students with humility and understanding. Interestingly enough, students often mislabel me as one of the "haves," and maybe I now am, but I will always carry with me the lessons from having not. Regardless of what my pay stub may say and although I may no longer count as part of the working class because of the recent Google search I just conducted I am still of and from it. It is still who I am at my core. The greatest transition I have ever experienced in my life was not the transition to college, the transition into the profession, or the transition into parenthood. It has been this transition into earning enough to qualify for an income bracket that comes with a paradigm I do not identify with whatsoever.

"Do they even make these anymore?" I am often asked by tentative passengers who brave my worn-out Saturn Vue. I laugh it off, but the reality is they don't. They stopped making them the year they laid my father off, the same year they closed the plant that moved my family and hundreds of others to that rural Tennessee town more than 30 years ago. My life in so many ways is tied to that plant, to that car, to that father, to that way of life. I am too much in some spaces and not enough in others, of a class that no longer claims me, and I am still stuck somewhere between privilege and poverty hoping like hell I don't get caught driving in the rain.

Narrative Analysis

Although they did not grow up in abundance, each contributor discusses access to the basic necessities and having enough. This sense of enough is captured in Sara's story growing up on a military base overseas where all needs were provided. Concerning needs being met, there was a sense of sameness: same type of housing, health facilities, and schools. In this framework of everything being the same on base, Sara was not exposed to various social class identities until her family moved to the United States. At that point, she became conscious of class stratification. Jacinda's story is similar in that her parents worked to provide a decent life for their family, and, with the exception of not having certain name brands, they were a fairly normal family within their community. In being raised within a working-class community, most families shared similar social classes (and racial identities), thus upholding this sense of sameness.

There is a shared perspective that in higher education social class is not discussed in any real way beyond financial aid or money, if even that. There is an assumption everyone knows, and they perform middle-class–plus rules, norms, and behaviors. This disregards those from poor and working-class backgrounds who are, essentially, unaware of a different playbook. Both Jacinda and Sally discuss the notion of "fancy" related to people and dinner events and their unfamiliarity with any of it. In this different social class world, each used the example of needing to learn which fork to use during a professional dinner and inevitably using the wrong one. This small example of the fork is not so small for those outside of the middle- and upper class ways of being. We show up differently and, depending on context, are not always welcomed. Sally shares that although she now has a seat at the table, she also still downloads coupons and earns a salary less than the cost of some of her students' cars. She exists somewhere in the middle.

In this social class shift, Sara and Sally also discuss a shift in and connection with their families. As Sara knows, social class is beyond economic capital, in which both of her sisters exceed hers; she still has greater capital, with educational capital from her degrees and in other forms, such as being part of the academy, an entity that was built on and seeps classism. Sally reframes her lens of imposter syndrome and rather than feeling like an imposter in higher education, her "true feelings of imposter syndrome came from the visits home . . . where I was worried I would be figured out by those I left behind" (p. 91, this volume). She became exhausted in her concern about how her dad would receive and interpret all of the markers of her current social class, not something to be taken lightly in her place between privileged and poverty.

Life in the middle is not always easy, and yet each writer figures out how to make it work. In this place of success and struggle, they role model tenacity and authenticity in figuring out how to be part of higher education on their own terms.

6

THE SENIOR
ADMINISTRATOR
PERSPECTIVE

*Narratives by Mamta Motwani Accapadi,
Thomas C. Segar, and Jeremiah Shinn*

The academy's class mobility narrative, upward mobility bias, and socialization process might be assumed strong enough to persuade those with a poor or working-class origin to remove all semblances of their background to have a long and fruitful career in higher education. But roots run deep; people often retain values and practices established earlier in their lives; and systemic challenges tend to endure. In this chapter, Mamta Motwani Accapadi from Rollins College in Florida, Thomas C. Segar from Shepherd University in West Virginia, and Jeremiah Shinn from Boise State University in Idaho share their stories and reflect on how their social classes of origin continue to arise in their higher education work, even as senior administrators. These individuals illustrate the blending that class straddlers may experience as they exist and persist in the academy.

Mamta Motwani Accapadi's Story: What We Do: Navigating Social Class as a Vice President

I had never thought about the complexities of social class until I began reflecting on navigating my own career journey as an educator. I grew up with a pull-yourself-up-by-your-bootstraps mind-set, and I was taught that mind-set. I believed that mind-set with all of my being: "Working hard is what we do." Although I never heard those words spoken in that way, they were the norm and expectation of my siblings and me growing up.

Daughter of Immigrants

To understand my social class journey, I need to share a piece of my parents' immigration story. My parents came to the United States in 1970, at a time when the country had lifted restrictions for immigrants from Asian countries due to a shortage of engineers, doctors, and nurses in the labor force. My father, having an engineering degree, came to the United States first, and my mother arrived shortly thereafter. Living in New York City, they settled in Jackson Heights, a neighborhood of immigrants, and began to pursue their American dream. Although many of their peers went into the stereotypical professions attributed to people of Indian descent (e.g., doctor, engineer), my mother found employment as a cashier in a department store and my father as a security guard. Even then, my parents thought they were fortunate—they sent money back to India, and the dollar to rupee conversion meant they were able to support their entire family, even on their hourly salaries in the United States. They came to the United States to raise a family in a country where their children could have access to education in a way they did not have.

I was born in December 1974. My mother had a C-section and went back to work the day she was released from the hospital—two days after giving birth to me. When I asked my mom why, she smiled and said, "Because you could get paid overtime working around the Christmas holidays, and I didn't want to miss that opportunity." This pattern would be the story of our childhood.

My family eventually moved to Houston, Texas, where my father was employed for a brief time as a mechanical engineer. By this time, we were a family of five with three children. Just as my parents were finally experiencing stability, my father was laid off from his job. Throughout our childhood, he was on-and-off employed, and as a result, my mother worked double shifts, sometimes even triple shifts, as a key-punch operator to keep us afloat.

The Race-Class-Culture-Gender Paradox

As a child I had no awareness that my parents struggled so much. I didn't realize that I was on the free lunch program in elementary school. In fact, I felt quite privileged. After all, we were not unfortunate like the people in India that PBS often showed on television. I had gold jewelry, a common thing for Indian families. None of my friends at school had gold jewelry, so it never occurred to me that I grew up in a working-class home.

My mother was very strict, and I assumed all of the decisions—from type of clothing, to school supplies, to restaurants, to the activities we engaged in after school—were based on the austerity that came from her cultural values and, thus, my cultural upbringing. Although some dimension of that assumption was true, I had no idea that our economic circumstances informed those decisions. I never had a lack of any kind of resource, particularly if it had anything to do with my education.

As the eldest child and as a daughter, it was my job to take care of my siblings. In the mornings, I set the breakfast meals for my family while my mother was getting my brothers ready. On the weekends, I was in charge of sorting the family laundry and would accompany my father to the Laundromat every Sunday, where we washed and folded our clothes. "Working hard is what we do." I never saw it as a sacrifice; in fact, I just assumed all people lived the way we lived. I was never allowed to work outside of the home because the expectation of me as a daughter was to serve the home. I grew up in a culture that believed daughters were the family's wealth and reputation, and you don't tarnish that reputation by making daughters work.

The Accumulation of Wealth

Because both of my parents were first-generation college students in India, they had no idea how to navigate the U.S. educational system. In many ways, although my mother had a strong personality, she deferred all financial decision-making to my father. We foreclosed on our house, severely impacting my father's credit history, and my father had no consciousness about a long-term savings strategy for me or my brothers.

Wealth is more than money. Wealth is an accumulated body of wisdom and experience that is passed on from one generation to another. My parents did not have this kind of wealth in India or in the United States. Although some families might have set up special college savings accounts or anticipated what the cost of college would be, my family had no idea. When it came time for me to apply to college, my mother learned for the first time that there was no real savings for me to go to school. Although this discovery was a shock to me, it was even more of a shock to her because she felt betrayed. For 20 years, she handed her paychecks to my father and assumed he was managing the finances appropriately. In fairness to him, he was doing what he knew how to do.

In any case, because of my academic accomplishments, I earned a full academic scholarship to University of Texas–Austin, and I worked throughout my undergraduate experience. I didn't know about or understand the concept of graduate school, but I did understand that if I wanted to continue my education, I would have to work to pay for it. For most of my graduate experience, I worked a minimum of two part-time jobs, sometimes even three, to pay for school. "Working hard is what we do."

Discomfort and Gratitude

I feel very uncomfortable sharing these pieces of my life story. The Indian part of me fears that somehow I am shaming my family. The upper middle-class part of me feels like I am trying to cover for what I have now. I continually question what it means to juxtapose my social class status as a child with my class status today, and if just by telling that story I am perpetuating a pull-yourself-up-by-your-bootstraps narrative somehow, regardless of whether it is unintended. At the same time, I feel so deeply grateful that I never realized our experience was different from most of my peers. I feel grateful that I have a work ethic that is clearly informed by my social class status as a child.

Surprisingly, navigating this journey across class status transitions has been humbling. I see, in one generation, how much wealth is passed on to my child compared with what was passed on to me. I know that my siblings and I will inherit my parents' retirement accounts and their home. The level of social class privilege I feel and see really challenges my own notions of access and equity. Recently, my nine-year-old daughter said to me, "Mamma, I just realized that I get most of the things I want, and all of the things I need." In her own way, she names her class privilege. Yet, in the same breath, she asks me, "Why do we not live in huge houses like all of my friends, and why don't I have a nanny?" In that breath, she names the enigma of the class conversation—that we somehow never arrive, and it keeps us from being honest about our class privilege.

Reconciliation

So how do we sit with the complexity of a fluid social identity status that has visible cues but may not be visible unless you know what to look for? How can I acknowledge the class status of my childhood while owning my class status today? I notice in myself a fear of sliding back. I regularly carry anxiety about how my employment status could change instantly, and this anxiety pushes me to lead an unsustainable work life. Because we all assess our social class status in comparison to one another, it is hard to come to an internal reconciliation about the fluidity of my class status but also the fact that I do not live in the class status of my childhood anymore.

The Intersections of Privilege

Although I could spend time focusing on the intersections of my subordinated identities, it is critical for me to be honest about how my privileged identities, when intersected, have a multiplier effect on my social class status. The more education I have received, the more access I have received, resulting in better professional opportunities. Having transitioned into middle age, I have agency over my actions and decisions in a way that young people and elderly people do not. These privileges have a positive multiplier effect on my class status, which then perpetuates a cycle of privilege from which I benefit as an individual and from which my daughter, in the generation after me, will also benefit. I think about how I can be more present and honest about my own privileged identities and carry less guilt. As a social justice educator, I feel like a fraud because I ask my own peers and I teach students to dismantle systemic issues and let go of their guilt, yet I hold on to my own guilt. The issues across different dominant-subordinate identities are unique, and there is no hierarchy of experiences of oppression, yet there is a haunting consistency of experiences that come with privileged identities.

Full Circle: Privilege, Power, and the Vice Presidency

Recently, over the past two years, I have really thought about how my class upbringing has shaped my professional pathways—both from a personal career trajectory and an operational approach within my position. On a personal level, I think about personal finances differently than my family. Although I have far more than I need, I realize that I carry a great deal of stress and anxiety around the fear of being unemployed and how I will take care of my family given that I am in a highly specialized position. Yet when I am in a calm space and can think about my privileged identities, I remind myself that my worst-case scenario might look like uprooting my family, giving up some conveniences, and experiencing some disruption to my life, but I would still be okay. In fact, I would still be beyond okay.

In my professional role as a vice president, I continually see how my upbringing has informed my approach as an institutional leader. I recognize this impact in three significant ways: (a) how I allocate and treat resources, (b) how I budget, and (c) the level of courage by which I am able to lead when it means asking for resources. First and foremost, probably any colleague would easily share that I am frugal. Earlier in my career, I used to take the leftover paper in our recycling bins and put it back in the printer so we used both sides of the paper. I didn't do this to be sustainable; I did this because it felt like a significant waste of resources to not fully use our paper. Similarly, when I ordered food for events, I would think about how portable the food might be for students to take home or when we might not use institutional catering services, which are often more expensive than ordering from restaurants. I spent so much time on decisions, trying to find a way to maximize every dollar spent, every resource possible, every moment fully realized. When I talk to my colleagues, I often ask, "Does this expense honor the tuition dollars our students will be paying off for decades into their future?"

Second and similarly, I am very conservative in how I budget resources. In my last two rounds of budget reductions, I have done whatever I can to absorb those reductions centrally so that direct services to students aren't significantly impacted. Yet I always try to spend less than I am allocated so that I can roll over funds to areas that need those resources. It is not unlike how I grew up. Just like I never knew our financial state growing up, I try not to create an environment for my colleagues to experience financial stress so they can serve our students in their fullest, most joyful ways. In many ways, my class upbringing taught me to prioritize what was most important, and I find myself leading with that same energy today.

Finally, I confess that I struggle with asking for resources. Although I am able to show the value of how my student affairs serve our institution, I feel deeply guilty taking the conversation the next step further and asking for more resources. I feel as if I have failed somehow—that I couldn't be creative or nimble enough to make ends meet or that I am contributing to an unsustainable business model. When I combine this with my identity as a traditionally raised South Asian American woman, it becomes even harder for me. I have always been told what amount of money I would have or not have in my personal life, so the idea of asking for money is deeply counterintuitive and uncomfortable for me. I have always believed that if I was good enough, then others would see, and the resources would come. So, when I don't see resources automatically allocated to my area, I have to work through my internal voice that tells me, "This is your fault because you didn't demonstrate excellence."

It has been freeing to openly discuss these reflections with my colleagues. At a time when more students and colleagues from working-class backgrounds are entering our institutions, openly discussing these topics allows all of us to interrupt our own life patterns and also hold sacred the experiences that have prepared us to be where we are today. We have the opportunity to claim the wisdom that has come with this identity.

Thomas C. Segar's Story: My Working-Class Family Background

I identify as a Black, cisgender, heterosexual, working-class male born in the United States as the descendant of slaves. Although I grew up 20 minutes from Baltimore, I lived in a small rural town outside of the city. My father worked as a pipefitter for General Motors, and my mother worked in food service in a high school cafeteria before I was born. She stayed home with me after I was born but cleaned houses occasionally once I started elementary school. When I was in middle school, my mother started working in a facility for adults with mental disabilities. She eventually took over the kitchen at that facility, where she prepared food for more than 60 people a day, by herself, for 20 years until she retired. My parents always had a hustle, whether it was my mother making Cabbage Patch look-alike dolls or my father doing side plumbing work. Cash was always exchanged, never checks, and every purchase my parents made during my childhood was also transacted in cash. Even the electric bill was paid in cash at the bank.

I lived the majority of my childhood in a house my father built with help from his friends. What I call a house could be described as a 3-bedroom, 1-bathroom apartment on top of a 3-car garage. In the 40 years since it was built, and to this day, that garage has never experienced a car inside of it, but it has housed tools, canned vegetables, and a washer and dryer. Before the apartment over the garage, we lived in a house located on the same lot that was built at the turn of the twentieth century with a stone-wall foundation and dirt basement. We had 1 full bathroom that my sister and I shared with our parents. Both houses exist about 50 feet from apart and still stand today.

We always had plenty of food. However, this meant my mother was a frugal shopper, and both of my parents were always watching for sales. Frugality meant my father would exchange cash for food stamps, which substantially extended the spending dollars and provided cash to mothers on public assistance who needed dollars for things food stamps just couldn't buy. Many conversations at the table—and we only had one table for all meals, which was located in the kitchen—were about what was on sale that week and where the best deals could be found.

We never wasted or threw away anything until it was completely used. I don't remember us ever throwing away food. We ate leftovers until they were gone. If they were not eaten, then they were frozen and presented again later. Leftover rice became rice pudding. Leftover baked chicken received new life as chicken stew or chicken soup. On the rare occasion that we had steak, there were seldom any leftovers, and usually that steak became my father's lunch. Besides beans, we seldom bought food that came from a can or a box like macaroni and cheese, frozen dinners, or Hamburger Helper. Prepackaged food never entered the shopping cart because the additional cost held no value when my mother could make something far better for a fraction of the cost. I remember seeing commercials for all kinds of food products that would never be found on our dinner table.

Only as I write and reflect do I realize how much I have held on to my working-class values. I have incorporated many of my parents' shopping and lifestyle habits into my life as a married adult with a middle school son and a high school son. More important, I have come to realize that these habits are not universally embraced. Yet I do eat leftovers until they are gone or I freeze them.

Even with a PhD and working as a vice president at a university, I repair most of the broken stuff around the house. A big part of that comes from being around my father and learning from him and his friends from the time I was 4 years old until my father's death, when I was 26. I struggle with what I perceive as unnecessarily spending money because a part of me believes that money should be saved or donated, not spent when I can make a repair for far less money. It's not about scarcity, but it reflects a strong belief in using talents and labor to save money. Nonetheless, I have to remind myself that time is a commodity, and at this point in my life, that time sometimes holds a higher value than money.

Social Class Identity and Higher Education More Broadly

Higher education over the past 100 years has mostly reflected the needs and interests of the middle and upper classes. I have a set of old yearbooks from the institution where I work dating back to 1924. Although the institution has more working-class students than anywhere I have ever worked, most students would identify as middle class and find the institution to feel like a place where they belong. However, the yearbook photos depict images more readily associated with fraternity and sorority life and other involvement that comes with a hefty price tag and might exclude students who have to work to pay for school. As I look at those photos, I ask, who has been left out of the picture?

Being left out often happens for poor and working-class students in subtle ways. For example, off-campus student activities events and even on-campus special programs that require students to pay out of pocket to participate create a clear division between socioeconomic classes. Similarly, student activities departments expect students to freely contribute their time to serving on activities boards with no means of compensating for any of their time, even when these same student activities board members provide staff support for events the rest of the student body attends and enjoys. Most student activities programs should be covered by the student activity fee folded into the cost of attendance.

Faculty members who judge working-class and poor students who have to work jobs during evenings and weekends demonstrate a high level of privilege and a sense of being out of touch. These same faculty members often express expectations around how students should be dressed when they come to class or establish requirements for students to pay for course- or academic major-specific supplies and fees out of pocket, actions that come from a complete lack of understanding of students' experiences. Any expenses (e.g., equipment, material, or supply) directly associated with a course or program of study should be included within the financial aid calculations of the cost of attendance and billed through the institution to reduce students' out-of-pocket expenses.

Rising costs of higher education and many states' divestment from higher education continue to make a college degree less attainable than in previous years. Institutional financial aid often rewards the middle- and upper middle-class experience with merit-based aid for families whose expected family contribution as calculated by the Free Application for Financial Student Aid (FAFSA). This metric means these students can likely pay for most of college and do not need institutional merit aid, which becomes more of a recruitment and admissions yield strategy than a means of making college more affordable for those who need it. Poor and working-class students face high expectations about being open to assuming large amounts of debt to complete college and, at times, have lower standardized test scores, making them ineligible for merit-based aid.

Events such as Family Weekend can create a great deal of stress for poor and working-class families. Not only do these students feel out of place, they feel even more foreign when their families come to campus. Family Weekend programs center on the middle-class experience by simply assuming all families from every background can and should take time off from work and stay in a hotel or travel a great distance for a short period of time. These events often provide limited or no opportunity to participate remotely, so students for whom travel and lodging falls outside of their family's budget have to endure the weekend alone while students whose families have the means enjoy a weekend of activities, only to see poor and working-class students with no families present.

Social Class as a Senior-Level Professional

I have held tightly to my working-class roots—or perhaps those roots have held tightly to me, which keeps me grounded. This grounding has created a heightened sensitivity to social class so I notice how often class gets left out of the dialogue about the way students show up. Perhaps more concerning, I have observed how race often serves as a proxy for class, suggesting that White students are not poor or working class but students of color generally are. Yet that assumption fails to grasp the lived reality of poor and working-class White students and middle- and upper middle-class students of color both facing discrimination and feeling like they do not belong but for different reasons.

Personally, I have noticed the ways in which senior-level colleagues describe how they spend their time and discretionary income. What they describe and the associated details share little in common with how my current household or my family of origin spends time and discretionary income. I have much less in common with donors, alumni, and local business owners who have an interest in the institution and with whom I have needed to collaborate. Most senior-level professionals appear to more readily connect with these individuals, and the connection appears to be one of class and race; class and race seem equally salient when it comes to these relationships.

Specifically, donor events can be awkward and have required me to round a learning curve. This has meant understanding and figuring out dress, social norms, and how to simply interact with anywhere from 50 to several hundred donors, alumni, and business partners. Social class often informs how one has learned to navigate such environments and how one has come to develop a sense of belonging. Over the years in my role, I have forced myself to engage in these environments and to adopt the belief that I belong because the perspective I bring, based on how I show up, does add value. To be clear, that belief had to be adopted, because I certainly wasn't born with it.

Colleagues don't understand the student experience, where students are coming from, and their challenges. Even when working in a state with many poor and working-class students, I notice statewide higher education policies that run counter to the needs of all students. For example, some colleges require 60% of tuition payment within the first 2 weeks of class, not permitting payment options that would spread the cost over a semester. Instead, schools promote third-party payment plans that at best allow students to spread costs over 2 months, with final payment due before the middle of the semester. Students must apply for these plans at least a month before the semester begins. Early application requirements and the short payback time frame often result in only middle-class students and their parents taking advantage of these payment plan options.

I have strived to bridge what appears to be a separate world between working-class and poor students' college needs and the college experience my colleagues seek to create for students. At times I ask myself whether I have done enough and whether I could do more to influence cost and culture on my campus to communicate affirmation and a sense of belonging. We invest little time discussing the realities of social class for students and have not responded nimbly enough to adjust practices, policies, and programs to be inclusive and responsive to poor and working-class students. I hope this book and our personal stories inspire a call to action for higher education administrators.

Jeremiah Shinn's Story: Fortitude and Irreverence

During my career, I have been fortunate to work with decent people in supportive environments and to progress into a role on campus that would indicate I have achieved at least some measure of professional success. I have spent more than half my life living, learning, or working on a college campus, and I consider my higher education experience to be the greatest privilege I can imagine, second only to my marriage as the most consequential thing to which I have ever dedicated time and energy. If ever there was a person who should have felt like a higher education insider, it is me. However, throughout my education and career, I have often felt like an imposter in the academic environment. I have routinely wondered whether I was just lucky to have avoided that one ill-advised opinion, poorly timed remark, or flawed logical argument that would identify me as a fraud and hasten my eviction from the ivory tower. Although I admit it sounds dramatic and it is certainly disproportionate to the reality of my experience, it nonetheless represents how I have felt at many junctures during my experience in the academy—the feeling of being an uninvited guest.

I was born and raised in a small Arkansas town by a young, single mother of three who did everything she could to shield us from the reality that each day was a struggle. I grew up in a family and an environment that is most accurately defined as working class, both financially and culturally. As a kid, I was involved in countless conversations about fishing, muscle cars, and baseball, but rarely a conversation about literature, economics, or the world beyond Pope County, Arkansas. I regularly attended Sunday school, Bible school, and hunter education courses, but not geography camp, band camp, or other experiences that would present an occasion for me to periodically spend time learning on a college campus. Attending college wasn't something that was necessarily expected or promoted in my family. There was no hostility toward college, and I do not recall being discouraged from attending, but I always sensed that it was something for other people. As I was growing up, college was a nonissue in my daily life, so I never seriously considered that I might attend college until a few of my peers began discussing dorms and majors as we approached the end of high school.

I consider myself fortunate to have inherited some of the best qualities of both my parents. From my father, I inherited an innate curiosity and a love of knowledge for the sake of knowing. I recall childhood visits with him being like a protracted game of trivial pursuit. There was always a story and set of related facts that brought dynamism and depth to even the most mundane places, things, and events. I carry that love of research and propensity for trivia with me today. From my mother, I inherited fortitude and a healthy dose of irreverence. She did not (and does not) play by anyone else's rules and has always approached life with a can-do attitude and an unwavering sense of confidence that she could do anything (and also that I could do anything). She always assumed she belonged wherever she wanted to belong, and she encouraged me to assume I did too. I did not ask for these qualities nor did I work to develop them in myself. I simply inherited them in near a perfect proportion that I am convinced is a reason I was able to overcome some fairly daunting structural and cultural barriers and ultimately succeed in my education and career. The circumstances of my birth did not predict that I would be sharing this story in an academic publication. Fortunately, DNA and good luck conspired to provide me with a few of the necessary tools to take advantage of some great opportunities—opportunities that others might have taken as a given by virtue of their own family history and formative environment.

I first began to recognize social class during the sixth grade. In my hometown, there were six elementary schools (grades K–5) that funneled into a single middle school (grades 6–7). When we arrived at middle school, it was apparent that students' starting balance of social capital (or how cool they were) was generally determined by the elementary school they had attended. I recall being incredulous that it mattered so much where you had gone to elementary school. Of course, it was a simple proxy for where you lived, and where you lived was a simple proxy for your socioeconomic status, so it makes sense to me now that I have a more informed and nuanced understanding of how the world works. Unfortunately for my friends and me, we had attended the elementary school that ranked fourth or fifth out of six in terms of social standing and prestige. We were neither outcasts nor treated poorly, but I remember something in my gut telling me that I would have to work a little harder to achieve the status that some of my classmates enjoyed by virtue of having attended a more prestigious elementary school. They seemed more naturally able to navigate this new environment. To this day, I do not believe they understood the stratified dynamic that existed, but it existed nonetheless, and those of us from the less prestigious elementary schools felt it, even if we could not articulate it.

I always heard my grandparents, aunts, and uncles talking about being "country bumpkins" when they were in school. They talked about feeling inferior to the folks in town, and they warned me not to get my hopes up when it came to participating in high school sports. I distinctly remember someone in my family telling me, "The kid whose daddy works at the bank or the insurance agency . . . that's who'll be playing on Friday night when you get to high school." Because I had always heard some version of this story and because I saw it playing out daily at school, it was difficult not to assume my fate was somewhat predetermined, at least as it related to something as socially important as playing high school football. I recall many working-class kids giving up sports or not trying at all. I still wonder whether they were hearing the same words from their grandparents, aunts, and uncles I was hearing from mine. Over time these words can reframe the expectations you have for yourself and cause you to view the very attainable as somehow out of reach. Thanks to the fortitude and irreverence I attribute to my mom, and thanks to her constant reminders that I was as good as anyone else, I managed to climb from a lower tier elementary school nobody and B-team fullback to starting wide receiver and student council president just a few short years later. Yet in doing so, I was never able to shake the distinct feeling that I was crashing someone else's party, even if I had amassed sufficient confidence to partially offset it.

My working-class background remains a foundational part of my identity as a human and a higher education professional. During my education and career, it has always been there, quietly shaping how I experience institutions and practices that were built by and for people with different backgrounds and experiences from mine. I also acknowledge that it differs from my other identities, in that nobody I meet today would assume I had a working-class background unless I disclosed it. Further, I do not believe my working-class identity has had much outward impact on how I have been perceived on campus, what I have been able to accomplish, or how I navigate my professional career. Although I have mostly adopted the dress, the neighborhood, the preference for organic foods, and the love for international travel that is more typical of an upper middle- or professional-class identity, I have also retained some of the feeling of not quite fitting in and of constantly crashing the party that I willed myself to fight against from the sixth grade until I graduated high school.

Graduate school was a particularly exasperating time for me as I grappled with what it meant to challenge my own cultural norms and to (for the first time) be around faculty and peers who had a fundamentally different worldview and set of experiences than I did. The transition from the small regional university in my hometown to one of the preeminent public universities on planet Earth was almost more than I could endure. My undergraduate institution felt like it was made for me. It was home. My graduate institution felt like it was made for someone else. Just as I had observed when I entered the sixth grade, it was obvious to me that my classmates were far more adept at navigating this new world than I was. It seemed so familiar to them. They seemed to know what to say and how to act. They sounded smart. They discussed concepts that were foreign to me and made declarations that called everything I had ever known into question. I hated it there. Not because I was excluded, ridiculed, or marginalized and not because I was academically or intellectually unprepared to be there. I hated it because I did not understand the rules, and I was exhausted by the burden of trying to fake it. But fake it I did, just as I had done before.

Although there have been times in my career when I have felt like an imposter on the verge of being discovered, those times have become fewer and farther between as I have progressed and amassed professional and social capital. I acknowledge that I have become a member of the in-group. I now feel more confident that my colleagues and peers believe I belong and know I have something to contribute. Still the higher education landscape is littered with vestiges of elitism and barriers to entry. Obsession with Carnegie classifications, rankings, athletic conferences, and one's own academic pedigree all serve as not-so-subtle reminders that our core values and incentive structures are not nearly as egalitarian as our most well-intended musings might indicate. From time to time, I encounter an individual or a situation that wakes up the sixth grader or the first-year graduate student in me—someone or something so blatantly and myopically elitist that I cannot help but revert to my place of frustration, and my natural inclination summons my innate fortitude and irreverence while guarding against being found out. Conversely, because I have developed a degree of comfort in this new culture, I no longer regularly notice the little things—the tiny, nuanced pieces of evidence that formerly served as constant reminders that this place was not meant for me. This is why it is vitally important for me to know the students on my campus, to hear their stories, to understand their struggles, and to remember that struggle does not only occur under the weight of blatant violence, oppression, or marginalization but also under the weight of 1,000 subtle reminders that they too are crashing someone else's party.

We have work to do if we are to create environments that are actively inclusive of students who might not fit the traditional definitions of at risk. We have to do this work with the knowledge that for college students who possess other dominant identities, the marginal identity of social class can be relatively easy for them to hide, assuming they acknowledge it to the extent that they are compelled to hide it. One of the interesting things about social class identity is how tempting it can be to fake it as a member of a different class, to not ask for help, and to go at it alone without a supportive community. To do otherwise might feel like making an excuse. It was never an option for me to make sense of my reality in a way that felt like an excuse. To do so would betray the self-reliant, bootstrap mentality of the working-class culture that will always serve as my anchor.

When members of the working class go to college, they can encounter an unfamiliar world that was not built for them. But as they learn and grow, they often discover that the world they left—their home—is not built to understand or appreciate who they are becoming as a result of venturing beyond that which has always been normal, right, and familiar to them. Like most working-class and first-generation college students, I am proud of my family. I am proud of the values I learned and the relationships I built in that small Arkansas town. I am thankful for the family, friends, teachers, and neighbors who believed in me enough that I was able to believe in myself. I have no doubt that I am here because I was once there. At the same time, I am also extremely proud of my education and career. I am proud of the fact that I have broadened my worldview, learned to think critically, and grounded myself in an intellectual community. I am proud to have changed my mind on a number of important issues, and I am proud to have brought a degree of clarity and practicality to some unnecessarily intellectualized conversations related to real human experiences. Finally, I am thankful to the colleagues and professors who have consistently and warmly welcomed me into this strange new environment and, like my mother, reminded me I belong here as much as anyone.

Narrative Analysis

As we take in these three individuals' stories, we should first note that, although they may be few in number, some senior administrators in the academy come from poor and working-class backgrounds. So, if you are reading this as someone who shares that background and aspires to serve in a similar capacity, know that is possible; and if you are reading this from a different lens, know that the senior administrator on your campus may take actions you don't quite understand because their social class worldview differs from yours.

Our senior administrators describe for us some of their childhood experiences and then offer insights on how that upbringing melds into their present-day roles. All of them share the multitude of influences that taught them about their social class, noting family as the most promi-nent instructors. Although they hold different racial and ethnic identities, Mamta and Jeremiah both name the bootstrap theory that was present in their households and communities, the belief that it is up to individuals to work hard enough to alter their own circumstances and the disregard for any systemic barriers that might hamper that. Thomas mentions his own parents' work ethic, holding multiple jobs at once, and talks about food as a symbol of social class in his household, utilizing coupons and making the most of leftovers. Jeremiah also examines how location and school rank, even at the prek–12 level, can impact one's social and cultural capital and, correspondingly, how a student is perceived by peers, teachers, and administrators.

Mamta, Thomas, and Jeremiah discuss how these values and messages from their backgrounds manifest in their perceptions of higher education and their roles as senior administrators. Jeremiah offers his dual pride in his upbringing and the people involved in it and in his opportunities to grow through education but notes that, despite acquiring some middle-class ways and preferences, imposter syndrome can consistently lie below the surface. Mamta describes how she notices her social class background influencing her feelings and decisions around divisional budgeting and resource allocation. Similarly, Thomas explains the awkwardness that can arise at donor and fund raising events because of differing social class worldviews and types of navigational capital. Mamta also acknowledges the vulnerability it takes to talk about social class, particularly when someone experiences a clash between their class of origin and their current, or attributed class, or both. This complexity of identity and context can instill feelings of fear and guilt, both of which Mamta describes. Additionally, all three administrators reference other dimensions of their identities that interact with their social class—namely, race, culture, and gender. This highlights, yet again, that social class is not experienced in isolation and, thus, is influenced by and through its combination with other aspects of our identity.

The three individuals explore how the academy does—or does not—serve students from poor and working-class backgrounds. Thomas points out an array of barriers we create between students and their academic and cocurricular engagement, including time, costs, financial aid policies, and the conflation of racial and class identities that often results in inaccurate and harmful assumptions about students. Mamta focuses on the financial hurdles she faced and how current students encounter similar or additional monetary obstacles in pursuing higher education, noting the reality that many must maintain several jobs at once to stay enrolled. Jeremiah highlights the classist practices of stratification that occur through Carnegie classifications, *U.S. News & World Report* rankings, and athletic conference alliances. He also cautions that all of us—those from poor and working-class backgrounds included—can become less aware of how social class shows up on campus as we become more comfortable with and immersed in the middle- and upper class conditions of our institutions. Thus, it is imperative that we remain vigilant to social class.

The stories of Mamta, Thomas, and Jeremiah provide us with insight on how even ascension to the highest administrative ranks of the academy does not automatically translate into fitting in. The rules of the game may still trouble us even if, or perhaps more so when, we understand them. They also call us to pay attention to the people in our campus community, learn their stories, and lobby for changes that will include social class identity in the diversity conversation and increase equity for those from poor and working-class backgrounds.

7

THE NONTENURED
FACULTY PERSPECTIVE

Narratives by Loren Cannon, Raul Fernandez, and Tori Svoboda

Let's be honest, status in higher education is a social class setup and faculty positionality embodies it. Nontenured faculty play a critical role on campus, yet their often large course loads and lower pay than that of their tenured colleagues are critical reflections of who receives what type of treatment. Unfortunately, being undervalued is something seemingly familiar for nontenured faculty with poor or working-class roots. Nonetheless, they are dedicated to student learning and success and work diligently to reflect it. This commitment to learning and community is represented in the stories of Loren Cannon at California State University, Humboldt; Raul Fernandez at Boston University; and Tori Svoboda at University of Wisconsin, La Crosse. We can learn from their willingness to engage the influence their social class of origin has had on their approach to working in a system that is not meant for them and their methods of managing the dynamic with clarity and compassion.

Loren Cannon's Story: Looking the Part

My experience of social class, in higher education and elsewhere, involves a dynamic interplay of elements that affect my relationship with those with whom I come into contact at work and also how I view myself. The often invisibility of class differences means that I can have a hard time recognizing the origins of my responses to certain social events, assumed norms, or ways of being in the world. These responses are sometimes related to my class background, whereas at other times my economic history combined with other aspects of my life experiences, rather than being invisible, shows up in nearly every aspect of my personal and professional lives. This history is both invisible and yet ever-present. As a White middle-aged man with a doctorate in philosophy and a background in mathematics, it is within the academy that I should, in some ways, feel quite at home. In some ways, I do. Yet there is an underlying feeling that my presence in the academy is somehow accidental, that I slipped in the back way, that if they knew my pedigree I'd be shown the door. In fact, my first college teaching position teaching mathematics at an urban community college came with the recurring dream of this theme. In the dream, a college administrator comes to my office and explains that I have been found out and thus must leave. My dream self responds with acquiescence, seemingly recognizing that this meeting would be inevitable, and I begin to pack my office belongings, knowing that I am not the kind of person who should have my own office, let alone one at a college.

I suppose some families discuss social class openly, but in my experience, the ideas I gleaned from my parents and early life experiences about the realities of economic privilege or vulnerability were unstated, opaque, and sometimes pretty bizarre. For instance, I noted as a young child that employees at fast-food restaurants wore the same uniform. From this, I inferred that those who, for instance, worked at McDonald's were a certain kind of person. At times, these ideas developed into a form of childhood imagining that people were determined or destined to do certain jobs because of their family background. It is almost like I imagined the United States to have a strict caste system in which one is born into one's profession, whether it is shoemaker, farmer, or McDonald's burger flipper. I would wonder, then, what sort of job I was born to do.

My father worked for the United States Postal Service. My earliest memories involve our family moving to Denver, Colorado, as a result of my father's employment transfer. Although I knew to be thankful of my father's steady government job, it was also obvious that his experience with the United States Postal Service was full of frustration and disappointment. My father soldiered on despite what seemed like deep dissatisfaction, waking up at 3:30 a.m. every workday and having really nothing left to offer his family in terms of support or attention after work. I never got the message that my dad regarded his work as meaningful, fulfilling, or something he was proud of. It was simply a means to a paycheck. It was equal parts life sustaining and life draining.

One ordinary day in October 1975, my father went to work as usual but did not return home. He had a fatal heart attack on the job. The post office, which seemed to be the source of so much grief for my father, was also the source of the government pension that kept my family afloat after his death. My mother struggled in many ways with her sudden and unexpected role as a single mother (my brother and I both still lived at home, ages 12 and 11, respectively). Shortly after my father's death, we downsized, and my mother went on the job market. With a high school diploma and work experience that was several decades old, she managed to land a job at the local county library reshelving books. As a true bibliophile, my mother found the job had its perks, but the pay was minimal (I made more as a lifeguard at a local pool) and being on her feet all day aggravated her arthritis. She was later promoted to library clerk, with a minimal salary increase. My family again was thankful that a mostly stable government job allowed us to pay the bills, but my brother and I were left largely to fend for ourselves as my mother, like my father before, seemed perpetually exhausted.

Being conscious of social class requires being conscious of a kind of difference. This requires being in settings in which this difference is observable. It involves getting out of the mind-set of "This is just how the world is" to "This is how the world is for us" and having a certain kind of characterization of who is included in this "us". Because most everyone I knew had two living parents, I knew, of course, that my father's death was an anomaly. However, knowledge of the economic ramifications of this event came to me only occasionally and unexpectedly. As we downsized into a smaller home, many of my schoolmates seemed to be moving into ever larger ones. Overnight, their homes seemed to grow extra garages and family rooms, and even in the winter their homes were heated to what felt like tropical temperatures. As I watched my peers grow seemingly richer, I watched my elder sister struggle to raise her own children in a kind of poverty that made my lifestyle seem rich in comparison. I related to my extended family more than I did to my classmates. These ideas led me to believe that my family was not fancy and our lives weren't filled with fancy things or fancy houses, and that there was a lot of fancy out there; it just didn't include us.

The idea of being fancy included going to college. Although I was academically inclined, I struggled with the expectation that I would attend college. This expectation seemed at least presumptuous if not outright arrogant. My mother was quite gifted, as were all of my siblings. Why in the world did I think I'd be successful when they didn't even get the chance to go to college at all? Besides, I would think at many insecure moments, do they even let people like me go to college? My state's flagship university intimidated me; it seemed a huge place that was a kind of playground for people who were uncommonly beautiful, in that alpine outdoorsy kind of way, and exceedingly rich. I also assumed they were much smarter than I was because that probably just came as a perk when one was both beautiful and rich anyhow.

I went to a school that had recently (temporarily) lost its accreditation and so was nicknamed "University of No Credit." My high school swim coach had gone there, and she thought I might have a chance on the team. I was accepted, gained an athletic scholarship in my first quarter as a walk-on, and kept it for four years. Going to school was a job, and swimming was part of that job. The students who "partied," engaged in what seemed like childish "floor wars" at the dorm, went on fancy vacations, and seemed, unlike myself, not to be deathly afraid of failure were baffling to me. I majored in secondary mathematics and had a Spanish minor: a prudential choice of emphasis when bilingual education was popular and there was a shortage of algebra teachers. Although I have an affinity and a respect for mathematics and perhaps for languages, my choice of study was my attempt to set the stage for later economic security.

My path from an assumed career in secondary education to that of working as a faculty member at a community college, and now at a state university, was steady and methodological. Earning an MS in theoretical mathematics paved the way toward my (tenured) community college position, and my doctorate in philosophy gave me the credentials for my present position. At each stage of my career, I attempted to ascertain whether the feelings I had of failing to belong were because of an inferior character, intelligence, or my own personal experiences and my subjective response to the same. It took decades for me to understand that although I didn't seem to have the same social capital as my academic colleagues I was no less capable. I am most often described as a hard worker, which is true. Although I can't overstate my personal commitment to teaching, scholarship, and service, being hardworking is a habit that began decades ago as a result of recognition of vulnerability and a need for security.

My experiences in higher education have surely been produced by being a first-generation college student from economic insecurity, but of course my experiences also affect the way in which I understand the world and myself. My Whiteness has undoubtedly privileged me in any goal I wished to undertake with regard to my education and professional life. I have never reported to a non-White supervisor and only rarely, in 11 years of college, had a person of color as an instructor. My class background has simultaneously fueled my capacity for success while making me hesitant to believe that such success was really possible, until it had been fully attained. Having one's nose constantly on the grindstone may lead to success, but it doesn't allow one to recognize when it is time to seek assistance, in the form of either an institutional program or a colleague, for doing so would only confirm suspicions (my own and possibly others) that I wasn't meant to be here in the first place. Similarly, a focus on avoiding economic disaster through personal effort rarely gave me the opportunity to become comfortable with small talk, easy comradery, or self-advocacy. Last, my queerness is an inextricable aspect of my experiences in the academy. As a student I shunned most social events because I felt I should be studying and also because I wasn't sure how to hide my queerness in my university's suffocatingly straight and cisgender context. As a faculty member, I have been actively shunned by fellow faculty colleagues and have endured a litany of microaggressions as a constant part of my career. Contrastingly, more recently I have also been seen as cool or even trendy by students and faculty members alike—sometimes even to the point that my identity, as a transgender man, is seen as a strange and unexpected progressive windfall for which the university can brag, "We even have one of those!!" In many ways, the ubiquity and dominance of my Whiteness, combined with the relative rarity and peculiarity of my gender history, seems to hide, if not erase, the fact that social class has been and continues to be relevant to my experiences.

My insider-outsider status is ever present. As a White middle-aged married man, I look the part of an academic philosopher; I look to be an insider. Yet when my transgender history is known, it is not unusual that I am deemed not a real man and instead some kind of phony or counterfeit replica. This kind of response by nontransgender colleagues is not uncommon for transgender individuals across the country and is both disrespectful and identity-denying. In a different way, my social class experience has led to years of feeling an imposter of a different kind—that my family is simply not the kind of family to produce academicians. Because global travel often necessitates knowledge of new languages, traveling between different social spaces requires learning various dialects and ways of communicating. I know that I speak somewhat differently with my family of origin than I do with my colleagues at work; I had to learn a different dialect when I changed disciplines from mathematics to philosophy, as I did when I began living as a man after four decades of living as one whom most perceived as a woman. There is yet a different dialect for explicitly queer or trans spaces. Although learning to communicate in different contexts is something to be valued, it can also represent a division or even fragmentation of self. The question "How am I to communicate to you?" (as a brother, as a trans guy among others, as a faculty member of invisible class and gender history, as a White middle-aged man buying a part at an automotive store . . .) starts to feel like "Who am I to you?" or even "Who do I need to be for you?"

I have worked at my present institution now for more than a decade. In many ways, I am an insider: Many assume that I am on the tenure track or received tenure long ago. It isn't unusual that I feel the need to out myself as "just" a lecturer to tenured colleagues who don't know my professional status. The moniker of hard worker has followed me to my present position, and I have built a curriculum vitae that includes professional publications, presentations, and community and academic service work that would be more than sufficient to earn the title of full professor. I have done this both because of my own values and because my status lacks the security of a tenure-line position. My department has requested a tenure-line position for more than a decade but has been turned down by the administration. Budget concerns are stated as justification for the denial, but the practice of not funding tenure-track lines and instead hiring lecturers (adjunct faculty) is a national epidemic. We presently live in a context in which upward of 70% of classes taught at our nation's colleges and universities involve non-tenure-track faculty. Lecturers like me regularly teach twice as many students for less than half the salary of a tenure-line instructor in essentially disposable positions.

My experiences in higher education have involved both belonging and not belonging—existing in a dialectical and fluid relationship. My extended career track (gaining my PhD at age 41) happened in large part because of my hesitancy to believe that academia could ever be a home for someone without a family pedigree of academic achievement. Now I find that my father's legacy of being part of a union is crucial to my own academic labor being valued in a way that provides any degree of security for me and my family. I was wrong when, as a young child, I believed that social class determined profession. Perhaps what I was noticing then was the presence of hierarchical structures and their capacity to reproduce themselves across professions and exploit those positioned on the lower rungs of the institution, whether that individual is sorting the mail, shelving books, or teaching courses in philosophical ethics.

Raul Fernandez's Story: I'm Not Even Supposed to Be Here

It was game 7 of the 2013 National Basketball Association (NBA) finals, and the Miami Heat had just bested the San Antonio Spurs in what was already being called one of the greatest playoff series of all time. The postgame celebration was well under way when NBA superstar LeBron James, with a championship trophy in one hand and a most valuable player trophy in the other, was being interviewed by ABC's Doris Burke.

Just two years earlier, in a highly publicized announcement, James left the Cleveland Cavaliers and his home state of Ohio for greener pastures in Miami. At the time, critics lambasted "The Decision," and some irate fans literally set his jersey on fire. Meanwhile, Cavaliers owner Dan Gilbert publicly chastised James for his disloyalty—a move seen by some as illustrative of the paternalistic attitude of the NBA's nearly all-White ownership toward its mostly Black players.

In this context, Burke asked James, "How, when everyone is coming at you, do you keep your head and perform at the level you do?" I was vaguely paying attention until I heard his response. "I can't worry about what everybody say [*sic*] about me," said James. "I'm LeBron James, from Akron, Ohio, from the inner city. I'm not even supposed to be here." It was that last line that immediately resonated with me: "I'm not even supposed to be here."

James was a multimillionaire superstar athlete with two championships under his belt—not exactly the most relatable figure for your average student affairs professional (I was working in student activities at the time). However, having become acquainted with his personal story, I knew we had come from similar humble beginnings: he in Akron, Ohio, and me in New York City.

With that one line, "I'm not even supposed to be here," and the shrug that followed, James was saying something about how elusive success can be for any low-income person of color. He was also saying there's a certain attitude that those from our shared background have about the challenges and criticisms we endure—in the larger symphony of our lives, it's all white noise.

Tracking Success

Success in academia has many measures, but none is more closely attended to by college presidents than the rankings, which are informed by retention and graduation rates. By the latter measure—college completion—success has been particularly elusive for Latinos. Just 11.1% of Latino adults hold bachelor's degrees, whereas only 3.9% hold master's degrees and just 0.7% hold doctorates (U.S. Census Bureau, 2016). The figures are even bleaker for Latino men from low-income, first-generation backgrounds—people like me.

I knew none of this as a child. I was born in 1977 to working-class parents in New York City. My mother was born in Ponce, Puerto Rico, and moved to the city as a teen. My father, who is also Puerto Rican and has some Mexican lineage, was born and raised in New York. They met while attending the State University of New York at New Paltz. Neither completed their studies. They got pregnant with my sister one year into college and, after years of odd jobs, made ends meet working for the transit system—my father cleaning trains and my mother cleaning buses.

I spent the first years of my life in Spanish Harlem, also known as *El Barrio*. It was and largely remains a neighborhood of poor and working-class Puerto Ricans. Many of these *Nuyoricans* were born in the city, and some, like me, knew just enough Spanish to get by. After the apartment where I lived as a baby burned in a fire, we moved into a new federal housing project called Taino Towers. Marred by disputes over money and construction, the complex of four 35-story buildings sat vacant for 3 years before finally opening in 1979 (Goodwin, 1979). Its name was a nod to the indigenous people of Puerto Rico who were decimated by the violence, enslavement, and smallpox brought to the island by Columbus and his compatriots. I spent my formative years there.

I started pre-K at Manhattan's P.S. (Public School) 96 at age 3 and received excellent marks in math, oral expression, and the arts, although just good in social behavior and study habits. These grades and similar marks in kindergarten led a teacher to recommend me for the Talented & Gifted (TAG) school on East 109th Street. I didn't know it at the time, but this moment was pivotal for me. The small measure of promise I showed as a child provided access to public education that was excellent, specialized, and (most important) free of charge—first at TAG, then Manhattan East, and finally at the Bronx High School of Science.

It's instructive to think about other pathways that my classmates may have taken. My family moved to the South Bronx in 1986, just as the crack epidemic was spreading across New York. Had I not been tracked into specialized schools, my default high school would have been Adlai Stevenson—a failing school plagued by gang violence, with a graduation rate of just 30%. It was closed for poor performance in 2009 (Robbins & Meyer, 2013). Compare that with Bronx Science, which counts among its alumni 2 Nobel Prize winners and recently boasted a graduation rate of 100% (New York City Department of Education, 2016).

Bronx Science is phenomenal at preparing students for the hard sciences if you show up to class—something I neglected to do much of during my junior and senior years. As a result, I struggled in math and science during my first year at Boston University (BU). I did excel at English and writing and decided to transfer to the College of Communication. I explained all of this to Chip, the head of BU's Science and Engineering Program, but he refused to let me transfer out, saying that I'd backdoored my way into the university. Still rough around the edges, I unleashed a slew of expletives on him, punctuated by, "Do you really want someone like me in your program?" He didn't, and he signed the transfer papers right there.

That part was easy. Getting my folks to go along with the switch was not. In the end, my father refused to pay for the rest of my time at BU, saying, "I sent you there to be an engineer. If you want to do something else, you can pay for it yourself." I took a semester off to work security at a high-rise downtown and slept on a couch in an apartment shared by my fraternity brothers. Established in 1931 to support Latin American students studying abroad in the United States, Phi Iota Alpha Fraternity evolved over the years to serve Latinos from low-income backgrounds. Those men supported and encouraged me to return to BU. I took out tens of thousands of dollars in loans to make that happen—a choice that I'm still paying for today. I struggle to rationalize that debt, which limits my ability to invest in the future, while I continue to benefit from the network of BU-related friends and colleagues.

I found myself in the field of student affairs quite by accident. I was working at a public relations firm when the dot-com bubble collapsed in 2001. My firm laid off most of its employees, although I was kept on and promoted likely because my salary was so low. Then came 9/11. The firm all but shuttered its doors, and I was left to collect unemployment. With a collapsed economy and few job prospects, I moved in once again with fraternity brothers, this time in Miami, Florida. While there, I did what many people do when the economy tanks—I went to graduate school. While at Barry University, I was a graduate assistant and resident assistant, which led to an interest in working in higher education and, ultimately, a job in student affairs back at BU.

Course Corrections

I had a rough run in my decade of work in student affairs, having encountered so many people who just don't get students from backgrounds like mine. There's a sense among some that we need to treat all students equally regardless of race or social class identity. Although that sounds nice on the surface, this color- and social class-blind attitude does nothing to address the inequities that folks with the grit and good fortune to make it to our institutions have endured and are still facing.

My own experience tells me that just a minor course correction can have an immeasurable impact on a life, and that educators are in a unique position to make that impact. I haven't talked much about my sister. She didn't get the same opportunities. No one tapped her as talented or gifted. She went to the usual schools, became disillusioned, got into trouble, and eventually ran away from home. She had two kids and works for the city, just like my parents. Same family, different opportunities, different outcomes. I've thought a lot about this over the years. It came to mind when I completed my doctorate and again when I became a faculty member. What would my life be like if I didn't get tapped and tracked into a resource-rich program at such a young age? Statistically, not writing this.

It's not just me who knows these stats. So do my colleagues and students. A faculty member who is Latino and male from a low-income, first-generation background? Good luck finding one of those in your average academic department. I don't particularly enjoy being the only one. In fact, I encourage every Latino higher education professional I meet to consider getting a doctorate and joining the faculty—something that was done for me some years ago.

Balling Out

I don't have imposter syndrome, that feeling where you think you don't belong, but it is odd to realize that my faculty colleagues all have doctorates and many are experts in their fields. We have flexibility in what we choose to research, how we teach our classes, and even what we wear to campus. It's that last one that can really show your social class status. What a person chooses to wear when there are few restrictions can be telling. I really overthought this for the first year. What will they think if I don't wear a blazer to this or wear jeans to that? However, over time, I just stopped caring what others thought and developed my own look: mostly jeans, with black sneakers, a button down, and a cardigan. Good enough? Honestly, who cares? What matters most (or at least should) are the work and our contributions to it.

BU's president came to visit with our faculty recently. We were advised of a process whereby we would funnel questions to our department and committee heads, who would be the only ones allowed to ask questions during the visit. President Brown concluded his opening remarks and offered to take questions. Ignoring the rules, I stood and asked him about support services for students with Deferred Action for Childhood Arrivals status. I felt the stares of other faculty members who must have been wondering whether this rookie faculty member didn't understand the process. Of course I did, but I'm here and he's there, and I've got a question about a group that I don't think anyone else is going to ask about. So I broke the rules, with no regrets, and I look forward to doing it again soon.

Some might think I should count my lucky stars. Do nothing to risk the title and treasure that's seldom bestowed on someone with my background. I just don't see it that way. Being one of a few gives me a sense of responsibility to speak up and advocate for others. It's true: I'm not even supposed to be here. But I am, and while I'm here, just like James, I plan to ball out.

Tori Svoboda's Story: "I Could Always Go Back to Being a Bartender"—Musings of an Ambivalent Academic

Like many other kids who grew up in poor or working-class families, I learned early on that to get by in school I'd have to adopt new ways of speaking, writing, feeling, thinking, and being. My earliest memory of school is being labeled as a free-and-reduced-lunch kid. We had to stand in a different line and wait for the full-paying students to go first. I remember the shame, ridicule, and judgment coming from others as well as arising from deep within me.

Being in the free-and-reduced-lunch line or receiving charitable help of any kind always felt awful. I was grateful for the help but fully aware of how systems and people in them had a way of making you feel like shit. People like the lunch lady who wanted to make sure we didn't "steal all the food." People like the teacher who asked me to retake a gifted and talented test because she was surprised I did so well. People like the social worker who said, "Do you want to be adopted or go back to foster care?" knowing both choices were undesirable. These folks may have had good intentions, but their gaze elicited shame. Clearly some held contempt for my family, others held pity, and none held joy. They didn't see us as their equals, just as unfortunates.

Perhaps they bought in to the so-called American dream, which suggests anyone can get ahead with hard work and ingenuity. If folks are poor, then their own bad choices are to blame. I understand the appeal of the argument (see Vance, 2016, for a contemporary version of this approach). To be honest, my own family is an example. I have two mothers, four fathers, and seven siblings from being in foster care, then adopted, and always in "broken" homes filled with drug/alcohol addiction and violence. School officials knew we were from the wrong side of the tracks, and I kept proving it.

My first detention in third grade was for telling a dirty joke, and I realized then that coarse language was not to be uttered in school. My next detention, in fifth grade, was for hitting another girl who said my family was trash and they only adopted me so they'd have cheap labor. I learned that violence was unacceptable, but only if it was seen. My first suspension came after someone reported I had alcohol in my locker. It wasn't even mine, but when caught, I wasn't going to rat out a friend just to save my hide. Loyalty was a value I learned from family, even if being loyal to those you cared about brought personal harm. Plus, I knew the school officials wouldn't believe me because by then I was living on my own. When people talk about college being the first time a student lives independently, they aren't talking about kids like me.

Truth be told, school has always been a safe haven because I love getting lost in books and learning. However, it has also been a site of contestation because I'm always treated like I should feel lucky I'm even allowed in. Critical pedagogues like McLaren (2016) would call my experiences being schooled rather than educated, and Bourdieu (1989) names this type of schooling as symbolic violence. Even well-meaning educators, perhaps like those reading this book, often collude with education systems designed to (re)train young people from working-class backgrounds to eliminate any traces of their home values/language and encourage assimilation to a middle or upper social class norm. The assimilation training that started during my K–12 school years was only amplified in college.

College

Most of the people in my small rural community did not go to college. Many men followed their folks into farming or blue-collar factory work, whereas women tended to go for secretarial positions. Few of us went to college, and even fewer finished. I started college the summer after high school graduation because I needed a place to live and learned I could stay in a residence hall of a regional college if I took summer courses there. I transferred those credits to a regional state school because it offered me a scholarship. I knew nothing about college majors, college options, or college financing. I had no idea that people shopped for colleges, that some were more prestigious than others. I had no clue, but I quickly learned.

People say social class is invisible, but it was on full display during move-in weekend. I pulled up in my 15-year-old rusted car with a few garbage bags of clothes. Others had their parents drop them off, bringing in storage bins full of goodies. After that first weekend, I found that other people at college assumed I was middle class—likely because I was perceived as White and learned how to class pass with clothes from thrift shops and more proper language. Students, faculty, and staff at college didn't know my family history, and because of my cisgender and racial privilege, I could fit in as long as I kept my mouth shut. The idea of being seen as the norm was tough because I had become accustomed to my identity as an outsider and didn't want to give it up. Hurst (2010) found working-class students often became renegades, assimilating to new environments and abandoning home, or loyalists, staying true to roots and home communities. I tried to be both, functioning as a double agent.

On the one hand, I loved college for all the different things I could learn and the opportunity to connect with people from racially and socially diverse backgrounds. On the other hand, I had "tells" beyond clothes or language that would give away my background. Other students joined clubs/organizations, but I didn't because I prioritized work. Others talked about studying abroad, but I believed that was just for rich kids who wanted to party abroad. Others talked about internships and networking as if we all had families connected to professional networks. My folks, who achieved sobriety and later success, would be able to provide that type of network today, but back then? Not so much. These days, social media is my big tell, as people see posts from my loved ones and are surprised that not everyone I love is a college-educated liberal progressive.

So much has been written about the experiences of first-generation low-income students, I hardly need to repeat these stories. Like many others, I straddled classes, speaking a different language at school than at home. I dealt with the "hidden injuries of class" (Sennett & Cobb, 1972), fully understanding that moving up the socioeconomic ladder was not a smooth journey. My friends and family were incredibly supportive, but the support was often served with a side of resentment. "Oh, college girl, think you're better than us?" they'd wonder aloud. College did teach me to think I was better than those who lacked formal educations, and I'm ashamed to still carry that with me.

Student Affairs

I finished my undergraduate degree in 4 years by working several jobs and enrolling in classes every summer. It was the only way to make up for lost credits when I transferred from a quarter-system to a semester-system institution. I went to graduate school for counseling and fell into student affairs backward while in that program. After a 20-year career in the field, half of which included teaching as an adjunct instructor in a graduate student affairs program, I changed lanes to become a full-time lecturer, then an assistant professor.

I enjoyed teaching part-time in a graduate program, and I was told that our leadership would no longer support staff teaching more than once per academic year. Teaching is what gave me the energy I needed to make it through grueling days as an associate dean. I was successful by many measures, but I found myself more and more resentful of the economically privileged students and colleagues with whom I worked. When several people sent me a job listing for a full-time lecturer position at a nearby state school, I applied. I took a $42,000 pay cut to take the position. Gulp.

I figured if I didn't like it, I would find another administrative position. I didn't have a partner who could make up the difference in earnings, but I had paid off my student loans and credit card debt. My partner comes from a similar working-class background, and we both knew that we had already lived on far less and could do so again. If nothing else, I could always go back to bartending, something I did while in graduate school. When my partner said, "Go for it," I did.

I was disappointed that after having an established career I was tracked into new teacher orientations, which assumed I had just completed my graduate degree and had never taught before. It was as if everything I had done over the past 20 years no longer mattered. Indeed, it hasn't mattered in the tenure process at all. Plus, because I entered as a lecturer and not an assistant professor, I was expected to teach all of the courses that others didn't want. This meant I had more courses, more new course preparations, and larger sections. After a year, I applied for 2 assistant professor positions. I was offered one at a private school, with a starting salary $25,000 higher and fewer teaching obligations, but I chose the one at the public school because I felt a greater fit with the institution, which enrolled more low-income and first-generation students.

Untenured Faculty Perspective

The longer I work in higher education, the more open I am about where I come from and what I return home to each night. People often assume that because I have my doctorate I'm now fully entrenched in the professional upper class. I certainly am when it comes to my educational capital. However, as I found in my dissertation research (Svoboda, 2012), the professional middle-class identity is like an ill-fitting suit. Underneath, embedded in my skin and bones, is a working-class identity. My partner and most of my friends remain working class. I'm more comfortable at a meat raffle in the local bar than I am at a faculty senate meeting. (For those not familiar, meat raffles are held in local so-called dive bars, and you buy a paddle for $1 and hope to win a few pounds of sausage or roasts or whatever they acquire.) I didn't leave my home fully behind, and I know that where I'm from isn't embraced by those with whom I work.

I frequently encounter others (faculty, staff, and students) who find my backstory either amusing, confusing, or both. Their eyebrows arch when I explain I never visited colleges while in high school, especially when they realize I was a high school student before the Internet or Google searches existed. They chuckle when I reminisce about comfort foods such as butter and sugar sandwiches, bouillon cubes eaten like sugar candies, or hamburger rice hot dish. They laugh heartily at my self-deprecating jokes, intended to blunt the edge of judgment when my unsophisticated self appears. It's the game we play. They'll tolerate me as long as my inappropriate presence is smart enough to pull back and retreat when I've pushed too far. When I push too far, reveal too much of myself, then I become the "inappropriate other" (p. 418, Trinh, 1997).

At a recent professional writing retreat, a prominent editor nearly spit out his coffee when I shared that if this tenure thing didn't work out, I could always go back to being a bartender. "That's so . . . , so . . . , um . . . , that's so . . . refreshing?" he finally sputtered out. He giggled and slapped his knee, as if I had told him a dirty joke. He later told me that "nobody is talking about class in higher education," which meant he thought either I was a nobody (because I had been writing and presenting about it for nearly a decade) or I wasn't anybody who counted (which seemed more likely because I notice that those in highly selective institutions look down their noses at those from less well-known colleges).

Just last week, in two faculty retention meetings, women were told they needed to sell themselves more, to be more visible. "Get out of the kitchen and take credit for what you served!" Ugh. I was told the same thing and chose not to go up for promotion this year because I didn't feel like I had done enough or could sell it enough. This feels like a case of gender and class combined, with little acknowledgment that when faculty of color or White women faculty express confidence they are mistaken as being arrogant. Once again, the individuals are seen as problematic rather than the system. The system demands conforming to a value that is 100% against everything I was taught about the importance of being humble, hard-working, with your nose down. To be seen as a show-off is one of the worst things you can do, and now you're telling me I won't get tenure or promotion unless I do it? That's just the way the system works?

I call bullshit. The whole system of ranked and contingent faculty is nonsense, with clear disparities along gender and racial lines, and what would be clear disparities along social class lines if we ever tracked how many faculty were former Pell Grant recipients or free-and-reduced-lunch kids. I'm often told, "Just play the game . . . and once you get tenure you can work to change the system." Really? I'm not sure I see evidence that those who get the prize ever look back over their shoulders at the working conditions of those behind them. If that were true, then more progress would have been made to provide adequate pay for contingent faculty, as well as to rewrite bylaws to acknowledge diverse approaches to teaching, research, and service. The good news, for me, at least, is that I'm in my 40s now, and perhaps with age (and racial or other privilege) comes the wisdom that I do not need to be as invested in trying to prove my competence. My future is not tied to this job. It is just a job, not my life. If I don't earn tenure, I have other options. I may not have been as confident in this truth while I was still paying off student loans or too young to see a future other than the one others had laid out for me. Still, as I've said, I can always go back to being a bartender. What's wrong with that?

Narrative Analysis

Even as educators with the necessary credentials (e.g., a doctorate), an underlying notion still exists that these faculty members are not systemically meant to be part of the academy. Tori discusses her class-straddling experience as a middle-class professional while personally returning home to her working-class life. She shares, "I know that where I'm from isn't embraced by those with whom I work" (p. 125, this volume). When she shares stories of her class of origin with colleagues, she is tolerated to the degree of their comfort. Loren feels that his being present in the academy is somehow accidental, and if his pedigree were known, he would be "shown the door" (p. 113, this volume). Bottom line, Raul begins and ends his story with the idea that given his class of origin as a low-income person of color, he is "not even supposed to be here [working in academia]" (p. 121, this volume). All three people carry with them an awareness that, although they can be part of the minimally middle-class life of academia, their "kind" is essentially not welcomed.

They knew it was their responsibility to pay for their education because they could not rely on their families to do so. Whether through an athletic scholarship or bartending, it was necessary for each of them to work to pay for their educational endeavors. Loren and Tori share the experience that while other students were involved in cocurricular activities or on extravagant vacations, their priority was working to pay for school. Once Raul changed his major, resulting in his parents no longer financially supporting him, he took time off from school to save enough money to go back. While not being part of the mainstream tapestry of students (i.e., from a middle- or upper class family), all three pushed forward for their first degree through hard work and dedication, with more degrees to follow.

In the precarious role of lecturer, Loren and Tori have had to teach more courses, sometimes those that others did not want to teach. This results in more course preparation as well as larger sections. Regardless of the amount of professional publications and presentations and community and academic service, Loren has been committed to the same institution for the past decade and has yet to receive the approval for a tenure-track position, accompanied by the typical reasons cloaked in budget constraints. The structure of non-tenured, tenure-track, and tenured professorship is a continued reminder of what the "lesser class" has to do to earn a living, often with much less salary, academic freedoms, and protection resulting in a greater risk of job loss.

Tori and Loren have a different relationship with the concept of imposter syndrome related to social class compared with that of Raul. Both Tori and Loren share that they do not come from families that produce academics and can fit in as long as they don't stretch the boundaries too much. There is a clear difference in language and behavior between their backgrounds and how they should exist on campus. Luckily, as the years have passed, there is less need to show up toeing the class line. Raul avows that, although he does not carry the imposter feeling, he does recognize he holds privilege in this current social class status with work flexibility, his research, and his ability to dress business casual on most any given workday.

Because some of their identities are mentioned within their stories, each impacts them differently. For Raul, there is an innate connecting of his social class identity with that of his Latino identity. Throughout his story, he weaves in his racial identity or, minimally, being a person of color and the importance of such. Within Loren's story, he shares that his White identity has provided certain privilege in his career trajectory while his "queerness is an inextricable aspect of [his] experiences in the academy" (p. 115, this volume) and is seen as being cool and trendy. Through this multifaceted lens, he has an ever-present sense of being both an insider and an outsider.

This triad of nontenured faculty understands the importance academia has had in their lives; despite being part of a system inherently structured to exclude them, they share a passion for education. They are able to pull from their social class of origin to show up with integrity, dedication, and drive to meet the demands placed on them in their positionality for student learning and support.

8

THE TENURED
FACULTY PERSPECTIVE

Narratives by Nancy J. Evans, Rudy P. Guevarra Jr., and Larry D. Roper

Tenure is often seen as the Holy Grail—the pinnacle of an academic career that gives someone license to say and do almost anything within the academy. However, things are never quite as they seem. The spoiler alert here is what tenure doesn't do: supersede deeply ingrained biases that people have when looking at or interacting with someone. Therefore, classism is still present, along with other isms, no matter how much or how long you have proven yourself worthy to be in higher education. Yes, even among the tenured and emeritus (i.e., honored folks who retain influence and privileges on retirement) faculty, social class influences how they are allowed to engage with and challenge the academy. In this chapter, we will learn more about negotiating social class identity from three faculty members who represent the three points beyond tenure—associate professor, full professor, and professor emeritus—through the stories of Nancy J. Evans, professor emerita at Iowa State University; Rudy P. Guevarra Jr., associate professor at Arizona State University; and Larry D. Roper, professor at Oregon State University.

Nancy J. Evans's Story: My Life in This Fine Place So Far From Home

In 1995, Dews and Law edited *This Fine Place So Far From Home*, a collection of essays by working-class academics, which captures the voices of the often-silent members of academia whose experiences as faculty are different from the lives they led growing up. These essays resonate with my lived existence as a tenured college professor who left my hometown of 800 people in upstate New York to attend college and later joined the ranks of the professoriate, living and working in a "fine place" that is "so far" from the home in which I grew up. In this brief reflection, I share a bit of my background as the disabled daughter of working-class parents, a first-generation college student, and a faculty member.

Growing Up

Home for me was a working-class family in a rural area of upstate New York. Farming and factory work 30 miles away in Schenectady were the main occupations of people in the area. My father, who left school after the sixth grade, was a tenant farmer. As is true in many working-class families, my father believed in traditional gender roles, in which the man was the family breadwinner and the woman stayed home to care for the family. My mother was the daughter of Norwegian farmers. She had completed a hospital-based nursing program and worked prior to her marriage. As my father desired, she did not work outside of the home after she married. When I was starting sixth grade, my father decided he needed more stable employment and secured a job working for the county highway department repairing roads, driving snow plows, mowing grass on the sides of roads, and doing other tasks related to the upkeep of county roads. We moved into town, renting one side of an old duplex until my father saved enough money to put a down payment on a house trailer, which we moved into just before I began ninth grade.

Living in an area made up of small towns and farms, where almost everyone around me was at about the same economic level, I never realized that we were poor. It was only after I left my hometown and compared my background to those of others that that realization hit me. Poor meant not having the money for extras such as movies, dining out, or going on vacations. It meant eating a lot of fish sticks, canned spaghetti, and government surplus cheese. It meant wearing clothes that my mother made. It meant my father charging Christmas presents and paying off the bills for the rest of the year. Three experiences made my life different from the lives of most working-class kids: (a) contracting polio when I was 4 years old, (b) being tutored at home in 8th grade, and (c) enduring the unexpected death of my father when I was 14.

Polio

I contracted polio during the last major polio epidemic in the United States. Between the ages of 4 and 12, I was in and out of hospitals having numerous orthopedic surgeries and rehabilitation. Most of my treatment took place at Albany Medical Center (Albany Med), which was about 30 miles from my home. My parents visited me as often as they could, but the expense of traveling back and forth from the hospital created a real financial strain on my family. Their inability to visit me more than once or twice a week also meant that I spent a lot of time alone when I was hospitalized. Although not ideal, I do think the self-reliance I have counted on all my life was built during those early years.

Although Albany Med was a reputable hospital and my orthopedic surgeon was well regarded for his work with polio patients, my mother always regretted that we did not have enough money for me to be treated at the Mayo Clinic in her home state of Minnesota. She believed that I would have received better care there that could have prevented the extensive paralysis I experienced as an aftereffect of polio. I doubt whether I could have avoided this outcome, but it saddens me that it bothered my mother so much throughout her life.

My Tutor

At age 12, I underwent the last orthopedic surgery I was to have. It involved surgery on both legs and required me to be in a full-body cast for several months while my bones healed. As a result, I could not attend school. My school principal arranged for one of the school's teachers to come to my home every evening to tutor me through eighth grade. A second-generation Hungarian, she was both inspiring and outspoken, in addition to being very funny. She saw my academic potential and challenged me to do my best. She also stood up to my father, who saw no point in women going to college, and convinced him to let me enroll in the college-prep track in high school. I am sure without her influence I would have been in the business track, destined to be a secretary at best. She remained my ally and mentor throughout high school and during my college choice process. I owe her a special debt of gratitude for instilling in me the importance of clear, concise, and well-constructed writing that contributed to my ability to produce meaningful published work.

Death of My Father

The death of my father in a work accident was a shock. The secure environment I had experienced, in which my father was clearly in charge, disappeared. My mother had to learn to drive, handle finances, and make decisions she was unused to making. She also returned to working as a nurse. Our financial situation improved as a result, but my brother and I were left alone through the night while my mother was working and during the mornings and evenings when she slept. As a result, we experienced an emotional void and had to take responsibility for our own actions and decisions during our teenage years.

Undergraduate Experiences

Because of my disability, I was eligible for the services of New York State Vocational Rehabilitation. They would pay for my college education if I attended a college in New York State and followed an educational program of which they approved. I decided on SUNY-Potsdam (Potsdam State), a college that did not seem concerned about my disability (as my first-choice college had been), assuring me I would be able to negotiate its flat campus. I wanted to follow in my mentor's footsteps and become a teacher, but Vocational Rehabilitation did not believe I could stand in front of a classroom all day and would not approve this career goal. Because I could not afford college without their assistance, I changed my plans and began college with no specific career in mind, which they, for reasons I could not understand, approved.

Attending Potsdam State was not a huge challenge for me because it was in a small town in rural northern New York, and many of its 5,000 students were from working-class backgrounds. I did well academically and was active on campus—involved in student government, campus radio, and a sorority as well as civil rights and anti-Vietnam War activism. I graduated in the spring of 1970 with no plans for my future. I had had no career counseling, nor did I have role models other than teachers and nurses, two careers that Vocational Rehabilitation had ruled out. After spending a year back home with my mother while I unsuccessfully searched for any job I could get, I sought advice from the dean of students at my college and decided to enter graduate school to prepare for a career in student affairs.

Graduate School, First Jobs, and Doctoral Study

My master's degree program in higher education-student affairs at Southern Illinois University presented challenges I had not experienced at my small undergraduate college. I was now supporting myself with a graduate assistantship. I knew that my mother could not provide much in the way of extra financial support, and I was therefore very limited financially. That meant no extra money for eating out, ordering pizza, attending events that cost money, or vacationing over breaks, nor could I afford to attend conferences or join professional associations. When I was given the option to complete my master's program a year early by enrolling continuously (summer, fall, spring, and summer) rather than for two academic years, I jumped at it because I would save money and could start working earlier.

Finding a job was a frightening proposition for me because I had been unsuccessful at doing so after I finished my undergraduate degree. I did not want to live with my mother again, and I was not physically able to do the kind of temporary jobs that others could do while continuing to job search. I therefore took the first job I was offered—as assistant dean of students at a small private college in rural Missouri. Although the job was engaging—a generalist position overseeing housing and student activities—I was lonely and had no peers my own age. If I had not been so scared about not finding a job, a characteristic of many working-class and disabled individuals, I would have recognized when I interviewed that isolation would be an issue.

The college eliminated my position after one year. In the late summer, with my self-confidence at a low point, I finally found a residence life position at Stephens College. Stephens, a private women's college in Columbia, Missouri, was a totally new experience for me. At that time (early 1970s), it was transitioning from a traditional "finishing school" for wealthy young women to an academically focused liberal arts college preparing young women for careers. As such, the students in my residence hall came from a variety of socioeconomic backgrounds and had quite varied perspectives and goals. As an example, my three resident assistants included a woman on a full academic scholarship from upstate New York whose father ran a gas station, a woman from Pittsburgh who was majoring in dance, and a woman from Virginia who was majoring in equestrian science and boarded her horse at the campus stables. Rather than seeing their differences as problems, I strived to use them as resources to help me understand the various viewpoints and issues that arose among the 95 diverse women who lived in the hall. I must admit, however, that when my hall president—a bright and engaging woman from Texas—told me that she would be taking a week off to attend her cotillion at home with her father flying her both ways in his private plane, I was not sure how to respond.

Working as a live-in residence counselor was a physically demanding and confining position. I found late-night calls and being constantly on call to be stressful and tiring. So, after two years in the position, and after testing the waters by taking a few psychology courses at the University of Missouri (MU), I made the decision to apply to their doctoral program in counseling psychology. Before I was really sure this was the career path I wanted to take, I was accepted and decided to enroll. Again, my decision was influenced by my need for security. I was also flattered that a program as competitive as Missouri's would accept me.

To ensure that I could support myself and pay for my studies, I spent two years of my doctoral program working part-time in the student activities office at Stephens College. Although this arrangement worked for me, it did prevent me from becoming close to my doctoral classmates who spent all their time on the Missouri campus. It was also a factor when third-year required internships were awarded; partially because the faculty did not know me as well as other students, I was not awarded an MU Counseling Center internship. With help from my adviser and because of my own resiliency, I secured an internship at the University of Iowa Counseling Center, requiring that I complete my dissertation off-campus but providing me with a wonderful learning opportunity.

After completing my doctorate, I worked for a few years as a counseling psychologist at the counseling center at Bowling Green State University (BGSU). I learned a bit about educational capital when I secured an adjunct teaching position in the College Student Personnel program at BGSU—my doctoral adviser and BGSU's College Student Personnel program chair had been classmates at Columbia University. I also discovered that I much preferred faculty life to the life of a counseling psychologist. After two years at BGSU, I left my job and secured a temporary faculty position at Indiana University.

Faculty Experiences

I have experienced a lot of dissonance as a faculty member from the working class. Although I am now financially secure and have the money to do pretty much whatever I want, I still think, and sometimes act, as if I were still a member of the working class, which can sometimes be uncomfortable and other times beneficial. Most of my faculty colleagues and many of my students have had middle-class or affluent backgrounds. They take for granted the resources that have been available to them throughout their lives, such as second homes, lavish vacations, travel abroad, private schools, new cars, and the latest electronic gadgetry. When they begin discussing all the material benefits they had as children and teens, I think back to my upbringing, where a vacation was visiting relatives in another state, which happened only twice, as I recall. The fancy hotels in which professional conventions and meetings are held still overwhelm me, as do the homes of some colleagues.

However, being from the working class has made me more sensitive to the varied backgrounds of my students. I understand that many of them did not have the money to hop on a plane to attend an on-campus admissions interview, and I have advocated for phone or Skype interviews for these students. I have encouraged the student organization to sponsor free events, such as picnics or socials at students' houses. I have also frequently brainstormed with students about inexpensive ways to attend conferences and encouraged attendance at less expensive state and regional conferences.

As I approach retirement, I worry about whether my husband and I have enough money to continue to live comfortably, although our financial adviser has told us we are doing just fine. We still live in a modest ranch-style home, drive vehicles until they wear out, and look at the prices on the menu when we eat out. In my mind, these are good things. Some of the working-class values I hold dear are being careful with money, looking out for those I care about, and staying humble, even in this fine place that is now my home.

Rudy P. Guevarra Jr.'s Story: We Got You

If you had told me during my high school years that I would be a professor one day, I would have said, "No mames!" For reals. I had a different life path planned for myself, and it wasn't being a professor. At that time in my life, I was involved with gangs and trying my hand at making music. The year was 1990 and that was my dream, or so I thought. After years of getting into trouble, working a lot of meaningless jobs, and the music thing not being what I thought it was cracked up to be, I had to rethink what I wanted to do with my life. I remember being told once by a former high school teacher that if I got my shit together I would be a good teacher. That comment always stuck with me, but I never gave it much thought until I started to think about my future and what my calling was.

My life lessons would soon be a way for me to navigate academia. The thing about running the streets when I was younger was that I learned a street hustle that served me over the years. It enabled me to see how academia was one big hustle. I had to both play a strategic game and enter a world that was never meant for people like me. My hustle now would be clocking grants and fellowships, grinding hard, professin', networking with my people (of all backgrounds), and making sure I would survive this profession with what I learned outside the ivory tower.

I also realized that being involved in music and performing had given me skills that would serve me well in the classroom. I still get nervous before every lecture, but it was the same feeling I had before a performance. Thus, teaching to me became a performance. It gave me the same high that I got being onstage. Although the delivery was not the same, I was still able to let my voice be heard—to share the knowledge that we were all exposed to and articulate what we were learning in a way that made sense; was real; and, best-case scenario, was transformative. In those moments, I knew I found my calling. Even today when I walk on my campus, I feel a sense of peace and happiness knowing that I get to make a living doing what I love. It is a privilege that comes with its own set of challenges, frustrations, and responsibilities, but for those who come from similar backgrounds, we know that our presence in the academy is crucial. Many first-generation college students, for example, see us and can relate to our familiar faces, our mannerisms, and the struggle that we all share when it comes to fighting for social justice and equity. Looking back, I realized that everything I went through as a teenager and into my early 20s was preparing me for this path. My experience is my own, and although for some it may seem unique, it is not. There are many others out there like me who now occupy these positions, and some of you reading this right now also have a similar story. This is mine.

Making Moves

High school was whack. I skated by and graduated, and then I attended one semester of community college before dropping out. I obviously wasn't ready. After realizing my life had a different path for me and I needed to take advantage of the opportunities my parents sacrificed for, I went back to community college after five and a half years. This time I was older, was a bit wiser, and had a fire inside and determination to get through and move on to a four-year university.

Finding My Place

I was hungry for knowledge and read a lot, but at times I felt intimidated to speak because I thought I sounded too raw, too "ghetto," compared with the other students who for the most part did not look like me at all. My friend Liz, who also attended Southwestern Community College and transferred with me to the University of San Diego (USD), made me feel like I could do it. She encouraged me. She was at times the one friendly face in some of my classes. Her presence made me feel at ease in a sea of Whiteness and, most of all, privilege. I found several ways to survive this environment. One was my relationship to the campus community. Because I was a transfer student and older than many of my peers, I didn't have to stay on campus. I commuted, maintaining my connection to my family and communities, which enabled me to endure. Another was my connection with people on campus to whom I could relate. I joined *Movimiento Estudiantil Chicanx de Aztlán* (M.E.Ch.A.) and made friends with students who belonged to the Black, Filipina/o, and Pacific Islander clubs. This space and those friends (many who were also from San Diego) were crucial to my survival at USD because I had a place to go where I could be me and feel at ease in the elitism that was part of the larger campus environment.

My professors were also important for my intellectual growth and were some of my earliest mentors. Learning from and visiting them during office hours enabled me to see how much they cared about their students. They inspired me. For example, one professor in particular unknowingly showed me what I wanted to do with my life. His name was Gonzalez, and he was our Chicano history professor. I looked forward to every class meeting. He would come and start every class with a story, hooking us from the get–go and having us hang on to every word of his lecture. Gonzalez was an amazing storyteller and he inspired me. One day I went to his office hours and sat down. I was nervous because he seemed so professorish. I was intimidated as I tried to formulate my question. I immediately blurted out, "So, how can I be like you, Holmes?" He looked at me seriously, pushed his glasses in with a smile, and said, "Well, you have to go to graduate school." I then replied, "What is graduate school?" That was when our mentoring relationship began, and I started to prepare myself for what my future would be: entering graduate school and becoming a professor. Gonzalez's guidance and friendship enabled me to see what kind of professor I wanted to be, which was a storyteller and a historian. Along with Gonzalez, I found additional mentors to work with and learn from in my Introduction to Ethnic Studies class. They all influenced and inspired me to become the teacher I am today. Those classes prepared me to find my voice and make my next move: graduate school.

Building a New Community

I couldn't believe I made it to graduate school. When I first made it to UC Santa Barbara (UCSB) in 2000, I was excited to experience this next chapter out of my life as a PhD student in history. My excitement, however, soon ended. When I went to the department to check my mail, another graduate student (who was White) asked with a look of suspicion whether she could help me. I turned and said no, trying to stay composed. When I went home, I spoke to my partner at the time about this and started getting angrier. Some would suggest that maybe my peer was just trying to be helpful. I call bullshit on that. Unless you are in a situation where your presence makes others feel uncomfortable and you are constantly viewed with suspicion and even fear, you can keep your opinions to yourself. This is a familiar feeling I've experienced many times throughout my life, and it was not a question of genuine assistance but one of, "Who are you and why are you in this office looking through that mailbox [which happened to have my name on it]?"

It would not be the last time I was made me to feel uncomfortable and marginalized at both UCSB and in the larger town of Santa Barbara. In those moments, I've been mistaken as a janitor or some form of "the help," a trespasser on campus, and other stereotypes that I would experience being racialized as Latino (I'm mixed Mexican-Filipino). This was not uncommon when I entered a space that did not consider people like me as belonging to these institutions. In fact, I felt so uncomfortable in the history department that I actually spent more time in Asian American and Chicana/o Studies, where I had an office as a teaching assistant and found more acceptance.

In graduate seminars, I also began to close up because of this marginalization, coupled with a growing discomfort because many of my peers reflected yet again this nondiverse population that for the most part also smelled of privilege (I believe I was one of six active graduate students of color in the whole graduate student population in my department at the time). Unlike the majority of my White peers, I did not come from a privileged background, and I was not as well read in the discourses and theories that were posited in our graduate seminars. The majority of these books were written by authors who I could not relate to, but I had to do the reading as part of our required courses. I did feel a sense of insecurity that I didn't know these authors and concepts, whereas most of my other peers did. I felt like, despite all that I had read, I still didn't know enough. I started to question myself. Do I belong in graduate school? Did I make a mistake coming here? Am I smart enough to make it and get my PhD? All of these thoughts of self-doubt were part of my own personal imposter syndrome. What could I contribute to these conversations as a homie from San Diego, California, who grew up in working-class/poor neighborhoods and did not have access to the same resources or privileges growing up as many of my peers?

With time, I began to see that my life experiences were an asset in graduate seminars that no amount of reading and theorizing could replace. For example, I remember in one graduate seminar my peers were theorizing about race and racism, but in my opinion, they had no clue what those concepts actually meant to people who had experienced them. My professor saw my frustration and then called on me. I asked my peers whether any of them ever knew what it was like to actually experience racism and made to feel unwanted in a space because of the color of their skin. Did they know what it was like to experience violence at the hands of the police because you fit a certain profile and you were helpless to defend yourself? Did they know what it was like to be a victim of a hate crime because they were not White? None of them could answer me. It was then that I knew my voice not only mattered but was a crucial part of these conversations. I also knew in that moment I would survive graduate school because I came with a certain life experience that many of my peers had no clue about or could speak with authority base on a lived experience. Their privileges shielded them. Those experiences, as painful as they were, became my assets in an institution and space that existed on a solid bedrock of elitism. Moreover, I came to UCSB knowing what I wanted to write about: my family and my communities back in San Diego. They were invisible in U.S. and California history despite their historical contributions and growing presence. I was determined to write my communities into existence. My voice would tell the story of Mexicans, Filipinos, and mixed-race Mexipinos in San Diego. They mattered, and I would show the world why. As I went through my graduate program at UCSB, I also relied on my family for their love and support. It was my balance against a world that I felt like I didn't really belong in.

As with my undergraduate experience, I reached out to the professors I was working with in the history department such as Zaragosa Vargas and Paul Spickard, as well as those in Asian American, Black, and Chicana/o studies, to seek their guidance and start building mentoring relationships with them. They became my mentors, friends, and strongest advocates for my work. What also made my time at UCSB meaningful was the community of friends I helped build to ensure that we would watch each others' backs and support each other through classes, exams, and the campus environment. I met many of these students in seminars run by Spickard and Vargas, who had a diverse group of students from other fields, who in many ways were also marginalized in their home departments and were seeking a like-minded community. It's great how we can find amazing people to connect with in some of the most isolating and conservative places.

We slowly began to build a community of people of color and White allies who were like-minded in terms of social justice and equity. We built our own community to change the culture of academia. These friends were from sociology, education, English, history, and so on. With that community, we were able to build a network that spent time together socially and also helped each other. As new graduate students came in, we offered a welcoming environment where they could build friendships and mentoring relationships. This group of friends and mentors provided a welcoming space for us to not only survive but also thrive. When asked how I got through grad school, I always say my family, network of friends, and the mentoring I received from my professors. In those spaces of community, I also found my voice as a teacher, writer, activist, and mentor.

I am a product of these friendships and mentoring, and now I pay it forward to my students, both graduate and undergraduate, from my home institution and others throughout the country. I know that for those of you reading my story there are others like you who are going through the same thing, feeling the same insecurities, and questioning your presence at your institution, wondering whether you also belong there. Let me reassure you: You do. Your voice and presence matter. The specter of imposter syndrome will always be present, but you must endure and prove to yourself that you belong right where you are. Your journey led you there, and your voice will be a testament to both your struggles and success in this profession. As long as we can accept that these spaces were not ever meant for us but we are here, we got in because we were qualified and need to be in these spaces to contribute to the conversation and transform it. Most important, we must hold the doors open for subsequent generations of scholars from underrepresented communities so that academia can be another space that is reflective of our society. As you travel along your own personal journey, find those people with whom you can build a community. They will be your chosen family, friends, mentors, and colleagues in this profession who will support your endeavors as you all rise together to become the gate smashers of the ivory tower and transform what education was meant to be: transformative, equitable, and inclusive. You are not alone. We got you.

Larry D. Roper's Story

I am always caught a little off guard when I am referred to as a first-generation college student. Clearly, as the first in my family and the only one among my generation of cousins on both sides of the family to attend college, I was certainly a first-generation college student. However, this descriptor jumps over the fact that neither my parents nor grandparents were high school graduates. As a result of this family circumstance and inherited legacy, my initial challenge was not solely developing a vision of college as a future destination but rather envisioning myself as a high school graduate.

Simply stated, I was born into and grew up in a world of poverty and racial segregation. At the time I was born, my father, mother, and 3 older siblings were living with my grandmother in a 946-square-foot house. For the first 8 years of my life, my immediate family, including younger siblings, lived in this house along with my grandmother and other relatives who were unable to afford to live on their own. At various times, up to 15 people lived in that tiny house. My father worked as a tire builder for Goodyear Tire and Rubber Company, and my mother and grandmother both worked as domestics, cleaning the homes of and preparing meals for affluent White families in the suburbs of Akron, Ohio, my hometown. Although the adults in the household worked long hours, they struggled to feed and clothe all of the children in our home. We often endured long stretches of time with various utilities being shut off because of our inability to pay the gas, water, or electric bill. I grew up accustomed to wearing poorly fitting and tattered clothing. Often during winter, I would sit through a full day of school with wet socks and cold feet because I had to walk through the snow or rain with holes in the soles of my shoes. I grew up not getting regular medical and dental care. As a result of this neglect, today I am undergoing significant, invasive dental work to correct the structural damage to my jaws that was caused by having teeth unnecessarily removed during my childhood.

My family life was complicated by the fact that my father was an alcoholic. His addiction resulted in him being largely absent from our home, being unreliable to contribute financially to our family's well-being, and not being present to perform a parenting role. When he was present, he was generally emotionally inaccessible and engaged in outward conflict with my mother.

When I was nine years old, my parents moved our family out of my grandmother's place and into our own rented home in the same neighborhood. When we moved into our own place, the conditions of our home life and the instrumental aspects of life worsened. We had less food security, starker living conditions, and fewer daily supports. When I was 12 years old, my father died of a combination of lung cancer and the toll taken by his alcoholism. At this time, my family was thrown even deeper into poverty. To this day, I can still vividly recall the despair I felt about the prospects for my life because of the weight of poverty and the bleakness of my surrounding conditions. We experienced eviction, stretches of time on public assistance, and the embarrassment of standing in line to pick up government surplus food. Miraculously, a series of events happened during the two years after my father's death that positively influenced and altered the course of my life.

Although my mother dropped out of high school in her junior year, I never doubted her intelligence or commitment to ensuring that my siblings and I graduated from high school. When I entered junior high school, she began studying to complete her General Education Diploma (GED). While growing up, I often heard my mother express to others her desire to complete her GED and her hope of pursuing a career as a secretary. Following the completion of her GED, my mom was able to get funds from a federal program to take courses at Hammel Actual Business College, a small school based in Akron. Over the next few years, I watched as she worked diligently going to night classes and doing homework while still awaking early six days a week to take the bus to the suburbs for a long day of work.

When my father passed away, I was in eighth grade. One day early in that academic year, my English teacher, a demanding but caring woman named Elizabeth Witt, asked me go to her room after school to discuss a paper I had written. When I arrived at her room, she extended her arm to present me with the assignment I had turned in. My eyes were immediately drawn to the unexpected amount of red markings that were immediately visible on the page. My initial shock was abruptly interrupted by her words. "You're a better student than this," she said. "You're a better writer than this, and I will not accept anything but your best anymore." Miss Witt proceeded to present me with her perspectives on the importance of doing my best, the value of education, and the importance of being a good writer. That interaction and the subsequent relationship with and support from Miss Witt increased the intensity of my academic effort. It is also important to note that Miss Witt was the first White person with whom I forged a meaningful relationship.

The next key event occurred in the athletic arena. I was fortunate to play peewee football for a team that was coached by a recent college graduate who, as circumstance would have it, rented a room in the house next door to my grandmother while he was a student. One of his requirements of players was that we bring our report cards for him to check that we were being good students, even though our team was not affiliated with the school system. He praised me for my good grades. Yet his biggest influence was when he said to me, "Young Mr. Roper, you will go to college someday." I was stunned when Mr. Neal said those words. I had no concept of college and absolutely no vision of college being part of my future. However, in the weeks, months, and years after his comment, I began to talk openly about going to college whenever people asked me what I wanted to be when I grew up.

The driving values that I learned from the adults in my life were the importance of education, community, family/kinship, and work ethic. These themes have been dominant in my consciousness and recurring in my personal and professional lives; my hope is that these are the attributes that others perceive to be characteristic of me. Watching my mother work to get her GED and business college diploma and then enjoy a 30-year career as a clerk/typist at the East Akron Community Action Agency inspired me to believe that education could be the pathway to dream fulfillment. The care and sense of community that I gained from my relationship with Miss Witt and Mr. Neal helped me to understand the power of human connection and the value of mentorship. Each of the three adults who were so pivotal at the defining phase of my life modeled and preached the imperative that I cultivate the capacity for hard work.

My background of growing up in poverty has had a profound impact on my identity, consciousness, and leadership. I believe that, because of my life experiences, I have a particular sensitivity to issues of social class, hierarchy, and privilege. My experiences equipped me with a survivor mind-set—a belief that no matter the difficulty of the situation with which I am confronted, there is a viable path forward.

I firmly believe that because of the people and messages that showed up in my life during the time when I was gripped by despair I have been endowed with a high level of hopefulness and tools of resilience, which to me are tied to the power of education and undeniable value of caring relationships. When I look back on my life and career, I am often at a loss to explain how I arrived at the place where I am today. As I stated earlier, my first horizon to conquer was seeing myself as a high school graduate. Never did I imagine that I would be the recipient of the pride that my mother and grandmother exhibited when I completed my PhD.

Although I have embraced my role and opportunities as a first-generation faculty member, I have not always felt at ease with this identity. I have generally felt capable and worthy of the various leadership roles in which I have found myself, which have included professor, interim dean of liberal arts, and interim director of the School of Language, Culture, and Society. However, I consistently feel uneasy about the level of entitlement and privilege afforded to faculty relative to other members of the academic community. I am particularly uncomfortable with the degree to which the prominence given to faculty is used to silence and marginalize the voices and contributions of others. During my experience in higher education, I have been nagged with one persistent thought/question that is tied to experiences in my early life and the frame through which that life prepared me to view the world: "How would the brilliance and wisdom of my mother and grandmother be treated if they were on a college campus?" The challenge and responsibility I have assigned myself is to teach, lead, and build community in a way that creates space to uncover the brilliance and encourage the contributions of others regardless of position or academic preparation.

I am struck by the performance of hierarchy, power, and privilege in faculty culture. Faculty meetings are constructed in ways that individuals can assert privilege based on rank; the silencing of junior faculty and instructors is astounding. In many situations, those at the rank of instructor are not invited to participate in faculty meetings, nor are they afforded votes in departmental decision-making processes. It still amazes me that the assumptions underlying faculty culture are so widely accepted. In my various academic leadership roles, I have used processes to push back on accepted norms and practices with mixed results. My concern is that the culture to which campus community members have acquiesced does not serve us well today and absolutely will not serve our needs and demands for the future.

The current condition of our world, the issues that are emerging daily on our national landscape, and the complex demands facing our institutions reveal the need for creativity, connection, and healing. I believe the responses we seek will come through the broadest possible engagement. If we are to ensure that our institutions have access to the best possible future, we must transform faculty culture to make it more open, less class oriented, and more collaborative. Members of our campuses yearn for relationships, meaning, and value.

The heart and spirit that the significant adults in my early life modeled and instilled in me have influenced me to believe there is an abundance of brilliance, talent, and potential on our campuses. Our challenge is to influence the culture to increase the voice and visibility of those who are pushed to the margins because of our current power structure. If we are successful in this awesome cultural transformation, I believe we will position ourselves to bring the value the world badly needs from higher education.

Narrative Analysis

Hailing from different parts of the United States and various community types, Nancy's, Rudy's, and Larry's stories illustrate that people from poor and working-class backgrounds live everywhere, and their explanation of how social class combines with other identity dimensions—particularly gender, ability, race, and ethnicity in their cases—underscores the distinct yet similar ways classes of origin can be experienced. Their stories illuminate the triumphs that folks from poor and working-class backgrounds can realize in the academy, along with some key factors that contributed to their success, and offer their calls to action on furthering social class equity in education.

Roadblocks existed for all three individuals in their pursuit of education. Nancy's bout with polio required her to receive homeschooling for a year of middle school, and her resulting physical disability caused her top-choice college some concern, which led her to attend a different institution. Rudy viewed high school as "whack" and dropped out of community college on the first go; then he felt uneasiness in courses because of differences in his communication style—which he describes as too raw or "ghetto" for the academy—before finding people and organizations that helped him feel more at home in educational institutions. Rudy also documents the racism and elitism he experienced in graduate school—both overtly from peers and covertly through the curriculum—and how it resurfaced some insecurities for him. Larry notes that he was the first in his family to graduate from both high school and college, which means there was limited knowledge within the family to forecast for him what those experiences would be like or help him navigate those spaces.

Each of these folks honors the contributions of family members, peers, and educators in aiding in their educational endeavors. Rudy mentions his family friend, Liz, several student organizations, and numerous faculty members from his undergraduate and graduate programs as support systems and safe havens. Nancy credits her eighth-grade tutor for convincing her father that women could be college bound and serving as a guide in the process of getting there. Larry acknowledges his mother's role modeling, his teacher's high expectations, and his coach's foreshadowing of college prospects as foundational to him earning a PhD. These stories tell us that educational success is a team effort, with a charge of asking ourselves: who are we supporting, Who are we not, and why?

Nancy, Rudy, and Larry also inform us of how social class, along with other identity aspects, remains present in their work and lives and compels them to advocate for other people from marginalized communities in their roles as scholar-practitioners. Nancy discusses the financial shift and security that faculty life has provided her while also owning that she retains some behaviors and preferences from her working-class background and continues to find certain academic spaces uncomfortable. As such, she views it as her role to advocate for others, particularly students, and for justice across identities. Rudy talks about using his voice to call out the bullshit, paying the support he received forward by serving as a role model and building communities to change the culture of academia. Larry reveals how classism and elitism manifest in faculty culture through entitlement, hierarchy (especially faculty rank), and power and encourages us to push back, even though it is a fight, to get to places of creativity, connection, and healing.

All three of these tenured faculty urge us to act—to do something to reduce elitism, classism, and other isms in higher education. If we can do as Larry suggests and put aside our egos and power plays to uncover others' brilliance, then maybe we can find comrades in the effort to achieve Rudy's vision that we "become the gate smashers of the ivory tower and transform what education was meant to be: transformative, equitable, and inclusive" (p. 140, this volume).

9

THE EXTERNAL
EDUCATOR PERSPECTIVE

Narratives by Briza K. Juarez, Edward Pickett III, and Roxanne Villaluz

The academy provides a lifetime career for some and a professional touching point for others. These external perspective narratives share the common thread of difference in career choice and reflect making difficult choices based on life context and passion. There is much to be learned from leaving the known of higher education and trying something different. Taking the leap, so to say, is found in the stories from Briza K. Juarez, now a full-time parent with a small business; Edward (Eddie) Pickett III, now a college counselor and 11th/12th-grade dean at a high school; and Roxanne Villaluz, now a baker and worker-owner of a bakery and pizzeria. Many times we can feel locked into a job because of the known, and although there is nothing wrong with that, these stories teach us that it is okay and possible to do something different. Add the layer of misalignment of values and classism that exists in the academy, and sometimes the choice is less difficult for those from poor and working-class roots. Let's take from these lessons and create a path that works best for you.

Briza K. Juarez: Sometimes Stability Is a Full Fridge

I don't remember exactly when I realized my family was poor. I remember knowing we weren't rich, but I think I knew we were poor in elementary school during daily lunch. But that story begins long before I came to exist.

I grew up in Oceanside, California, a picturesque beach town at the northernmost end of San Diego County. It's home to Marine Corps Base Camp Pendleton and has a diverse ethnic and racial population. The neighborhood I grew up in is known as South O, and it was a happy place to grow

146

up. I remember playing with the neighborhood kids on the street and chasing after the ice cream truck. My father worked in construction and my mom was at home with us until I was in the first grade. My elementary school was fairly diverse largely due to the children bussed in from the barrio that my grandparent's home was in.

In elementary school, my father, when he worked, made enough money to disqualify us from free lunch, but he didn't regularly work. I remember my mom packing our lunch, a peanut butter and jelly sandwich, and on occasion a burrito from leftover dinner. We never had snacks or a drink in our lunch bags. I also remember eating lunch with my friend Rhiannon. She would always share her chips and snacks and never made me feel like it was charity, but she always packed extra, and I was always grateful.

My parents had the kind of relationship that burned everything in its path, including each other. When my mom collected the courage to leave my father, she had $42 to her name. Forty-two dollars and 3 children. She had lost her job when my father started a heated argument with a coworker at the job she had secured for them. They were both let go that night. The next day, she decided she couldn't save her children and continue to carry my father. So, she asked her friends to help store some of our belongings. We moved in with my aunt and slept on the floor of her spare bedroom. I was in the sixth grade then and a few months away from middle school.

My mom quickly started taking any job she could to save money to move us out to a home she could afford. My mother's friend Rosario, a woman who had taken her under her wing when she was 17, had a newborn with colic. She was always giving us a helping hand and mothering my mom in a way she had never had. She told my mom about a rental her daughter-in-law had that was a Section 8 home, for which my mom had to apply for government assistance to rent. I remember going with my mom to the numerous appointments with the social worker and her embarrassment as she kept telling us that it was just temporary until she could rent an apartment on her own. We moved into the rental in the barrio my grandparents had lived in, the same one that had children I had known in elementary school.

My mom made good on her promise, and we moved into a different apartment about a year later. To say money was tight is an understatement. Once a week we would have enough money to eat 25-cent hamburgers from McDonald's. We couldn't afford the cheese upgrade, but she would buy a 99-cent order of French fries for us to share. I didn't have a jacket that winter, and instead I wore a grey sweatshirt with a hunting dog on the front. I wore it every day. I didn't think anyone noticed until a girl whose father was a Marine mentioned the dog on my sweatshirt. I remember the conversation vividly. I knew then that others knew we were poor.

By mid-sophomore year of high school, my father was working semi-regularly and would give my siblings and me cash every week. He never paid child support, and my mom never took any of the money he gave us because she said his money always came with too high an interest rate. I wasn't wise with the money; in hindsight I should have saved it. Instead, I bought all the clothes I liked and went out to eat with my friends. My relationship with my father ended abruptly the night of my high school graduation party. I didn't speak to him again for a decade.

When applying for universities, I knew I wanted to attend a four-year institution and forgo attending a community college as I didn't want to delay getting a bachelor's degree. At the time, the only people I knew who attended community college never went on to pursue a bachelor's degree or attended for multiple years before transferring to a four-year institution. I remember thinking it would not save me money if I dragged it out for years, and I knew I would be motivated to complete my degree within four years if I was paying the tuition. I earned scholarships to cover tuition my first semester. I got a job a few days after graduating from high school at a temp agency and knew I had to make enough money to cover books and the next semester's tuition before January.

While in college, I had anywhere from one to three jobs to pay for my tuition and books. I lived at home, and my mom would help me pay for books when she could. I paid my way through college, grinding away at one to two on-campus jobs at a time and an off-campus job in retail or as a bank teller.

Through mentors met at those on-campus jobs, I was introduced to the student affairs field. At the time I was a business major, and I had every intention of following a path into the corporate world. Then one day during a class on business management, the conversation turned to the *maquiladoras* (factories) that were found just south of the border in which U.S. companies used to turn a higher profit on the backs of their Third World neighbors. The conversation quickly turned to higher profit margins from the cheap labor force. I thought of my Tia Lupe, my mom's sister. She worked in a maquiladora for 60-plus hours a week, and her wage was $60. I remember she told me and my mom that she was lucky to have that job, despite the fact the work was hurting her back and her eyesight was deteriorating. She told us it was one of the higher paying jobs in town. I told the professor that the cheap labor force were people, with families, working for pennies. I changed my major a few days later.

My first on-campus job was for the admissions office as a peer counselor. I was tasked with advising prospective students and going to recruitment fairs at high schools and community colleges. I was so happy to find a job that would allow me to meet with students who were interested in attending a four-year institution, most of whom would be first-generation college students.

I became a minority undergraduate fellow with NASPA and was able to attend conferences and develop my intention to pursue higher education as a career. Through this fellowship, I landed my first professional job in higher education, an internship at the University of California, Santa Cruz (UCSC). It was a summer internship in housing. I was working with another intern, a grad student from the University of Southern California named Minh. We became fast friends, and that internship showed me the need for people of color to work in higher education. The resident assistants we were supervising were a diverse group, and one of the students and I bonded over our shared experience as daughters of immigrants.

After graduation from college, as I was working as an assistant resident director at my alma mater, I received a call for a job at UCSC. I took the job and moved 500 miles away from my family to another picturesque beach town—this one with a median income triple that of Oceanside. When I first moved, I lived in a tiny granny shack studio behind a Victorian house a block from the beach. It was small, but I loved hearing the sound of the ocean lull me to sleep, and the barking of the seals woke me up in the morning.

After a few months, Minh also accepted a live-on position at UCSC and invited me to live with him on campus. Our arrangement was that I would buy the groceries as we lived on campus for free as part of his compensation. I kept the refrigerator stocked and the pantry full. One day Minh told me I did not have to go grocery shopping that week because the fridge was packed. I started crying as I realized that my middle-class income afforded me a full fridge. I was so traumatized from growing up without a full fridge that I was packing it full before I was eating its contents. I still think of that lesson to this day.

Minh and I often spoke about our experiences as the children of immigrants, and we both found the students with whom we most identified and who sought us out were first-generation students. These relationships with first-generation students kept me motivated in higher education, even with all the political and racist issues I dealt with regularly.

Santa Cruz is an affluent and racially homogeneous town. It also has a politically progressive community, but it is cloaked in White savior complex. Twenty minutes south of Santa Cruz is Watsonville, an agricultural community with a large, mostly poor Latino population. I often found myself driving south to leave the Santa Cruz bubble for tacos and entrance to a world I knew more intimately.

After four years at UCSC, I was extremely burned out and decided to leave higher education. Originally my plan was to move back to Oceanside and find a job in higher education in San Diego County. However, I left in the middle of a recession that cut higher education budgets with a resulting hiring freeze. Instead I found a job in the private sector and thought I had left higher education for good.

I went to work in human resources for a company specializing in contracting for public utilities. I was promoted into a management position with required travel around the country visiting different projects. My schedule had me traveling every other week, 24 weeks of the year. One of the last projects I was assigned to was in rural Louisiana. I enjoyed the work but found my mind wandering to the areas I was working in and the folks we employed. I met a man who was applying to be a meter reader after having been a professional player in the National Football League (NFL). He was injured early in his career and was left without a job. There was a juxtaposition of all of the opportunities that could have been for him against the work he would be doing reading meters in his tiny hometown.

The stress of traveling became more challenging as I missed my new husband, which led me to apply for a job at University of California, San Diego (UCSD) on a whim. The prospect of returning to higher education was both exciting and daunting. When I got the job I was ecstatic, although not excited about the significant pay cut.

I returned to student affairs with a position at UCSD. My commute was an hour or longer if I missed the 10-minute window, so I would often arrive 15 minutes before the office opened. During these early mornings, I would visit with the custodian who maintained our offices. I chatted with her and got to know her. She was from my mom's hometown, Tecate, and she would tell me about her son stationed overseas in the service. Sometimes she would lament about the issues the custodial staff faced with the housing department. I learned of the unfair treatment that the largely Latino staff faced, especially the repercussions of any issues brought to management. I also learned about the unfair policies faced by student staff employed by the housing department, often going hungry because their resident adviser contracts would not allow them to work more hours outside of their jobs, which meant they could not make ends meet on their meal stipends.

During my second pregnancy, I had multiple complications that jeopardized my ability to carry my daughter to term. I was on bed rest for six weeks. During that time, a lot of soul-searching and meditation led me to realize that what I most wanted was to stay home and care for my children. After my daughter was born, we discovered medical issues requiring multiple specialists and therapists. My husband and I cemented my decision to leave my career and stay at home with our children.

To say that I don't miss higher education would be a lie. I miss the daily interaction with students and witnessing the "aha!" moments of self-realization. I miss meeting with students of color, particularly first-generation students, who would seek me out to discuss issues they faced and hear the perspective of someone who had been in their shoes. I miss the conversations about missing home, often neighborhoods that were significantly more diverse than the populations of their college lecture halls. But I don't miss the concealed, and too often not concealed, classist and racist issues prevalent in the culture. I don't miss seeing the folks who held director and higher positions on campus all share a similar background and the few people of color in leadership positions.

These days I'm happily at home with my children and have my own small business. I don't know if I will ever return to higher education. I will keep the lessons I learned of acceptance and opening my eyes to see the multiple identities that make up each person we meet. I'm grateful for all of the folks who helped open my eyes and my mind to all the possibilities a little girl from a poor family never imagined and helped me find a way to keep my refrigerator full.

Edward (Eddie) Pickett III: Filling Our Plates

Many people have said to me, "Your life was so hard." But honestly, I never saw it that way. Although my reality was certainly challenging, I was always cognizant of my peers who were in similar or worse situations. I am a first-generation college student and Black man who grew up with a blue-collar background between Oakland and Berkeley, California. I was born to a 19-year-old mother and a 20-year-old father who have both battled drug and alcohol addictions. Because of this and other reasons, my 3 siblings and I lived between my parents and grandparents in the early years and later between my grandparents and dad. I have such deep respect for the role my grandparents played in my life and the lives of my siblings, providing the stability that we needed. One thing I became certain of while growing up is that I would not become any of the negative statistical trends associated with my background. I did not know where my journey would take me, but I was constantly told college was the best step to change my reality.

I walked into my first year at Pitzer College in Claremont, California, thinking that my college years were going to be like Nick Cannon's experience attending a historically Black college and university (HBCU) in the movie *Drumline*. Little did I realize I was attending a predominantly White institution (PWI), and my social class would play as large a factor as my race.

There were plenty of moments when I felt my background as a lower income Black student was less than, and I neglected telling most of my college friends and administrators about my social class and family background. I did not want to be defined or judged by stereotypes of working-class Black people. When asked what my parents did for work, I would say, "My dad works at the Oakland Airport," and I would conveniently leave out the fact that he was a custodian.

Why did I feel the need to hide or downplay where I came from? My dad had a union job, and both of my grandparents had blue-collar jobs as well. Although we were not poor, having blue-collar jobs across the bay from San Francisco did not allow your finances to stretch as far as they would in areas with a lower cost of living. In the years after college, many of my friends and I have talked about being on financial aid in college and some of the struggles, but it was not a conversation we were equipped to have back then.

Entering college, I thought I wanted to be an engineer because I liked science, technology, engineering, and math subjects and heard the profession made a stable income; that dream ended after one semester of college physics. Instead, I found my future career through my work outside the classroom in the admissions office. The work fit my outgoing personality, and it better equipped me to tell my story and begin to understand the higher education landscape for people like me.

There is no shortage of studies showing that high-achieving low-income students are underrepresented at elite institutions from organizations such as the Jack Kent Cooke Foundation, the Lumina Foundation, the Schott Foundation for Public Education, and the National Bureau of Economic Research, to name a few. Gaining an excellent understanding of the complexities of access into higher education was my academic inspiration for applying to graduate programs in higher education administration. I wanted to know why there were so many colleges, but people from my background (people of color and/or low income) were not attending them. I found plenty of insights on college access in graduate school and continue to stay informed on the issue by reading studies such as Bailey and Dynarski's (2011), which notes the growing gaps between children from high- and low-income backgrounds, or the report by Shapiro and colleagues (2017) that shows the continued large gaps in 6-year completion rates between White and Black students—a 24 percentage-point difference (62% and 38%, respectively).

Seeking to understand college access intellectually was a driving force behind my application to graduate school, but it was also a choice motivated by my lived experience. I wrote the following paragraph as the closing to my graduate school personal statement, and I'm including it here because it is a true articulation of my path and who I hoped to be for my family.

Through positive and negative experiences alike, I never doubted my ability to succeed. I have become mentally stronger because I learned to view my negative experiences as hurdles in life that many young people do not have to face. I kept myself busy by playing sports, attending after school outreach programs, and spending time with my younger siblings. Being a part of the [working] class meant that I did not grow up with much of what individuals from more fortunate circumstances might take for granted. Thus, a master's degree would not only benefit me professionally, but on a deeply personal level. Lastly, achieving this goal will allow me to continue to be a positive role model for my younger siblings and a living and close-to-home example of the possibility of academic and professional success in their own lives.

Looking back at this statement, I realize how my words about making a difference for my family, and not just myself, are rooted in the first-generation, working-class experience.

Leaving graduate school, I found myself actively choosing to stay on the East Coast to work in the admissions office at Tufts University, where I eventually rose to the position of director of diversity recruitment. Tufts will always have a fond place in my heart because my office had some amazing people, and it is where I began and solidified my career in the college admissions field.

Since the moment I stepped onto the Pitzer College campus in 2004, I have spent nearly half of my life in selective private colleges and universities. These institutions include Pitzer College, Massachusetts Institute of Technology (MIT), Boston College, and Tufts University. All of these colleges except for MIT were on a 2017 *New York Times* list of 38 colleges and universities that had more students enrolled from the top 1% of the income scale (>$630,000) than the entire bottom 60% of incomes (<$65,000). I would never say that I fully adapted to these environments, but I learned to get by in an educational setting where I was by far a minority. I had to adjust to new systems and code-switch often, which prepared me for many professional interactions. I learned to work with the system to make change and create opportunities.

To make change, I've had some difficult conversations with peers and colleagues along the way about college access for people like me. Too many times I have found myself in a room where people make assumptions, not always subtly, about people from different racial groups or the working class not "wanting to get an education," or assuming they do not have the work ethic to persist through college. A lot of the time those same people do not acknowledge the journey that the student took just to be present at that college or university. If one issue happens at home or with financial aid, then that student might not have a place to turn for help. I have been close myself. I never registered on time because the little bit of a bill I had to pay was coming from my work-study or summer earnings. That was more than 10 years ago, and tuition has increased over the rate of inflation in the time between.

When I found myself in that situation, I did not know where to look for help, so I can both imagine and know from data that many students are still in that same boat. In my undergraduate and graduate studies, I did not speak up often when people made assumptions about working-class citizens because I did not have the language to respond effectively. I now have the language and data, and I look at these conversations as a possibility to make change.

At Tufts, I finally started to raise my hand and share that the people some of my colleagues were making assumptions about are people like me. That usually silenced the room. In my younger days, I would try to make people feel comfortable after such statements. Not anymore. Why should I be the person to comfort someone who makes me uncomfortable? In those situations, I usually stay calm outwardly. I have developed a pretty thick skin, leaving me able to deal with such comments and not internalize the assumptions as fact. I prefer to acknowledge their comments, let them stew in the awkward silence, and allow myself time to think about my next steps in the conversation.

The approach that works best for me when addressing assumptions and stereotypes is to ask questions that tap into why people hold these beliefs. From there, it is a little easier to break down the myths with facts. These tough conversations are an opportunity for learning on both sides. I have found answers about how people have come to these conclusions, what in their background shaped this, and how I can begin to help them see another way. Most often I have found that the assumptions were bred from lack of life experience with people in marginalized groups.

A college campus is a great space for these difficult conversations to happen because students are meeting people different from them, many for the first time. Although I recently left higher education to work in a high school, I still enjoy creating an environment where we can have difficult conversations on socioeconomic status or race and ethnicity. Reflecting on my own experience in college, I know these conversations are needed.

I was on a panel a few years back in which I was asked to finish the sentence, "College is . . .". I was intrigued by how different people on the panel answered the question, so I returned to my office and asked my colleagues and some students the same question. Most people tried to include as much information as possible into one sentence. The shortest and best answer (in my opinion) was from our beloved "hip dean," who said, "College is opportunity."

I try to reflect on this statement in my daily life. If college is truly an opportunity, then I will continue to strive to create those opportunities for people who may have to travel a little farther to get to the door of opportunity. I live by the saying, "If I eat, we all eat," and I think it articulates my upbringing best because it shows a collective mentality and responsibility to share the opportunities given. Unfortunately, buzzwords such as *tradition* and *culture* in these college environments have traditionally meant exclusion of many groups, people of color and working class included. I feel that I had the great privilege of learning in and working to reshape environments not originally made for me, and it is my personal and professional responsibility to pass the plate of opportunity to the next person. With that, we may be able to get to a point where stories like mine are not the exception but the norm.

Roxanne Villaluz: Moving Through Social Identity by Degrees

I was born in San Jose, California, in the 1970s just before the giant tech boom when San Jose was a proliferation of fruit orchards, vast fields of vegetables, packing and processing plants, and trucks rumbling along streets lined with giant warehouses. My working-class neighborhood was just down the way from a technological oasis decimating the land around it while displacing and removing the indigenous native populations in favor of coding and software engineers.

We were working class because the U.S. educational system refuses to honor and recognize the validity of foreign degrees and education, claiming the inferiority of not learning Western culture first. My father started out in the literal fields as a U.S. Department of Agriculture (USDA) inspector of fruits, vegetables, and processed foods. My mom worked on the assembly line at Hewlett Packard. Throughout my adolescence and into nearing my adulthood, my mom worked on many assembly lines and in many jobs that I did not understand at the time were supposed to be beneath us.

My mom worked as a cleaning person; she also sorted donations in the warehouse and worked on the sales floor for the Salvation Army. My mom worked many different jobs, doing similar things but at different places. And she loved every job. She enjoyed what she did, she appreciated and was close to many of her coworkers, and she never came home tired.

My dad spent his whole working career in the United States. He moved to the United States in his early 20s to escape the militarized dictatorship of Ferdinand Marcos. He spent his whole professional career working for the

USDA, uprooting the family as he pursued opportunities that would lead to promotion. He moved us to different cities and places. He moved for a better salary.

In 1978, my parents, my older sister, and I moved from San Jose to Fairfax County, Virginia to be closer to my dad's job in Washington DC. My dad's salary now made it so that instead of living in what would be considered the hood, the urban downtown area like we were in San Jose, we were now firmly ensconced in the middle class, living in the burbs on a cul-de-sac near a lake with a giant park at the end of the street. For four years, my life consisted of lawn darts, fireflies in bottles with punched-out lids, Brownies scouts, square dancing, croquet, and stilt walking.

In 1982, we were uprooted again and returned to San Jose, but this time there were five of us: my two parents, my older sister, myself, and my new little brother. Like the game Chutes and Ladders, moving back to San Jose would have been considered hitting a chute. But the way I understood needs and wants was simple: food, clothing, shelter, fresh air, and time to play. No matter where we lived and what social class we occupied, we always had these essentials.

We had a variety of clean clothes. We had food on the table. Most of the vegetables and fruits came from our yard or from a yard of someone our family knew intimately. We had clean water to drink. We had a constant and consistent roof over the entire family. Often that roof provided for many more people. While living in San Jose, our house had many family members coming in and out. Sometimes I shared a bedroom with my sister or grandparents depending on the circumstance. For me, San Jose was the most comfortable I had been.

In the summer of 1991, we moved to Fresno, California, and we jumped way up in social class. We went from the hood to mansion adjacent all on the same salary. The move to Fresno highlighted that the cost of living in an area and the amount of money someone makes is an important variable in what someone can afford: Social class is not only how much money you have but how much your money can afford to buy.

In all of this traipsing back and forth between cities, between social classes, I learned how to survive, how to get along and make friends in the in-between. Social class mattered only when it came to my split family. I grew up bifurcated: bicultural as an Ilokana American and biclass with my mom and her family in the United States being considered working class. Most of my cousins, uncles, and so on on her side worked trade jobs or jobs requiring only a GED/high school diploma. My dad and his family were upper middle class. Most of my cousins, uncles, and so on on his side worked trade jobs that required beyond bachelor's degrees: DDS, MD, CPA, JD, and so on.

I straddle this bisection as a professional cook/baker and as someone who possess multiple postsecondary degrees. I still identify as working class partially because of my salary and the type of work I do but primarily because I am proud of my working-class roots, my working-class ancestry, and my working class. I know that my education affords me access to the upper middle class and the mansion adjacent even if my salary is not comparable.

Higher Education Speak and Degrees Are My Cultural Capital

I have access with my Western education. I can take off my chef coat and baker's chapeau and don my scholarly robes and the clothes that say I have educational knowledge to become a different class. I had to learn how to move in and out of different classes through trial and error because my parents came from a different cultural understanding of class. Additionally, education as a form of class was something they were not equipped to teach me.

We have created that system. For students to gain access to postsecondary education, to get in, to participate in postsecondary education, they have to engage with terms such as *admissions, SAT, ACT, transcripts*, and *official/unofficial*; then they need to log into a student center to register for courses and face terms such as *prerequisites, cocurricular*, and *subsidized/unsubsidized loans*.

These students try to come to the university to apply, to get in, and to do the things, and our language makes it difficult to explain to their parents what they need to succeed. The fact that higher education requires translation and interpretation for people to participate sets us up to believe in and perpetuate the system of social class.

The prerequisites for college all point toward social class; for example, Advanced Placement (AP) courses for a head start on college credits can only be had by those with access to AP classes. In addition, money is required to take the AP tests to even attempt to get the credit.

The differing requirements for the variety of higher educational options are a social class system unto themselves: trade schools, two-year associate degree-granting institutions, four-year public institutions, four-year private institutions, and subject-specific institutions: ballet, photography, and fashion design. The requirements for each type of system match the access one is granted to social and cultural capital, and this social and cultural capital gives one access to different social classes. During my time at each of these different institutions as a student, staff member, and guest lecturer, I noticed the social class distinctions. Even when students managed to attend institutions of higher learning outside of their social classes, many students talked about imposter syndrome or not having done enough to be where they need.

Dialogue for Healing, Learning, Growing, and Digging Deep Into Classist Roots

The notion of imposter syndrome, or students feeling like they still need to prove something, was a common theme in a course I facilitated on class. The Critical Dialogues Across Differences (CDAD) facilitated course is designed to challenge students to think, converse, and share ideas with people from a diversity of backgrounds. The CDAD course on class I facilitated specifically required students to think beyond good, better, or best. We challenged them about progression as an upward motion.

We challenged students to think about a nonlinear progression of social class and success based on their own vision of what success looks like for them in their respective lives. We talked at length about the ideas of upward mobility—moving up, moving away—the idea that being successful is going away from where you come from. Students in the CDAD course on social class talked about being at a premier division I research institution as a step up from where they were in social class. Attending and being accepted into this university is about upward mobility for many students attending—going up and leaving behind.

Many of the students expressed the following sentiments: "I am successful. I have moved in social class because I am going to a better school that is more prestigious" and "I got into several state universities and community colleges—but then I got into this division I research institution and other similar types of universities are 'better' and more 'prestigious.'"

Throughout the different sections I facilitated, several students said that leaving their old neighborhoods, not having to live the way they did back home, signaled to them proof that they had begun their ascent upward in class. For many of the students, the model for what success looks like is having more money than their parents or other people in their neighborhoods or being associated with people who had more. Many of the students said that the type of school they attended almost guaranteed a step up because of the level of prestige. Consequently, even at a young age, people begin to learn the postsecondary hierarchy.

Social class success for many students, staff, and faculty members is about having enough money to purchase things that are not among our basic life necessities. Moving up in social class is about being able to live beyond one's basic requirements: being able to afford more than just the basic needs of water, clothes, food, and shelter (e.g., owning a larger home dwelling, being able to choose what types of foods to eat, and having access to a variety of different types of clothing). It is to be out of the reach of the past—being able to move out of one's old neighborhood, not having to return to where we began as children, but somewhere that appears better on the surface.

We know that we have moved out of the reach of the past when we are told that we have made it. The crucial question when the idea of making it would come up in dialogue is, "How are we defining *success?*" That was an important question for critical awareness because so many students were certain they had moved up but then began to struggle with the idea of moving up or making it when they started to talk about what success was for each of them. Often how they described success began to appear different from what they had been subconsciously working toward.

One way we began to talk about healing around our internalized classism was through art and dialogue. In one course, each student was asked to draw the idea of upward mobility versus progression in his or her life as seen through a class lens. When we drew upward mobility, all the students drew some type of mechanism that indicated they could only go up or down. In every scenario, people were inevitably stacked or above someone else—an automatic hierarchy was created. When the class drew the idea of progression, many students drew lines or structures that were horizontal, zig-zagging, or that moved in a variety of directions. They also showed people at varying places along these structures. Rather than people being above or below, they just appeared to be at different places. Many of the students talked about progression being three-dimensional so people were just at different points.

There were many discussions about not being proud of being from the ghetto or the 'hood. We challenged students to think about why being from the 'hood or ghetto was considered negative. Why are we told that we need to escape the worlds that raised us, taught us, loved us, and hated us? Examining our relationships with our neighborhoods and how others perceived our neighborhoods was a great space for growth and learning. We encouraged students to engage in dialogue around the following questions:

- Why are so many of us not proud of our neighborhoods?
- Where did we learn to be ashamed/embarrassed about where we come from?
- Why do we think that in seeking success and progression we must cast aside or not love/care about where we come from?

Facilitating CDAD allowed me to take time to be critical of how classism shows up for me and the ways in which classism is part of all the structures I engage with daily.

Even if You Want to Go Home Again, You May Not Be Able to Afford It

Social class is a complex identity, and for those with limited finances and resources, social class is stark. Social class determines whether you have social capital and tells you whether what you know and understand culturally can be cultural capital. In writing this essay, I continue to reflect on the opportunities afforded me as I move in and out of social class identities. I continue to reflect back on class and the academy. I often think about why and how in becoming or adopting a different class through my currency of educational degrees I inevitably and inadvertently feel detached and far away from so many people in my life. The moving in and out of class spaces is the experience of many students who come from backgrounds similar to mine, and yet we do not get an opportunity to talk about the effects of classism: internal and external.

As I think about my time in the academy and now outside of it, I have many wishes and hopes for the future. I hope that those within academia, those who have left it, and those attempting to join continue to be critical of our systems. I hope we continue to challenge how we understand accessibility through a variety of lenses and continue to create structures that no longer contain hidden culture or require people to sacrifice parts of their identity that bring richness into postsecondary institutions. Instead, I hope they continue to bring into consciousness and action the ideas that institutions designed to educate should create systems that are boundless and accessible to anyone seeking education and not based on what people can afford.

Narrative Analysis

The themes of family and stability were shared across all stories, and although stability was provided in various ways, there was a shared experience of steadiness as a result. Once Briza's mom separated from her husband, she promised her three kids she would save enough money for their own apartment. After working multiple jobs, she was eventually able to afford a home for her family. With Eddie's young parents battling addiction, his grandparents played a critical role in providing stability for him and his siblings. He valued the care they showed him during rough life moments as a kid. Roxanne writes about her parents providing the essentials of food, clothing, shelter, fresh air, and time to play. Regardless of geographical location or social class, she always had the essentials growing up.

When working in higher education, they each supported students from their similar social class backgrounds. In working at different institutions with varying professional ranks, Eddie knew the importance of combining his own class story with data to speak to the discrepancies across social classes and work on ways to best support poor and working-class students. Through this combination of storytelling and statistics, he was able to educate his colleagues in caring, effective ways. Despite the fact that he no longer works in higher education, he still makes the effort to create an environment involving critical conversations about socioeconomic status. During her tenure in student affairs, Briza connected with first-generation college students to provide familiarity and conversations about home.

All three ventured to different life journeys after working in the academy. Eddie's move remained in education, but he went to work as an administrator at the high school level. In this setting, he continues to push the difficult conversation as he recognizes the importance to do so, for both himself and those around him. In her self-identified bisection, Roxanne turned in her administrator role to become a professional cook/baker. In doing so, she recognizes she still has various forms of cultural capital because of her degrees and resulting educational knowledge. In this straddling of class, she continues to identify as working class because of factors related to salary, type of work, and connection to her working-class roots. After having her second child, Briza decided to stay at home with her kids, owning a small business as a side hustle. She misses aspects of higher education and is grateful for her connections and lessons from it.

The richness in these stories to take the leap outside of the academy is scary and liberating. They teach us that higher education can contribute to our lives in meaningful ways while also creating tension and exhaustion, and we have the privilege of choice for what best fits our lives and gives us joy. It doesn't mean going back to the academy is off the table, but instead it helps us realize that careers change and there are options we may have never considered possible.

IO

SHARED SOCIAL CLASS
EXPERIENCES AND THE
INTERSECTIONALITY
OF IDENTITY

W̶e intentionally pulled the thread of social class identity as it is rarely written about in forms beyond financial need in higher education. We want to provide a platform for those from poor and working-class backgrounds who are simultaneously included and excluded on college campuses. Because of our lived experiences within and outside of the academy, we recognize the vast social class inequities that exist. There are powerful, painful, beautiful stories to hear and learn from that are silenced, ignored, and disregarded. We pulled the thread for a place of connection and healing across social class because, let's be honest, social class elicits moments of anger, guilt, embarrassment, shame, challenge, frustration, and inadequacy. Of course, it also elicits moments of pride, strength, humor, courage, and joy.

We are also keenly aware that wholeness involves more than social class. Regardless of saliency or consciousness, our lives involve a complex synthesis of identities and experiences. Other identities intersect with social class forming the lens from which we interact with the world and vice versa. It is evident from the collection of stories in this book that context extends beyond social class, and centering social class provides the opportunity to consider how it influences wholeness.

Social Class Experiences Across Positionality in the Academy

Despite their different positionalities with the academy—from undergraduate student to professor emerita—the 24 contributing writers' narratives coalesce into 7 meta themes that highlight the persistent influence a poor working-class background may have for someone in higher education. These overarching premises include hard work, working hard, and the hustle; stereotype threat; the costs of pursuing higher education; imposter syndrome, class passing, and code-switching; increasing the social class conversation; making systemic changes; and paying it forward. Along with commonality, there are also differences in the stories that showcase how social class can be experienced in unique ways. Together these meta themes and distinctions form our key learnings from the narratives.

Hard Work, Working Hard, and the Hustle

The mere mention of *working class* conjures up language and descriptors in the narratives. Hard-working, working hard, and the hustle are all descriptors for figuring out how to make ends meet. Kevyanna explains that, for her, working class means she and her family all worked one or more jobs to support and contribute to family finances. Jacinda and Roxanne speak about their parents working hard to provide enough for their families, not needing anything beyond the essentials. Mostly raised in a single-parent home, Briza shares about her mother working hard and taking any job she could to save enough money for her family's housing. Both in a union, one employed as a custodian and the other at an automobile manufacturer, Eddie's and Sally's fathers worked long, hard days to cover family expenses. Although Loren's parents were seemingly unfulfilled in their respective government jobs, they worked long days providing the means to keep a roof over their heads and pay the essential bills.

The ethos of hard work has shown up throughout the contributing writers' college careers as well as their current work life. Summer jobs, work-study jobs, and off-campus part-time jobs were a way of life to cover college costs and, for some, postdegree living. The voices of current students reflect that of the professionals' voices. During the summer before starting college, Keyvanna worked a minimum wage job for more than 50 hours a week to help cover the costs of her first year in college. Téa found herself working in the dining hall, which angered her initially; however, the job soon became a place of care, comfort, and connection for her. Unlike most other areas on campus, the people and environment felt familiar to her. The same hard work ethos is part of Carmen's experience of having a job during high school to help supplement her family's income, Mamta working multiple jobs during undergraduate and graduate school, and Jacinda taking a second job after her master's degree to pay the bills. Needless to say, we work without question or hesitation to make ends meet.

The truth of the matter is that hard work—picking up multiple jobs, taking side gigs, doing what is necessary to get by—is all a hustle. For those from poor and working-class backgrounds, it is a part of surviving. Some people refer to their family's or their own hard work as just that: a hustle. Whether it is Thomas's mother making Cabbage Patch look-alike dolls for supplemental cash or Connie's father infinitely thinking of strategies to navigate family finances, the hustle is a cultural norm and just a way of life for those from poor and working-class backgrounds. In his role as professor, Rudy uses his skills of the street hustle in the academy, "clocking grants and fellowships, grinding hard, professin', networking with my people (of all backgrounds), and making sure I would survive this profession with what I learned outside the ivory tower" (p. 135, this volume). In the middle-class world, this would be referred to as *transferable skills*, the caveat being the hustle comes with a certain fortitude and way of being not often associated with or found in academia's career coaching.

Stereotype Threat

An unspoken, covert norm is that college is not for those from a certain social class. The ivory tower was not intended for kids receiving free or reduced lunch, kids who use swearing as an art form, and certainly not kids with family members struggling with addiction—those with a different vocabulary, a different dress, a different ethic. Raul's story, titled "I'm Not Even Supposed to Be Here" (pp. 117–121, this volume) and Loren's questioning moments of "Do they even let people like me go to college?" (p. 114, this volume) reflect this notion of belonging in the academy or, in this case, not belonging. Because we all learn messages related to social class from the get-go, such a narrative is both internal and external. Good or bad, these messages are internalized and outwardly expressed.

For some, college wasn't part of the equation. Given Larry's young lived experience in poverty, racial segregation, and generational lack of education, he was destined to not graduate high school, much less complete a PhD. It was only after key adults in his life pushed and exposed him to the idea of college that he considered it a possibility. Similarly, growing up with no exposure to college, the context of Jeremiah's working-class family included fishing, muscle cars, and baseball. None of that is bad, it's just not part of the middle-class dialogue and training that lend themselves to the world of higher education. Although his family had nothing against college, it "wasn't something that was necessarily expected or promoted in my family" (p. 105, this volume). That's the thing with poor and working-class families: College is not discouraged but instead it is not part of our daily lives.

For others, college was expected with limited or nonexistent social or cultural capital to navigate the system of academia. Even with college being encouraged, and for some demanded, they still found themselves as outsiders. Many dealt with years of internalized messaging of not belonging in the academy, which continue to surface despite their education and credentials. As a graduate student, Dylan struggles to find his "own social class identity in a system which I'm not sure I truly belong" (p. 56, this volume). Then when we fast forward to Loren's story in being part of the academy with multiple degrees, it is still taking him decades to understand that just because he had different social capital does not make him any less capable. Luckily, he has been able to reframe and recognize that his class background "simultaneously fueled my capacity for success while making me hesitant to believe that such success was really possible" (p. 115, this volume).

Despite stereotypes, questions from others, and internal self-doubts, we did it. We pushed through the narratives and statistics that college is not a place for those of us from poor and working-class families. We figured it out and came out the other side with one degree, if not multiple. We hold titles and positions not designed with us in mind. Within these accomplishments, do not make the mistake of equating the struggles and successes of our stories with pulling one up from one's bootstraps. Doing so dishonors the history and complexity of navigating through external stereotypes and assumptions, internal fear, and self-doubt.

Costs of Pursuing Higher Education as a Student and an Educator

Sure, money buys books, food, and electricity, but social class is much more than economic capital. It is about the various forms of capital that impact one's daily life: social, cultural, academic, navigational, and resistant (Yosso, 2005). All of this creates the haves and the have-nots based on which capitals are valued. Acquiring the sometimes less tangible forms of capital comes at a deep cost to poor and working-class folks. As Tori shares, "The system demands conforming to a value that is 100% against everything I was taught about the importance of being humble, hard working, with your nose down" (p. 126, this volume). There is an expectation to let go of your past and assimilate into a new, better one—the upward mobility bias. From the undergraduate student perspective to the external one, there is a cost in gaining a different, upward social class. Daniel states it best: "Sending a student to a university is a high-risk commitment for a working-class family" (p. 35, this volume). The cost encompasses resources—money, time, relationships, and emotional energy—and follows us into our campus jobs as administrators and faculty members.

Because most people go directly to money when social class is mentioned, we will do the same. Degrees cost money and a lot of it for poor and working-class folks. Yes, there are factors that play into the particular cost: type of institution, location, proximity to home, first-year live-on requirement, and so on. But for a poor or working-class student, most of it is overwhelmingly expensive regardless of those factors. Additionally, the myth that poor and working-class students receive a free ride is indeed that: a myth. Again, working hard and a lot is simply part of the game. Sixteen of the 24 contributing writers directly shared how they worked prior to or during their college experience to help with family expenses, to help pay for college, or a combination thereof. There was less time and opportunity for cocurricular involvement and unpaid summer internships as well as to simply be a student. For poor and working-class folks to reach the proverbial end of the rainbow of a degree includes costs (literal and figurative) not often part of the middle-class student narrative.

Economic capital is also part of the professional narrative. Make no mistake, higher education pays more than working the counter at a fast-food restaurant. However, there is a clear disparity factoring in degrees, work experience, and hours worked, particularly for those lower in the institutional hierarchy. The major factor in Armina's job search processes has been free housing connected with working in residence life. This opportunity eliminates the need to spend resources on finding and securing an apartment and hauling bulky, heavy furniture to the next destination. Plus, depending on the institution and position, moving expenses are likely not included or fully covered and definitely not offered to be paid up front, and moving can be expensive. Besides, is housing really free when living in a residence hall filled with college students and being on call at all hours of the day? Even after landing that first job out of graduate school, Sara and Carmen talk about living paycheck to paycheck, struggling each month to make ends meet. Again, for many, student loans kick in pretty quickly, and life's bills are expensive. It is not always economically easy to work on a college campus.

In pursuit of higher education, there is also the personal cost—to students' relationship with themselves and family and friends from their social class of origin. There is a tenuous balance between appreciating this new, often viewed as "better" current social class, and not operating as better than one's social class of origin. On Tori's journey, she found support from her family and friends sprinkled with the resentful comment, "You think you're better than us?" As Carmen continued her education, she was asked or perhaps was the target of statements such as "What, now you think you're all good?" from family members not having attended college. Although said in jest, these comments strike a nerve, are familiar, and follow us in our social class trek.

The personal cost to one's social class of origin is confusing and painful, especially when there is little to no opportunity to talk about it. From language to food to knowledge, life is different. There is a sense of loss in no longer quite fitting in back home and not being the same person after first stepping foot on campus. Téa vividly recalls her first interaction on campus involving lunch during move-in day. She, her mother, and her brother were in uncharted territory, from the thick, university-inscribed napkins to the fancy cheese ravioli. In that moment, she realized her journey in higher education was about more than her being a first-generation college student. It was about her entire family being first-generation to all things involving college and at an Ivy League institution to boot. Even with Dylan being keenly aware that higher education was his ticket out, he still lives with the tension of wanting to go back while knowing, if or when he does, he is not the same person as he was when he left for college, although his small hometown of Ohio remains the same. He simultaneously feels the opening and closing of the same door. For Brenda, it's an ongoing struggle in "learning how to bridge that gap between new educational horizons and family dynamics" (p. 75, this volume). Having a foot in different class worlds is a lifetime balancing act—sometimes with ease and sometimes with challenge but always with strategy and intention.

Imposter Syndrome, Class Passing, and Code-Switching

It is tricky and wearying to be confident and successful while navigating a place and system not built with you in mind. The dynamics of feeling inadequate, out of place, and self-questioning accompany poor and working-class folks in the academy. An "insider-outside status is ever present" (p. 167, this volume) as Loren puts it, and there are many moments of feeling like an outsider or experiencing the notion of imposter syndrome: not fitting in and being a fraud. In Roxanne's experience in higher education, "Even when students managed to attend institutions of higher learning outside of their social classes, many students talked about imposter syndrome or not having done enough to be where they need" (p. 157, this volume).

Battling imposter syndrome involves an infinite journey with questioning belonging and whether we are enough to be part of the academy. Again, because when it comes down to it, the system of academia actually tells us we do not belong. Brenda continues to navigate imposter syndrome in maintaining a perceived middle-class lifestyle combined with the question of what life would be like if . . . Facing a typical, daunting combination as a class straddler, Sally talks about her struggle of being an administrator with perceived social class capital yet still not having quite enough of it: "I have found myself at countless professional dinners, conferences, conventions, and so on where I quickly knew I did not fit in . . . . I was given a seat at the table (hooray, right?), I just didn't know which fork to use" (pp. 90–91, this volume).

It is revealing that even those more seasoned or higher ranked in the academy feel as if they never quite fit in. At the senior level, Thomas has much less in common with donors, alumni, and local business owners, resulting in his need to understand the norms from dress to social interaction. Jeremiah shares that throughout his education and career in higher education he has often felt like an uninvited guest, wondering whether he was just one of the lucky ones. As a doctoral student, Rudy was filled with questions of self-doubt and unease: "Do I belong in graduate school? Did I make a mistake coming here? Am I smart enough to make it and get my PhD? All of these thoughts of self-doubt were part of my own imposter personal syndrome" (p. 138, this volume). Although clearly holding various forms of capital associated with middle-class life, feelings of inadequacy and uncertainty related to being enough remain present.

Then there's social class passing, whether internally or perceived by others. The assumption is that one's current social class, which is often perceived as middle class, is what and who that person has always been. Armina shares this sentiment: "Regardless of what our household income stated . . . on the outside looking in, everything appeared as it should. I guess one could call it 'class passing' because outward presentation, perception, and image were upheld" (pp. 63–64, this volume). Tim knows students he works with only see the end product of his social class story. His degrees, position, and office surrounded by windows must mean he has made it. Both Connie and Sara talk about assumptions that people make about their class of origin based on material factors, degrees, and professional titles. Owning a good car and taking fun vacations are read a certain classed way, and rightfully so. Both come with social class privilege, and, admittedly, the luxuries are pretty nice. In the push back in class passing, Connie admits she too sees herself as a middle-class woman. The fortunate piece for Connie is that in this book it's okay to hold multiple social class identities. There is no need to choose only one, and there should never have to be.

Perhaps this perception of class passing is because we have become accustomed to, and good at, code-switching. Living within our poor and working-class roots while managing the academy's drastically different values, norms, and practices requires fluency. Loren and Tori share the sentiment of having to learn a different language and set of standards. Such fluency is a requirement to survive in the academy for those from poor and working-class families. Eddie talks about never fully adapting to academic environments but rather adjusting to new systems and code-switching. Jacinda knows that code-switching is part of her everyday life, noting, "I like hip-hop, I swear, and I code-switch . . . . I had to learn how to dress; how to wear makeup (properly); how to speak in different ways; and, of course, which fork to use at dinner" (p. 97, this volume). This fluency requirement is also needed to remain connected to the values of our social class of origin despite how different they may be from the expectations from the academy. Sally still downloads coupons for the grocery store every Saturday morning, and Tom still does most of his home repair, even though both can afford to live life differently.

Increasing the Conversation on Social Class in Higher Education

Social class is not generally discussed in or outside the academy. It is taboo and off limits. However, almost every touch point on campus involves social class in its multiple forms of capital, extending beyond finances. As Sara shares, "Most days I have to remind myself that social class is more than money because that is often where the conversation starts and stops in higher education". It is important to pay attention to the ways in which social class is talked about on campuses and the limitations of mere money forms such as financial aid packages and affordable programming. If we dig deeper, social class is about the dynamics found in the requirement for a meal plan, the types of food offered on campus, an (early) housing deposit, the expectation of long work days staffing late-night programs, happy hours for staff team building, and written and unwritten norms and practices at faculty meetings. Yet even with class firmly planted in higher education, story after story expresses the need to expand the conversation on social class so that those from poor and working-class backgrounds can feel like part of campus.

A result from the lack of social class conversation is feeling dismissed and unheard. Found within all of the undergraduate student and sole master's student stories is a shared sentiment of not being included—in literature, processes, and the ethos of the academy. Téa shares that in her poor social class identity, she is "begging to be noticed by the world, begging for the world to care about [her]." Kevyanna similarly relates in that the "feeling of being included and a part of the larger community is just as important [as admissions processes and maintaining good grades]." These powerful statements are a reflection that higher education is failing our students by ignoring the social class conversation. When we say higher education, we are not referring to a nebulous entity floating on campus. We mean all members on campus—administrators, faculty, staff, and students across all social classes. Yes, this includes us, and you, too.

Assumptions and messages made about and taken in by poor and working-class folks impact their college and on-campus professional work experience. As Eddie points out, "People make assumptions . . . the working class not 'wanting to get an education,' or assuming they do not have the work ethic to persist through college." This assumption, along with countless others, combined with the disregard of social class in the conversation, furthers isolation on campus. Internalizing these messages can result in the shame, fear, and guilt that Sara shares as part of her social class story, and we want better for members of any campus community. Let us share Armina's hope of being "unafraid to be uncomfortable by talking about social class" (p. 65, this volume). To create more inclusion within higher education requires college campuses to openly engage social class; otherwise poor and working-class folks will continue to be system outsiders.

Making Changes in/to the System

But why change the system if it is working? That question is part of most any discussion involving change, especially asked by those for whom the system is working. The stories throughout this book speak of the need for change. It is time to listen to members of our community. In Tom's experience, "We invest little time discussing the realities of social class for students and have not responded nimbly enough to adjust practices, policies, and programs to be inclusive to poor and working-class students" (pp. 104–105, this volume).

Given the aspirations of academia to do and be better with inclusion, Roxanne knows it needs to "continue to bring into consciousness and into action the ideas that institutions designed to educate should create systems that are boundless and accessible to anyone seeking education and not based on what people can afford" (p. 160, this volume). From the faculty lens, Larry points out, "If we are to ensure that our institutions have access to the best possible future, we must transform faculty culture to make it more open, less class oriented, and more collaborative" (p. 143, this volume). There is nothing wrong with gaps; the academy just needs to be open enough to transform them.

Sometimes we can get stuck in the how—to create change, to create inclusion, to act. Luckily, there is wisdom in the stories within this book, asking us to pay attention and notice that the steps are neither huge nor overwhelming. In fact, they are doable, and it's just a matter of having enough awareness and courage to put them into action. Armina has an easy fix: When her office requires an all-day training, she seeks funds to provide lunch. This may seem like an obvious act, but that is not always the case. There is often an expectation that those working on college campuses have the means to afford an occasional lunch, but that assumption is unintentionally classed. Interrogating that assumption alone can help change office culture. Graduate school interviews involve time and money. Nancy advocated conducting phone and Skype interviews. Some change is really not hard. Sally talks about leading with humility and understanding in advocating for poor and working-class students and professionals. She makes it her responsibility to be a voice amid those with six-figure salaries for a group of people often forgotten.

When Jacinda is asked about ways to increase diversity in professional organizations, her answer is always to "make them more affordable" (p. 87, this volume). It is a simple answer, and because academic-related systems are embedded in class(ism), it is not an answer always given or heard. Still, she keeps at it. Mamta reflects on the ways in which her social class upbringing has informed her leadership capacity and approach, particularly how she allocates and treats resources, how she budgets, and the level of courage by which she is able to lead when it means asking for resources. She prioritizes resources, and in discussions with colleagues, Mamta asks, "Does this expense honor the tuition dollars our students will be paying off for decades into their future?" (p. 100, this volume). It is both a caring and hard-hitting question that has power to generate critical conversation involving social class and class(ism).

Paying It Forward

Leave no one behind! That is the mantra of most of the contributing writers. From helping to supplement family and friends' income to mentoring students to interrogating current policies and practices in pursuit of creating more inclusive ones, there is a sense of responsibility to pay it forward. Increased access and acquired social class capital certainly extend beyond our individual self, and stopping there would be nothing short of selfish.

Sometimes giving back is about helping ends meet. Tim finds himself monetarily helping students when he can. He knows he has access to resources he didn't have as a student, and he finds some of his students in the same situation. That's the thing with people from poor and working-class families in the academy: There is a connection with the social class struggle. There is meaning and purpose in reaching back to our communities to pay it forward. Eddie talks about providing "opportunities for people who may have to travel a little farther to get to the door of opportunity" (p. 155, this volume). We are hopefully making it a bit easier for those coming after us. We recognize the support extended to us in our acquisition of degrees and own our responsibility to continue to build a path. Rudy works to "pay it forward to my students, both graduate and undergraduate, from my home institution and others throughout the country . . . . We must hold the doors open for subsequent generations of scholars" (pp. 139–140, this volume). Raul uses his voice (and privilege) to ask challenging questions in the advocacy for others. Larry talks of his personal challenge "to teach, lead, and build community in a way that creates space to uncover the brilliance and encourage the contributions of others regardless of position or academic preparation" (p. 143, this volume).

Unique Experiences

Because social class does not exist in isolation, unique experiences are found with other intersecting identities contributing to the writers' meaning of and navigation in social class. Race, gender, gender identity, disability, sexuality, geography, and family structure were mentioned intersecting identities that led to individuals' unique experiences. Some stories involved the impact of growing up in an urban or rural setting, whereas others included the current social class differences between their siblings, many times a place of contention and disconnect.

The lives of Armina, Roxanne, Daniel, Connie, Briza, and Mamta are grounded in their families' journey to the United States as immigrants. The importance of that experience has given them distinctive insight into social class and how they navigate it. They recognize their parents' challenges and the impact those challenges had on their childhood and social class worldview (Liu, 2011). Although some of their parents came to the United States with degrees and valuable work experience from their home country, they had to start from the beginning. In Roxanne's story, she shares, "We were working class because the U.S. educational system refuses to honor and recognize the validity of foreign degrees and education" (p. 155, this volume). They shared a similar uphill struggle with most poor or working-class families and had the added layers of difference in language, values, norms, and community.

As a child in a military family overseas, Sara adds a perspective missing in social class conversations in the academy. This combination is usually void in conversations in higher education because, unless it's a military affiliated institution, the two are designed to exist separate from each other. Insightful in her story is the sense of sameness found in the overseas military base. The same types of housing, hospitals, stores, and activities were practical and rightly so given the nature of moving for those in the military. Although there were differences in housing between officers and enlisted personnel, a military base can only have so many stark differences for a kid to notice.

College athletics was a means to an end for Loren. It was one of the ways he was able to afford school, and he worked hard to keep his athletic scholarship to attain his degree. When it comes to college athletes, athletic scholarships are often associated with athletes of color and understandably so given the number recruited for revenue-generating sports. Loren expands the social class conversation as a White student in college athletics.

Key Learnings

Sharing an intimate story about one's social class is hard enough, but doing so in a book involves vulnerability. This form of scholarship wrapped in storytelling allows us a depth of learning easily lost through mere numbers or statistics involving class-related issues. As we read each story, it became clear that digging into the stories of poor and working-class individuals included complex feelings and risk to their current capital. Being willing to share growing up with poorly educated parents, struggling to pay basic bills, or feeling like you don't fit in with your peers takes courage. These stories are counternarratives to academia's particular set of standards on the ways it recognizes social class, and our hope is that they help us engage social class in more authentic, vulnerable ways toward inclusion.

Social class involves a great deal of language—*poor, working poor, working class*, and *class straddling*, just to name a few terms. Terms are not easily defined and are used differently depending on the individual. Some people used the same term (e.g., *working class*), but their stories revealed a different meaning of that particular term. This tells us that we need to listen to folks' stories and how they define themselves, rather than ask them to check a box or assume we know what they mean when they name a term.

To be congruent with inclusion, the academy needs to start engaging social class; otherwise, we are doing a disservice with inclusion and social justice efforts. Plus, as reflected in the stories, not doing so is damaging to members of poor and working-class families. By *the academy*, we mean all players of the campus community—students, administrators, faculty, and all other members—and by *social class*, we mean all forms of capital it involves, not just money or economic capital. There is a critical need to place social class on the table with other areas of identity, particularly to better understand the dynamics that exist on campus for those from poor and working-class families.

Found within these stories are resiliency, courage, determination, and grit. There is a great deal to learn from the skills that poor and working-class students and colleagues bring to campus. Learning about their struggles and successes can better equip higher education to reframe the perspective; instead of viewing these individuals from a deficit lens, we can learn from the ways they navigate campus with success.

Social Class Is Not Experienced in Isolation

System Dynamics Related to Identity

In this collection of stories, social class is center stage because typically it is not. Even within social justice work, engaging this particular identity is perpetually at the margins. Class is not discussed in almost any personal or professional circle, or at least not directly or intentionally. We have been socialized to believe it is a taboo topic while being omnipresent, like air. As reflected through each story, social class forms a sense of self in ways potentially not recognized in the moment and yet impacts life along the way.

We know identity extends beyond social class. Identity is a social construct (Torres, Jones, & Renn, 2009), and in this construct, it is a reality regardless of whether we want it to be. Some of our identities are salient, grounding, and noticeable, whereas others live below the surface in ignorance, rejection, or secrecy. Identity is innate, salient, clear, ambiguous, set, and fluid. It connects communities and tears them apart, both within and across. When it comes to identity, we are referring to being a part of a group that is marginalized or privileged as a result of institutional and systemic policies, practices, rules, and norms. Identity is not just what we think and how we feel as individuals. It includes the groups we are a part of and the ways in which institutional and systemic structures interact with said groups (Tatum, 2013).

Let's pause here to clarify some terms because language alone is where we can find ourselves stuck or confused, which is not a place we want you to be. The literature interchangeably uses the terms *marginalized* and *subordinated*. These terms refer to social group identities that are institutionally and structurally oppressed. Examples include poor, working class, people of color, women, trans, and disabled, just to name a few. On the flip side, the terms *privileged* and *dominant* are interchangeably used and refer to social groups that institutionally and structurally oppress. A few examples are middle and upper class, Whites, men, and nondisabled (Kirk & Okazawa-Rey, 2013).

A challenge with identity work is that people often retreat to their individuality without considering the institutional structures in place, causing subordination or dominance. In other words, people respond by claiming they don't feel oppressed or privileged. (Johnson, 2001). Individuality allows denial of the ways in which subordination is automatically placed on or privilege is automatically granted regardless of individuality. In other words, it does not (just) matter who we are as individuals; instead, what matters are the social groups we individually belong to when it comes to the dynamics of subordination and dominance (Hardiman & Jackson, 2007). To add to this complexity are the concepts of intersectionality and intersecting identities.

Intersectionality

Intersectionality is both clear and ambiguous. Depending on who is writing and talking about it, it is referred to as a theory, term, or concept. Its foundation involves social identities and systems of privilege and oppression. Intersectionality helps us better understand how people make meaning of who they are as well as the institutional structures in place that create inequities. A lack of structural analysis undermines the influence that intersectionality can have to shift inequitable policies and practices (Collin & Bilge, 2016). Our work as educators is to understand intersectionality so we can engage and shift those institutional structures and systems toward social justice.

Intersectionality continues to change. Since its formal origin, it has expanded across social identities, systems of power, and academic and activist bodies, and stretched beyond the United States (Carbado, Crenshaw, Mays, & Tomlinson, 2013). Given the scope and audience of our work, we hope to honor the original author of intersectionality while also providing insight into its presence in the academy related to identity and higher education. We also know the scholarship provided is limited because it is in the particular context of higher education and identity, and intersecting identities extend beyond the walls of academia.

Legal scholar Kimberlé Crenshaw formally introduced the term *intersectionality* into the academic world. Her knowledge of the systemic dynamics of privilege and oppression related to social identities—particularly race, gender, and class—positioned her to understand the ways that people were treated related to multiple marginalized identity groups (Anders & Devita, 2014). She focused on ways that women of color, particularly Black women, were treated regarding violence with accompanied oppression in their gendered and raced identities (Cho, Crenshaw, & McCall, 2013). This intersection of marginalized identities highlighted "the need to account for multiple grounds of identity when considering how the social world is constructed" (Crenshaw, 1991, p. 1245).

Her analysis did not focus on just the individual experiences of women of color but rather on how those marginalization experiences were a consequence of group identities as a result of the institutionalized, structural oppression of racism, sexism, and classism (Crenshaw, 1989; Wijeyesinghe & Jones, 2016). Although their oppression was felt as individuals, it also involved a set of normalized and condoned behaviors, practices, and rules that targeted, placed, and treated poor women of color as less than those in their counterparts' privileged identities. If we circle back to social class, intersectionality involves the identities of class–gender, class–disability, class–race, and class–sexuality, to name a few.

In this mention of oppression, it is important to provide context. We are referring to oppression beyond bias, inequitable treatment, and discrimination. Oppression involves and emphasizes "the pervasive nature of social inequality woven throughout social institutions as well as embedded within individual consciousness" (Bell, 2007, p. 3). It is structural and rooted in norms, values, habits, practices, and behaviors that result in inequities between privileged and marginalized groups (Young, 2013). Oppression may manifest itself in different ways depending on the social identity and ism; but in the end, it establishes a power differential based on in- and out-group membership.

To move into the scholarship of intersectionality found in higher education, the distinction between our body of literature and that of Crenshaw is that it has evolved to include the intersections of both marginalized and privileged identities. Although "theory is never done, nor exhausted by its prior articulations or movements" (Carbado et al., 2013, p. 2), we hold dissonance in the shift from its original theory by Crenshaw given her multiple subordinated identities as a Black woman and the arduous work involved for her to even propose intersectionality to the academic (and legal) world. As often found in inclusion work, we are holding the both/and. We do not want to conflate intersectionality with intersecting identities or the multiplicity or combination of identities, and we want to recognize the arduous work also done by higher education scholars who have entered the subject matter with a different meaning. In sharing their work, we will use the language found in the literature with an understanding that for us intersectionality involves multimarginalized identities rather than across marginalized and privileged ones. Needless to say, this topic is tricky; messy; complex; and, for some, probably controversial. Then again, so is social class identity.

Intersectionality in Higher Education

Intersectionality has been added to and reframed in various academic disciplines. Given this book's content, we are offering how it has been theorized by higher education scholars to better understand and support college students in their development. Identity and lived experiences comprise our context or worldview (Liu, 2011), and understanding it helps us better recognize how we feel about our individual and intersecting identities and the world around us (Reinert & Serna, 2014). Similar to Crenshaw's (1991) work on intersectionality involving multimarginalized identities, Reynolds and Pope (1991) developed the multidimensional identity model to better support students in their identity development, focusing on multiple oppressed identities and potential ways individuals can choose to deal with or negotiate their multiple oppressions.

The model contains four options for what are termed *identity resolutions* within multiple oppressions. Options 1 and 2 focus on identifying with an aspect of self, with the first option occurring in a passive, accepted manner and the second in a conscious, active choice (Abes, Jones, & McEwen, 2007; Pope & Reynolds, 2017). Option 1 operates in a sense of unknowing.

Carmen shares in her story, "I didn't know what working poor was as a kid; I didn't know that's what we were. Many of my neighbors, my schoolmates, and the families with whom we spent time came from a similar financial background" (p. 57, this volume). Although her social class of working poor existed, she did not know the identity was structurally placed on her but rather, "It was just the way it was." In a social class lens, option 2 of identifying in active consciousness is tricky because of the lack of engagement, language, and knowledge to identify in a social class.

Options 3 and 4 involve multiple aspects of self, with one in a conscious, segmented fashion and the other in an integrated one. Within this third option, individuals are conscious of and accept their multiple identities but live them out in separate ways. Pope and Reynolds (2017) use the example of a Black gay man actively involved in his church and gay community. Within his Black church community, his queerness is unknown, and yet separately and simultaneously, he participates in the predominantly White gay community. Although this example represents an individual with intersecting identities, there is a sectioning of those various identities depending on his environment. Option 4 is the integration of an individual's multiple, intersecting identities. With this integrated sense of self, individuals combine and exist in all of their multimarginalized identities. They do not feel a sense of needing to choose one over the other but rather can accept and live as their intersectional self. Nancy's story represents this fourth option as she discusses her consciousness of her multiple oppressed identities. For Nancy, there is connection of being disabled, a woman, and raised poor in a rural setting, and one does not exist without the other in her sense of self.

The model of multiple dimensions of identity (Reynolds & Pope, 1991) builds on the concept of intersecting identities with the integration of marginalized and privileged identities and other components involved in one's life. This model "describes the dynamic construction of identity and the influence of changing contexts on the relative salience of multiple identity dimensions" (Abes et al., 2007, p. 3). The original model involved a core sense of self surrounded by one's particular life context (e.g., family background, past and current experiences) and dimensions of identity (e.g., social class, race, gender, and religion). No dimension exists in isolation from the other and instead can only be understood in relation to the other (Jones & McEwen, 2000). The newer version of the model incorporates meaning-making capacity to better represent the relationship between context and salience of identities and the relationship between identities and one's core sense of self (Abes et al., 2007). Found in Dylan's story is a grounded core sense of self with his intersecting identities of social class and race. He has an increased awareness of it as he talks about the complexity of his White poverty and the necessary self-work "to approach the nuances of simultaneous privilege and struggle" (p. 55, this volume).

Summary

Each contributing writer's story powerfully represents the reason for this book—to provide a venue to better recognize how social class is present in the academy and to more deeply understand its influence on the lives of those from poor and working-class backgrounds. Found throughout the stories are unique insights from individuals and a collection of voices that offer similarities to the ways in which the academy does and does not support social class inclusion.

Two things are apparent. First, social class needs to be included in social justice work in higher education. It needs attention and conversation. It will be uncomfortable and messy, but then again, so is any work involving identity. The second is the need for the academy to expand and engage social class beyond money. As evidenced through every story, marginalization happens in the subtle ways in which social class is felt by people from poor and working-class backgrounds. It involves the impact of using different language and operating in a different set of norms not valued in an academic setting.

To effectively create inclusion in the academy, social class has to be part of the work. Otherwise policies, practices, and norms will continue to marginalize students and professionals from poor and working-class backgrounds in damaging ways. In addition, doing so supports institutions of higher education to be more congruent with their mission and values related to diversity and social justice. It is simply good practice. So, let's explore how we can do this.

Increasing Social Class Consciousness and Inclusivity in Higher Education

M artin, Williams, and Young (2018) note that the "lack of attention to social class within our field has left many educators and students without a language, awareness, or understanding of social class as an aspect of identity" (p. 10), and they encourage us to "reconsider how campus systems, policies, and practices may inadvertently be marginalizing [folks from poor and working class] backgrounds" (p. 14). Our hope is that the stories in this book generate more attention on this dimension of identity, and we offer this chapter as first steps to begin or extend your language, awareness, and understanding of social class on your campus and in the field at large with the aim of more class equity in higher education.

Let's start by having you ask yourself: "How can I use my positionality as an educator, my knowledge of the system, and the opportunities I have had to help others navigate the academy? How can I serve as an advocate and empower others?" In this process, let's keep the following at the forefront of our minds: "Social justice is not done 'to' or 'for' someone else but is an action that is accomplished 'with' the other person or community members as equal partners" (Liu, 2011, p. 239).

Suggestions for Increasing Social Class Consciousness in Higher Education

Garrison and Liu (2018) highlight how self-awareness is "one key factor for increasing competence of student affairs professionals" (p. 25) and suggest that student affairs professionals should understand their worldviews, biases, and views on meritocracy and social class inequity because they can affect their services for students (Liu, 2011; Locke & Trolian, 2018; Pope, 2014). Love (2010) refers to developing awareness as part of liberatory consciousness. This act of self-awareness helps to develop "the capacity to notice, to give our attention to our daily lives, our language, and even our thoughts" (Love, 2010, p. 600). The following questions can guide self-reflection to garner more self-awareness:

- What have I been told about being rich and poor?
- How does my family social class background impact me?
- What are my significant memories of being different from others with respect to social class?
- What am I comfortable with regarding social class? What do I struggle with regarding social class?
- How is the culture of the college where I work different from my own culture with respect to social class?
- What kind of social class–related messages do I convey when interacting with students or developing services? (Garrison & Liu, 2018)

Once we have engaged in some self-work around our own social class identity, we can begin to raise our consciousness of how others may identify. Liu (2011) offers his social class worldview model, both the original and revised versions, as frameworks from which to do this. The model is explained in chapter 1, and Liu's implications for practice include being aware of our own worldviews and corresponding biases; considering that there are multiple ways that people make sense of and define their social class; understanding that people may still have some work to do around this identity and learning how to be with them in their struggle; utilizing one-on-one conversations with students and colleagues to grasp their social class worldview and how it influences their experiences, behaviors, and decision-making; and acknowledging the level of salience that social class identity has in a person's life. One practical way to do this is to not make assumptions because, as Elkins and Hanke (2018) teach us, people can be practicing social class code-switching on our campuses. For example, just because students wear name-brand coats or shoes does not mean they are affluent; they may have spent their scholarship money on that item to better blend in to your campus. Do the work to learn their story.

The key to all of this, however, is letting go of the idea that social class is a taboo topic and talking about it. Yes, it may seem or feel odd. Yes, you may step in it. Do it anyway. Because, as Liu (2011) points out, "Having some comfort in talking about social class and classism is just the foundation for becoming competent in [this identity area] . . . the real work is coming to an understanding of our own biases and worldviews" (pp. 209–210).

Suggestions for Increasing Social Class Inclusivity in the Academy

Concurrently with creating a more critical and consistent consciousness about social class in higher education, how can we create higher education spaces that consider social class identity and increase inclusivity for students, administrators, and faculty members from poor and working-class backgrounds? Here we offer a few suggestions based on the narratives in this book, the social class literature, our personal and professional experiences, and benchmarking with colleges and universities throughout the United States.

Recognizing and Naming Classism

As we have already discussed, class involves various terms and definitions, making it a bit ambiguous and elusive, when most often we prefer concepts involving work related to inclusion to be exact and clear, particularly for those of us in higher education. Consequently, this space of ambiguity allows an easy escape to avoid recognizing and naming classism on campus and in ourselves. Similar to self-awareness, mentioned earlier, awareness involving what is happening around us increases our competency. To create social class inclusion, we must be able to recognize and name class-related moments. Consider how social class and classism might show up within the campus contexts described in Table C.1.

As martinez (2012) offers, "It takes intentionality and patience to merely understand there is something to recognize; moreover, naming it is a whole other level of action" (p. 92). Putting it out there may feel risky or vulnerable. Take a deep breath and do it anyway. Let's remember, doing so is courageous. We must be able to point out why events such as orientation and family weekend are exclusive or the ways in which staff bonding over happy hour contains traces of classism (Ardoin & martinez, 2018). Naming it creates moments for learning, allows us to consider ways to be inclusive, and encourages action.

Upward Mobility Bias
Assuming everyone attends higher education as an attempt of "movin' on up" (in the words of *The Jeffersons* theme song), the proverbial social class ladder is a form of upward mobility bias (Liu, 2011). It causes us to presuppose that

TABLE C.1
Examples of How Class Permeates the Academy

As Individuals	In Departments	On Campus
Assumptions About Intelligence And Professionalism	Office Hours of Operation	Deposits for Registration and Housing
	Recruitment and Hiring Practices	
Expectations Regarding Attire, Language, Communication Style		Preorientation and Orientation Programs
	Involvement in Professionally Related Organizations	Family Weekend
		Spirit Days
Mentoring	Reimbursements	
		Student Involvement
Discussions About Housing, Dinner, Vacations	Potlucks	Internships
	Happy Hours	

the student or colleague from a rural or inner-city area doesn't want to return home. It makes us deem that underserved students need etiquette classes and colleagues from poor and working-class background need to be taught professionalism. It drives our belief that whatever social class is higher than us is better than us and that we should always strive for more. Try to recognize when this bias—which is a form of classism—arises for you and attempt to let it go. Then get to know people's stories about their social class, their myriad of life experiences, and what they may want to learn.

Jargon, the Hidden Curriculum, and Navigational Capital
Parts of the systemic, dominant structures in the academy are language and unwritten norms and practices not easily understood by those from poor and working-class backgrounds. Let's face it, phrases such as *systemic, dominant structures* and *the academy* represent such jargon. Higher education uses words and phrases that lose many people (Ardoin, 2018). Our role is to reduce or remove the jargon, which can be as simple as using the definition versus the jargon term. For example, we can say *academic area of study* instead of *major* or *time to meet with faculty* instead of *office hours*. Coupled with this, we need to discard the alphabet soup that is higher education acronyms. If we have to use an acronym (although we never truly have to, we just prefer to), we should at least be intentional about saying or spelling it out the first time we use it. We can also consider making a campus- or

department-based dictionary—in both hard copy and electronic forms—for all students, administrators, and faculty to access if, or when, they need it. These efforts would be relatively simple, with the potential for significant impact. It would also be a start to demystifying the academy's hidden curriculum, which includes all the norms, policies, practices, and communication methods, many of which are based in middle- and upper class ways, that higher education assumes people know.

Sharing college knowledge with poor and working-class students can be helpful, particularly as they enter the academy as prospective and first-year students (Ardoin, 2018; Locke & Trolian, 2018). This peek into the hidden curriculum can be converted into navigational capital for students as they begin to decipher terms, rules, and opportunities within higher education. Take nothing for granted. For some it is translating academic language and explaining which campus office is responsible for what. For others, it is teaching them the ins and outs of the cocurricular or leadership experiences on campus. Develop a resource list of questions and answers from how to manage coursework, work, and maintain a healthy personal life to how study abroad works and that actually if they work the system correctly, they can have such an experience if so desired. Discuss the concept of faculty office hours and the importance of utilizing them if they need help or have questions. In fact, work with them to ask questions and seek help when necessary; most students from poor and working-class backgrounds have been socialized to do otherwise. They come to campus with a keen sense of being able to navigate a system; help them translate those skills to a college campus.

Evaluating Policies and Practices

In our dominant identities, we often miss the mark of what is and is not working for those with subordinated identities. So, instead of guessing, let's ask students and families from poor and working-class backgrounds where we have created barriers for them; put them at the table where policy decisions are being made (Locke & Trolian, 2018). Find out what they understood regarding the application process and all that comes with acceptance. Ask about what practices made their support system feel comfortable moving them to and visiting them in college and what has pushed them away. Find out about their experiences in the dining facility, library, classroom, registrar's office, and athletic field, all of the touch points on campus. Talk about practices with each touch point and, equally important, ask how they are treated. Do so without explanation and judgment, and don't do it over a formal dinner with white linen, multiple courses, and ever-confusing flatware.

Take time to do your homework on your institution's relationship with social class. Learn about the history of social class on campus, what has changed, and what has remained the same. Become versed in the formula for financial aid and what policies are in place to support poor and working-class students paying for college. Take inventory of your office's practices around formal and informal time off, expectations in professional involvement, and what's considered a team player or go-getter personality. Better understand the policies and practices related to hourly or frontline staff. Admit there is already different treatment. We've recently become aware that some campuses without air-conditioning allow (many) administrators to telework from home in extreme temperatures during the summer but hourly or frontline staff need to remain in the office. Yes, it happens, and yes, it may just be happening on your campus if you're not paying attention.

Gathering Different Data

Knowing that colleges and universities often lack any data, or quality data, on how their community members identify in terms of social class, we should begin gathering different data. Soria (2018) notes that "a holistic, composite measure of social class is sorely needed" (p. 57) and offers how social class data collection can include nuanced, multifaceted data from more objective indicators, such as parental income, parental education (i.e., first-generation college student status), and occupational prestige, and more subjective indicators, such as asking people how they identify. Collecting both can be helpful in cross-checking and validating data, but consider if or how we are doing this (or not) with other dimensions of identity. Do we ask people to validate their race? How about their sexuality or religion? Then, why do we not accept how people self-identify their social class, particularly when research indicates that "students' subjective self-identification of social class can 'provide more reliable and predictive assessments than objective measures, especially in education research'" (Rubin et al., 2014, p. 198).

The point of all this is to ask students, administrators, and faculty about their social class and, then, to believe them. You can start this at the program or office level if your institution is not yet at a place to do it campus-wide. Any time you ask about identity, include social class in its broad form. Gathering data on social class will also allow you and the institution to know who is on your campus, support efforts to shift policy or practice, introduce new support systems and resources, and create more equity in the academy.

Learning About Campus and Community Resources

You cannot point someone in the right direction if you don't know the direction. The same is true for sharing resources. You have to know what they are before you can suggest them. With social class, it is key to know the campus and community resources that can help folks secure basic needs, connect them with others who share their social class identity, build their forms of capital, and celebrate who they are. This may require you to do some homework (i.e., information digging) about your institution and location. It may mean you need to walk or drive around to get a physical layout for where resources are and who good contacts may be (Liu, 2011). Where are there food pantries, when are they open, and is there public transportation to get there? Is the food ordered for events packable enough for those in attendance to take home leftovers? What are the free events on campus or in the community where people can build social capital and are those at varied times so people with job or caregiving responsibilities can choose events that align with their schedules? Is there a virtual space to connect folks who have similar social class identities; if not, might there be an opportunity to create one? Make the effort to learn the answers to questions like these.

Engaging in Education and Training

It will also be important to provide space for folks to come together to talk and learn about social class identity. Engaging people in dialogue within and across social class identities can be both challenging and powerful. Consider gathering people who identify as poor or working class, as well as those who identify as middle class, upper middle class, or affluent. Helping those with privileged class identities understand their own social class worldview, the privileges and power they have been afforded through social class, and the microaggressive behaviors they may exhibit can make a significant impact on how they understand themselves, the academy, and society, and it can encourage them to contribute to more social class equity. Incorporating other dimensions of identity into these dialogues will also be key in assisting folks in grasping how social class intersects with their race, ethnicity, gender, age, sexuality, religion, and ability.

In the true spirit of learning, be continual in the education around social class and classism. Don't let it just be a one-and-done effort. That will be counter to your efforts. Trainings are great and important—do them often and with enough time for more than learning theories and terms related to social class—but also include other ways to engage in and learn about social class. Read and discuss books, articles, blogs, and stories. Choose the most popular movie or television show and interrogate the ways in which class is involved. Believe us, there is plenty of content. It is just a matter of paying attention and having the courage to engage it.

Summary

We could write a whole book on strategies, and we recognize the influence of context. Thus, although we offer these suggestions as first steps, we know you will need to scale them to suit your particular campus or community. We just ask that you do what you need to do to talk about social class in the academy. It may be that the initial conversation you need to have is with yourself. What is your social class story?

REFERENCES

Abes, E. S., Jones, S. R., & McEwen, M. K. (2007). Reconceptualizing the model of multiple dimensions of identity: The role of meaning-making capacity in the construction of multiple identities. *Journal of College Student Development, 48*(1), 1–22.

Adams, M., Bell, L. A., & Griffin, P. (Eds.). (2007). *Teachings for diversity and social justice.* New York, NY: Routledge.

Anders, D. A., & Devita, J. M. (2014). Intersectionality: A legacy from critical legal studies and critical race theory. In D. Mitchell Jr. (Ed.), *Intersectionality & higher education: Theory, research & praxis* (pp. 31–44). New York, NY: Peter Lang.

Archer, L. (2003). Social class and higher education. In L. Archer, M. Hutchings, & A. Ross (Eds.), *Higher education and social class: Issues of exclusion and inclusion* (pp. 5–20). New York, NY: RoutledgeFalmer.

Ardoin, S. (2018a). *College aspirations and access in working-class, rural communities: The mixed signals, challenges, and new language first-generation students encounter.* Lanham, MD: Lexington.

Ardoin, S. (2018b). Helping poor and working-class students create their own sense of belonging. *New Directions for Student Services, 162,* 75–86.

Ardoin, S. (2019). Social class influences on student learning. In P. Magolda, M. B. Baxter Magolda, & R. Carducci (Eds.), *Contested issues in troubled times: Student affairs dialogues about equity, civility, and safety* (pp. 203–214). Sterling, VA: Stylus.

Ardoin, S., & martinez, b. (2018). No, I can't meet you for an $8 coffee: How class shows up in workspaces. In B. Reece, V. Tran, E. DeVore, & G. Porcaro (Eds.), *Debunking the myth of job fit in student affairs* (pp. 97–117). Sterling, VA: Stylus.

Arner, L. (2016). Survival strategies for working-class women as junior faculty members. In A. L. Hurst & S. K. Nenga (Eds.), *Working in class: Recognizing how social class shapes our academic work.* Lanham, MD: Rowman & Littlefield.

Astin, A. (2001). *What matters in college?* San Francisco, CA: Jossey-Bass.

Bailey, M. J., & Dynarski, S. M. (2011). *Gains and gaps: Changing inequality in U.S. college entry and completion.* Available from http://www.nber.org/papers/w17633.pdf?new_window=1

Barratt, W. (2011). *Social class on campuses: Theories and manifestations.* Sterling, VA: Stylus.

Bell, L. A. (2007). Theoretical foundations for social justice education. In M. Adams, L. A. Bell, & P. Griffin (Eds.), *Teachings for diversity and social justice* (pp. 1–14). New York, NY: Routledge.

Bell, L. A. (2010). *Storytelling for social justice: Connecting narrative and the arts in antiracist teaching.* New York, NY: Routledge.

Borrego, S. (2008). Class on campus: Breaking the silence surrounding socioeconomics. *Diversity & Democracy, 11*(3), 1–3.

Bourdieu, P. (1977). *Reproduction in education, society, and culture.* London, UK: SAGE.

Bourdieu, P. (1984). *Distinction: A social critique of the judgment of taste.* Cambridge, MA: Harvard University Press.

Bourdieu, P. (1986). The forms of capital. In J. G. Richardson (Ed.), *Handbook of theory and research for the sociology of education* (pp. 241–258). New York, NY: Greenwood.

Bourdieu, P. (1989). Social space and symbolic power. *Sociological Theory, 7*(1), 14–25.

Bourke, B. (2014). Positionality: Reflecting on the research process. *The Qualitative Report, 19*(33), 1–9.

Brown, D., & Swanson, L. (2003). *Challenges for rural America in the twenty-first century.* University Park, PA: Pennsylvania State University Press.

Carbado, D. W., Crenshaw, K. W., Mays, V. M., & Tomlinson, B. (2013). Intersectionality: Mapping the movements of theory. *Du Bois Institute for African and African American Research, 10*(2), 1–11.

Cho, S., Crenshaw, K. W., & McCall, L. (2013). Toward a field of intersectionality studies: Theory, applications, and praxis. *Journal of Women in Culture and Society, 38*(4), 785–810.

Coghlan, D., & Brydon-Miller, M. (2014). *The SAGE encyclopedia of action research.* Los Angeles, CA: SAGE.

Collins, C., Ladd, J., Seider, M., & Yeskel, F. (Eds.). (2014). *Class lives: Stories from across our economic divide.* Ithaca, NY: Cornell University Press.

Collins, P. H., & Bilge, S. (2016). *Intersectionality.* Cambridge, UK: Polity.

Cranton, P. (2006). *Understanding and promoting transformative learning: A guide for educators of adults* (2nd ed.). San Francisco, CA: Jossey-Bass.

Crenshaw, K. W. (1989). Demarginalizing the intersection of race and sex: A black feminist critique of antidiscrimination doctrine, feminist theory, and antiracist politics. *University of Chicago Legal Forum, 1*(8), 139–167.

Crenshaw, K. W. (1991). Mapping the margins: Intersectionality, identity, and violence against women of color. *Stanford Law Review, 43*(6), 1241–1299.

Creswell, J. W. (2013). *Qualitative inquiry and research design: Choosing among five approaches* (3rd ed.). Los Angeles, CA: SAGE.

Denzin, N. K. (1986). *Interpretive biography.* Newbury Park, CA: SAGE.

Dews, C. L. B., & Law, C. L. (Eds.). (1995). *This fine place so far from home: Voices of academics from the working class.* Philadelphia, PA: Temple University Press.

Duckworth, A. L., & Quinn, P. D. (2009). Development and validation of the short grit scale (GRIT–S). *Journal of Personality Assessment, 91*(2), 166–174.

Elkins, B., & Hanke, E. (2018). Code-switching to navigate social class in higher education and student affairs. *New Directions for Student Services, 162,* 35–47.

Fuller, A. (2012). In selecting peers for comparison's sake, colleges look upward. *The Chronicle of Higher Education*. Available from http://www.chronicle.com/article/in-selecting-peers-for/134228

Garrison, Y. L., & Liu, W. M. (2018). Using the social class worldview model in student affairs. *New Directions for Student Services, 162*, 19–33.

Gee, J. P. (1991). A linguistic approach to narrative. *Journal of Narrative and Life History/Narrative Inquiry, 1*, 15–39.

Goodwin, M. (1979). East Harlem's troubled Taino Towers set to open. *New York Times*. Available from http://www.nytimes.com/1979/02/09/archives/east-harlems-troubled-taino-towers-set-to-open-weve-got-to-get.html?_r=0

Hardiman, R., & Jackson, B. (2007). Conceptual foundations of social justice education: Conceptual overview. In M. Adams, L. A. Bell, & P. Griffin (Eds.), *Teachings for diversity and social justice* (pp. 35–66). New York, NY: Routledge.

Hesse-Biber, S. J. (2017). *The practice of qualitative research: Engaging students in the research process* (3rd ed.). Thousand Oaks, CA: SAGE.

hooks, b. (2000). *Where we stand: Class matters*. New York, NY: Routledge.

hooks, b. (2014). *Teaching to transgress*. New York, NY: Routledge.

Hurst, A. L. (2010). *The burden of academic success: Loyalists, renegades, and double agents*. Lanham, MD: Lexington.

Hurst, A. L. (2012). *College and the working class: What it takes to make it*. Rotterdam, The Netherlands: Sense.

Hurst, A. L., & Nenga, S. K. (2016). Introduction. In A. L. Hurst & S. K. Nenga (Eds.), *Working in class: Recognizing how social class shapes our academic work* (pp. 1–9). New York, NY: Rowman & Littlefield.

Johnson, A. G. (2001). *Power, privilege and difference*. New York, NY: McGraw-Hill.

Jonassen, D. H., & Hernandez-Serrano, J. (2002). Case-based reasoning and instructional design: Using stories to support problem-solving. *Educational Technology Research and Development, 50*(2), 65–77.

Jones, S. R., & McEwen, M. K. (2000). A conceptual model of multiple dimensions of identity. *Journal of College Student Development, 41*(4), 405–414.

Kirk, G., & Okazawa-Rey, M. (2013). Identities and social locations: Who am I? Who are my people? In M. Adams, W. J. Blumenfeld, C. Castañeda, H. W. Heckman, M. L. Peters, & X. Zúñiga (Eds.), *Readings for diversity and social justice* (3rd ed., pp. 9–15). New York, NY: Routledge.

Lambert, E. (2004). How can we better help student success? *The APCA Student Activities Journal.*

Lathe, T. R. (2018). *The working class student in higher education*. Lanham, MD: Lexington.

Liu, W. M. (2011). *Social class and classism in the helping professions: Research, theory, and practice*. Thousand Oaks, CA: SAGE.

Liu, W. M., Soleck, G., Hopps, J., Dunston, K., & Pickett, T. (2004). A new framework to understand social class in counseling: The social class worldview and modern classism theory. *Journal of Multicultural Counseling and Development, 32*, 95–122.

Locke, L., & Trolian, T. (2018). Microaggressions and social class identity in higher education and student affairs. *New Directions for Student Services, 162*, 63–74.

Love, B. J. (2010). Developing a liberatory consciousness. In M. Adams, W. J. Blumenfeld, C. Castañeda, H. W. Heckman, M. L. Peters, & X. Zúñiga (Eds.), *Readings for diversity and social justice* (2nd ed., pp. 599–603). New York, NY: Routledge.

Lubrano, A. (2004). *Limbo: Blue-collar roots, white-collar dreams.* Hoboken, NJ: Wiley.

MacLeod, J. (2009). *Ain't no makin' it: Aspirations and attainment in a low-income neighborhood.* Philadelphia, PA: Westview.

Martin, G. L. (2015). "Tightly wound rubber bands": Exploring the college experiences of low income, first-generation white students. *Journal of Student Affairs Research and Practice, 52*(3), 275–286.

Martin, G. L., Williams, B., & Young, C. R. (2018). Understanding social class as identity. *New Directions for Student Services, 162*, 9–18.

Martin, R. J., & Van Gunten, D. M. (2002). Reflected identities applying positionality and multicultural social reconstructionism in teacher education. *Journal of Teacher Education, 53*, 44–54.

martinez, b. (2012). Social justice begins at home. *Journal of Critical Thought and Praxis, 1*(1). Available from https://lib.dr.iastate.edu/jctp/vol1/iss1

McDonough, P. M. (1997). *Choosing colleges: How social class and schools structure opportunity.* Albany, NY: SUNY Press.

McLaren, P. (2016). *Life in schools: An introduction to critical pedagogy in the foundations of education* (6th ed.). New York, NY: Routledge.

McMillan, A. (2017). One of us: Some thoughts on sexuality. In N. Connolly (Ed.), *Know your place: Essays on the working class by the working class* (pp. 90–102). Liverpool, UK: Dead Ink.

Merriam, S. B. (2009). *Qualitative research: A guide to design and implementation.* San Francisco, CA: Jossey-Bass.

Mertens, D. M. (2015). *Research and evaluation in education and psychology* (4th ed.). Thousand Oaks, CA: SAGE.

Milner, H. R. (2007). Race, culture, and researcher positionality: Working through dangers seen, unseen, and unforeseen. *Educational Researcher, 36*, 388–400.

Mughal, D. S. (2017). Navigating space. In N. Connolly (Ed.), *Know your place: Essays on the working class by the working class* (pp. 69–77). Liverpool, UK: Dead Ink.

Mullen, A. L. (2010). *Degrees of inequality: Culture, class, and gender in American higher education.* Baltimore, MD: The John Hopkins University Press.

New York City Department of Education. (2016). *2015-16 school quality snapshot.* Available from http://schools.nyc.gov/OA/SchoolReports/2015-16/School_Quality_Snapshot_2016_HS_X445.pdf

Patton, M. Q. (2015). *Qualitative research and evaluation methods* (4th ed.). Thousand Oaks, CA: SAGE.

Polkinghorne, D. E. (1995). Narrative configuration in qualitative analysis. *Qualitative Studies in Education, 8*, 5–23.

Pope, R. L. (2014). *Creating multicultural change on campus.* Hoboken, NJ: Wiley.

Pope, R. L., & Reynolds, A. L. (2017). Multidimensional identity model revisited: Implications for student affairs. *New Directions for Student Services, 157,* 15–24.

Ramsey, P. G. (1991). Young children's awareness and understanding of social class differences. *The Journal of Genetic Psychology, 152,* 71–82.

Reay, D. (2005). Beyond consciousness? The psychic landscape of social class. *Sociology, 39*(5), 911–928.

Reinert, L. J., & Serna, G. R. (2014). Living intersectionality in the academy. In D. Mitchell Jr. (Ed.), *Intersectionality & higher education: Theory, research & praxis* (pp. 88–98). New York, NY: Peter Lang.

Relles, S. R. (2016). A call for qualitative methods in action: Enlisting positionality as an equity tool. *Intervention in School and Clinic, 51*(5), 312–317.

Reynolds, A. L., & Pope, R. L. (1991). The complexities of diversity: Exploring multiple oppressions. *Journal of Counseling & Development, 70*(1), 174–181.

Rothe, D. (2006). A stranger to paradise: Working-class graduate in the culture of academia. In S. L. Muzzatti & C. V. Samarco (Eds.), *Reflections from the wrong side of the tracks: Class, identity, and the working class experience in academe* (pp. 49–59). Lanham, MD: Rowman & Littlefield.

Rudolph, F. (1990). *The American college & university: A history.* Athens, GA: The University of Georgia Press.

Schwalbe, M., Godwin, S., Holden, D., Schrock, D., Thompson, S., & Wolkomir, M. (2000). Generic processes in the reproduction of inequality: An interactionist analysis. *Social Forces, 79*(2), 419–452.

Sennett, R., & Cobb, J. (1972). *The hidden injuries of class.* New York, NY: W. W. Norton.

Shapiro, D., Dundar, A., Huie, F., Wakhungu, P., Yuan, X., Nathan, A., & Hwang, Y. A. (2017, April). *A national view of student attainment rates by race and ethnicity–Fall 2010 cohort (Signature Report No. 12b).* Herndon, VA: National Student Clearinghouse Research Center.

Soria, K. (2016). Working-class, teaching class and working class in the academy. In A. L. Hurst & S. K. Nenga (Eds.), *Working in class: Recognizing how social class shapes our academic work* (pp. 127–139). Lanham, MD: Rowman & Littlefield.

Soria, K. (2018). Counting class: Assessing social class identity using quantitative measures. *New Directions for Student Services, 162,* 49–61.

Soria, K. M. (2015). *Welcoming blue-collar scholars into the ivory tower: Developing class-consciousness strategies for student success.* Columbia, SC: University of South Carolina, National Resource Center for the First-Year Experience and Students in Transition.

Stich, A. E. (2012). *Access to inequality: Reconsidering class, knowledge, and capital in higher education.* Lanham, MD: Lexington.

Stich, A. E., & Freie, C. (2016). The working classes and higher education: An introduction to a complicated relationship. In A. E. Stich & C. Freire (Eds.), *The working classes and higher education* (pp. 1–10). New York, NY: Routledge.

Streib, J. (2016). Lessons learned: How I unintentionally reproduce class inequality. In A. L. Hurst & S. K. Nenga (Eds.), *Working in class: Recognizing how social class shapes our academic work* (pp. 79–90). New York, NY: Rowman & Littlefield.

Stuber, J. M. (2011). *Inside the college gates: How class and culture matter in higher education.* Lanham, MD: Rowman & Littlefield.

Svoboda, V. (2012). *Constructing class: Exploring the lived experience of white female student affairs professionals from working class families* (Doctoral dissertation). Available from ProQuest Dissertations Publishing. (Accession No. 3520348)

Tatum, B. D. (2013). The complexity of identity: "Who am I?" In M. Adams, W. J. Blumenfeld, C. Castañeda, H. W. Heckman, M. L. Peters, & X. Zúñiga (Eds.), *Readings for diversity and social justice* (3rd ed., pp. 6–9). New York, NY: Routledge.

Thomas, S. L., & Bell, A. (2008). Social classes and higher education: A reorganization of opportunities. In L. Weis (Ed.), *The way class works: Readings on school, family, and the economy* (pp. 273–287). New York, NY: Routledge.

Torres, V., Jones, S. R., & Renn, K. A. (2009). Identity development theories in student affairs, origins, current status, and new approaches. *Journal of College Student Development, 50*(6), 577–596.

Trinh, T. M. (1997). Not you/like you: Post-colonial women and the interlocking questions of identity and difference. In A. McClintock, A. Mufti, & E. Shohat (Eds.), *Dangerous liaisons: Gender, nation, and postcolonial perspectives* (pp. 415–419). Minneapolis, MN: University of Minnesota Press.

Tzanakis, M. (2011). Bourdieu's social reproduction thesis and the role of cultural capital in educational attainment: A critical review of key empirical studies. *Educate, 11*(1), 76–90. Available from http://www.educatejournal.org/index.php/educate/article/view/251

University of California Admissions. (2017). *Blue and gold opportunity plan.* Available from http://admission.universityofcalifornia.edu/paying-for-uc/glossary/blue-and-gold/index.html

U.S. Census Bureau. (2016). *Educational attainment of the population 18 years and over, by age, sex, race, and Hispanic origin.* Available from https://www.census.gov/data/tables/2016/demo/education-attainment/cps-detailed-tables.html

U.S. News & World Report. (2017a). *How does SDSU rank among America's best colleges?* Available from https://www.usnews.com/best-colleges/sdsu-1151

U.S. News & World Report. (2017b). *How does UC Berkeley rank among America's best colleges?* Available from https://www.usnews.com/best-colleges/uc-berkeley-1312

U.S. News & World Report. (2017c). *How does UCLA rank among America's best colleges?* Available from https://www.usnews.com/best-colleges/ucla-1315

Vance, J. D. (2016). *Hillbilly elegy: A memoir of family and culture in crisis.* New York, NY: HarperCollins.

Waal, K. (2017). An open invitation. In N. Connolly (Ed.), *Know your place: Essays on the working class by the working class* (pp. 62–68). Liverpool, UK: Dead Ink.

Warnock, D. M. (2016). Capitalizing class. In A. L. Hurst & S. K. Nenga (Eds.), *Working in class: Recognizing how social class shapes our academic work* (pp. 173–183). Lanham, MD: Rowman & Littlefield.

White, J. W., & Ali-Khan, C. (2013). The role of academic discourse in minority students' academic assimilation. *American Secondary Education, 42*(1), 24–42.

Wijeyesinghe, C. L., & Jones, S. R. (2016). Intersectionality, identity, and systems of power and inequality. In D. Mitchell Jr. (Ed.), *Intersectionality & higher education: Theory, research & praxis* (pp. 9–19). New York, NY: Peter Lang.

Wilson, J. (2006). Working-class values and life in academe: Examining the dissonance. In S. L. Muzzatti & C. V. Samarco (Eds.), *Reflections from the wrong side of the tracks: Class, identity, and the working class experience in academe* (pp. 159–169). Lanham, MD: Rowman & Littlefield.

Yeskel, F. (2014). Introduction: Caviar, college, coupons, and cheese. In C. Collins, J. Ladd, M. Seider, & F. Yeskel (Eds.), *Class lives: Stories from across our economic divide* (pp. 1–12). Ithaca, NY: Cornell University Press.

Yosso, T. (2005). Whose culture has capital? A critical race theory discussion of community cultural wealth. *Race Ethnicity and Education, 8*(1), 69–91.

Young, I. M. (2013). Five faces of oppression. In M. Adams, W. J. Blumenfeld, C. Castañeda, H. W. Heckman, M. L. Peters, & X. Zúñiga (Eds.), *Readings for diversity and social justice* (3rd ed., pp. 35–45). New York, NY: Routledge.

AUTHORS AND CONTRIBUTORS

Authors

Sonja Ardoin is a learner, educator, facilitator, and author. She originates from "Cajun country"—the small, rural community of Vidrine, Louisiana, specifically—and is proud of her first-generation college student to PhD educational journey, with degrees from Louisiana State University, Florida State University, and North Carolina State University. A self-described scholar-practitioner, Ardoin made the move from full-time administrator to full-time faculty member in 2015 and currently serves as assistant professor of student affairs administration at Appalachian State University. Her career path includes experience in student activities, leadership development, community engagement, fraternity and sorority life, student conduct, and academic advising. Ardoin studies social class identity in higher education; college access and success for first-generation college students and students from rural areas; student and women's leadership; and professional preparation and career pathways in higher education and student affairs. She stays engaged in the higher education field through presenting, facilitating, and volunteering with national organizations such as ASHE, NASPA, ACPA, LeaderShape, Zeta Tau Alpha, Delta Gamma, and Peer Forward and reviewing for several journals. Ardoin is also a contributor to the NASPA Center for First-Generation Student Success advocacy group, the NASPA Socioeconomic and Class Issues in Higher Education Knowledge Community, and the AFLV Board of Directors. Learn more about Ardoin at https://www.sonjaardoin.com/.

becky martinez is a class-straddling mixed-race woman of color who loves engaging in social class and class(ism). She humbly comes from a family of farmers and blue-collar professionals and now finds herself as a first-generation white-collar professional and is still working through what that means. In her professional capacity, martinez is an organization development consultant and trainer with a focus on social justice, leadership, and organizational change with Infinity Martinez Consulting and a faculty member with the Social Justice Training Institute. Her work centers on dismantling systems of oppression through critical reflection and dialogue intertwined with theoretical models and key concepts. She is passionate about systems thinking while working with campuses, government agencies, and community-based organizations to be more equitable with their policies, practices, and procedures through an inclusion lens. Prior to consultancy, she was an administrator within the California State University and the University of California systems as well as private liberal arts colleges. She is a co-lead facilitator for the LeaderShape Institute, has been a certified trainer for the Anti-Defamation League and the Gay, Lesbian, & Straight Education Network, and a certified counselor-advocate through Peace Over Violence in Los Angeles. Connect further with martinez and her work at www.infinitymartinez.com.

Contributors

Mamta Motwani Accapadi currently serves as the vice president for student affairs at Rollins College. She has served as dean of student life at Oregon State University and worked in multicultural affairs at the University of Texas at Austin. She has held academic appointments in ethnic/Asian American studies, women's studies, and educational psychology. Her calling is grounded in commitment to mentorship, career advancement, and overall joy of underrepresented communities in higher education.

Constanza (Connie) A. Cabello serves the Stonehill College community as the assistant to the president for institutional diversity/director of intercultural affairs. Cabello plays a critical role in advancing the college's commitment to a diverse and inclusive community by promoting accountability, maintaining a holistic vision and approach to equity across campus, and providing communication to the community regarding the college's ongoing efforts. She enjoys presenting on the regional and national levels as a higher education professional and trainer. Cabello's strong training background allows her to work with organizations to develop cultural consciousness and strategize to reach individual and organizational goals. She has participated in transformational experiences such as the Social Justice Training Institute, the NASPA Escaleras Institute, and the NASPA Mid-Level Institute. Among her most rewarding experiences are coordinating the Student Social Justice Training Institute (at University of Massachusetts, Lowell), serving as a faculty member for the NASPA Dungy Leadership Institute (at the Ohio State University), and being a Latinx/a/o advocate for the inaugural NASPA Region I Ubuntu Institute.

Loren Cannon has been teaching at the college level since 1993, first in mathematics and later in philosophy. He holds a bachelor's degree in mathematics (secondary education), a master's degree in mathematics (theoretical), and a doctorate in philosophy with an emphasis on ethics and social theory. He has held his current position as a full-time (yet nontenure-eligible) lecturer in philosophy since 2006. He was awarded his university's Distinguished

Faculty Award for Excellence in Teaching in 2014 and has active research and service programs. His research interests include a number of topics within ethics and social theory, including trans (in)justice, collective responsibility, and environmental ethics. Cannon has presented widely on these topics in both formal and informal venues. His publications include articles in peer-reviewed journals, book chapters, textbook chapters, and more informal contributions. Cannon is White, of Irish working-class descent, a first-generation college student, and a cisgender-passing transgender man who is open about his gender history. In nearly all professional settings, he finds himself to be the only transgender person in the room.

Dylan R. Dunn serves as the coordinator of collegiate recovery at the University of Denver, working to ensure that students do not have to sacrifice their recovery from substance abuse and behavioral disorders to succeed in college. Dunn is an alumnus of The Ohio State University as an undergraduate student and Colorado State University as a graduate student. Dunn's time in higher education has largely centered on learning how to tell and live his story authentically so that he can empower students to do the same. Dunn spends his spare time listening to true crime and professional wrestling podcasts, creating art, and attempting to establish a work-life balance.

Daniel Espiritu is an undergraduate student at Chapman University majoring in political science. He hopes to make a difference in the world by combining his low-income background with his higher education.

Nancy J. Evans holds the title of professor emerita in the School of Education at Iowa State University, where she taught in and coordinated the student affairs program. She also taught at Penn State University, Western Illinois University, and Indiana University; served as a counseling psychologist at Bowling Green State University; worked in residence life and student activities at Stephens College; and served as assistant dean of students at Tarkio College. Evans holds a PhD in counseling psychology from the University of Missouri–Columbia, an MFA in theatre from Western Illinois University, an MSEd in higher education from Southern Illinois University, and a BS in social science from State University of New York (SUNY) Potsdam. Her publications include 11 books and monographs, among them *Disability in Higher Education: A Social Justice Approach* (Jossey-Bass 2017), *Student Development in College: Theory, Research, and Practice* (Jossey-Bass, 1998) and *Toward Acceptance: Sexual Orientation Issues on Campus* (University Press of America, 1999), as well as 40 book chapters and 45 journal articles. Her research has examined the impact of the college environment on the development of students with minoritized identities. Evans has received many awards from professional associations and educational institutions, including the Lifetime Achievement Award (2015), the Voice of Inclusion Award (2006), and the Contribution to Knowledge Award (1998), all from ACPA-College Student Educators International.

Raul Fernandez is the associate dean for equity, diversity, and inclusion and a lecturer in the higher education administration program at Boston University's Wheelock College of Education & Human Development. He is a nationally recognized leader on issues of equity and inclusion in education and is the creator of the popular Wide Lens film series at the Coolidge Corner Theatre. He teaches a graduate course on diversity and justice in education and studies the impact of school segregation on the racial dialogue gap. He serves on the NASPA Faculty Council and NASPA Equity, Inclusion, & Social Justice Division, and he also serves as an elected Town Meeting Member for the Town of Brookline, Massachusetts; as a board member for the Brookline Teen Center; and as an active member of Brookline for Racial Justice and Equity. He hails from El Barrio (Spanish Harlem) and the Bronx, New York.

Sara C. Furr is the dean of students in the School of Social Service Administration at the University of Chicago. Furr has more than 10 years of experience as a social justice educator, creating opportunities for students, faculty, staff, and community members to explore topics such as identity development; leadership development theory; and power, privilege, and oppression. She received her bachelor's degree in public policy from the University of North Carolina at Chapel Hill and a master's degree in higher education and student affairs from the University of South Carolina. Furr also has a master's degree in liberal studies with an emphasis on urban community development from Loyola University Maryland and a doctorate in higher education from Loyola University Chicago. Her dissertation, titled *Wellness Interventions for Social Justice Fatigue Among Student Affairs Professionals*, can be found at www.socialjusticefatigue.com. Her research interests include multiracial identity, critical pedagogy, and radical healing. In her free time, Furr enjoys spending time with family and friends; reading; running; being involved in the community; and teaching dance fitness, boot camp, and spin classes.

Rudy P. Guevarra Jr. is associate professor of Asian Pacific American studies in the School of Social Transformation at Arizona State University. Originally from San Diego, California, Guevarra attended Southwestern Community College before transferring to the University of San Diego, where he earned his BA in history. He also earned his MA and PhD in history from the University of California, Santa Barbara. Guevarra is a former University of

California Chancellor's Postdoctoral Fellow and current Ford Foundation Senior Fellow. His research and teaching interests include comparative/relational ethnic studies; Pacific Islander and Asian American studies; Chicanx and Latinx studies; migration, borderlands, and U.S. labor history; and critical mixed-race studies. Rudy is the author of *Becoming Mexipino: Multiethnic Identities and Communities in San Diego* (Rutgers University Press, 2012) and *Aloha Compadre: Latinxs in Hawai'i, 1832–2010* (Rutgers University Press, forthcoming). He is also coeditor of *Beyond Ethnicity: New Politics of Race in Hawai'i*, with Camilla Fojas and Nitasha Tamar Sharma (University of Hawaii Press, 2018); *Red & Yellow, Black & Brown: Decentering Whiteness in Mixed Race Studies* with Joanne L. Rondilla and Paul Spickard (Rutgers University Press, 2017); and *Transnational Crossroads: Remapping the Americas and the Pacific*, with Camilla Fojas (University of Nebraska Press, 2012). Guevarra is also a founder and director of the Latinx Pacific Archive (www.latinopacificarchive.org) with Alexandrina Agloro.

Jacinda M. Félix Haro has more than 15 years of experience in the higher education field, with work encompassing Title IX coordination and investigation, student conduct, crisis management, CARE team/student support, multicultural and LGBTQ education, diversity, and inclusion training, student advising, advocacy and engagement, leadership and involvement programs, fraternity and sorority life, student union work, residence life, and new student orientation programs. A first-generation college student and proud Nuyorican, Félix Haro currently serves as the interim dean of students at MCPHS University in Boston. Félix Haro received her BS in communication arts from SUNY New Paltz and her MAT from Sacred Heart University, and she is currently a student in the higher education administration PhD program at the University of Massachusetts Boston.

Timothy (Tim) M. Johnson serves as the director of student leadership and engagement at Guilford College in Greensboro, North Carolina. As a first-generation college student, a college degree was super important to both him and his family. As a native of Baltimore, Maryland, and now resident of Greensboro, North Carolina, he is a city boy at heart and appreciates being around people and the joy they bring. His hope is that his story and others do the same for you!

Briza K. Juarez spent 15 years working in the Cal State University and the University of California systems in higher education administration and is now a mother of two and a small business owner living in Southern California.

Armina Khwaja Macmillan is a learner, listener, educator, and optimist. Macmillan currently serves as the director for student conduct and integrity formation at Seattle University, with a background in residence life at Seattle University and Northeastern University. She holds degrees from the Georgia Institute of Technology and Texas A&M University. As a Muslim woman, a first-generation college student, a first-generation Pakistani American, and someone with an evolving class identity, Macmillan strives to critically examine her own identities as they relate to the world around her. She appreciates staying active and volunteering with national organizations, including Alpha Chi Omega, Phi Gamma Delta, and NASPA. In her free time, Macmillan enjoys pop culture, food, exploring the world, dreaming, and quality time with loved ones.

Sally G. Parish serves as the associate dean for student leadership and involvement at the University of Memphis, where she provides leadership and strategic direction to a department of 17 staff, 3 functional areas, and more than 100 programs a year. Prior to her current role, Parish served as the founding director of the Center for Leadership and Service and the Leadership Studies Minor at the University of Tennessee Knoxville. A first-generation college graduate of the University of Memphis (UofM), Parish also has her master's degree in higher education administration from Florida International University and is pursuing doctoral studies at the UofM. Parish is a certified strengths coach with more than 10 years of consulting and training experience in the corporate, education, and nonprofit sectors. She is active as an adjunct faculty member, is a board member for a local nonprofit volunteer center, and has been published on best practices of leadership development. Parish has also developed and consulted on departments, training programs, and academic programs at numerous institutions, in addition to serving as an invited speaker and facilitator at dozens of conferences, companies, and institutes. Most proudly, Parish is mom to daughter Nola and son Deacon, and she is a grateful wife to her supportive partner, Danny.

Edward (Eddie) Pickett III is a college counselor and an 11th/12th-grade dean at Polytechnic School in Pasadena, California. Prior to this role, he worked for six years at Tufts University, where he rose from admissions counselor to associate director of admissions and director of diversity recruitment. He earned a master's degree in higher education administration from Boston College and a bachelor's degree in media studies and studio art from Pitzer College. Pickett is the product of a blended family of six siblings, firmly believes it takes a village to raise a child, and is a first-generation college graduate. Outside of work, he enjoys researching the intersections of race and class; spending time with his wife, Joie; barbequing; and watching live sporting events.

Kevyanna Rawls is an undergraduate student at the University of Memphis, where she is double majoring in English and African American studies with minors in Spanish and sociology. She is involved in student government and dedicates her time to working with administrators to address issues that impact student life on campus. In her spare time, Rawls loves to spend time with her family, travel, and catch up on her favorite television shows.

Carmen Rivera currently serves as the talent manager for organizational development for the Division of Student Affairs at Colorado State University (CSU). One of the first things she tells folks is that she is from New Mexico, Santa Fe and Mora specifically. Where she's from is fundamental to who she is. She earned her bachelor's degree in Hispanic studies and Spanish from the University of Northern Colorado. She then went on to earn her master's degree in student affairs in higher education from CSU and is currently a doctoral candidate there in the higher education leadership program. Her higher education career began when she worked for the Upward Bound program. She worked in TriO for more than 13 years and then worked in international education as the director of student experience at INTO CSU for several years. Additionally, she's a faculty member for the Social Justice Training Institute, a co-lead facilitator for the LeaderShape Institute, and a consultant in the areas of social justice and leadership. One of her most important roles is raising her two super awesome sons with her super awesome wife. She loves 90's R&B, has an insatiable thirst for travel, and is obsessed with all things Frida Kahlo.

Larry D. Roper was born and raised in Akron, Ohio. Currently, he is a professor in the School of Language, Culture, and Society at Oregon State University, where he serves as coordinator of the undergraduate social justice minor and coordinator of the college student services administration graduate program. Previously, he served as vice provost for student affairs at Oregon State University from 1995 to 2014. A first-generation college graduate, he has degrees from Heidelberg University, Bowling Green State University, and the University of Maryland. He has held numerous positions in higher education during his career of more than 40 years. Roper currently serves as a commissioner with the State of Oregon's Higher Education Coordinating Commission, on the board of trustees of Heidelberg University, and as president of Jackson Street Youth Services (an agency serving homeless and vulnerable youth). Roper embraces his roles as husband to Dina and father to Ellis.

Thomas C. Segar serves as the vice president for student affairs at Shepherd University, where he also teaches in the College of Student Development and Administration graduate program teaching courses on the higher education student, higher education administration and legal accountability, and student leadership development. He has been an independent consultant to colleges, public school systems, and other educational organizations for more than 15 years. He speaks, writes, and researches on leadership, diversity, and social justice topics. Segar earned his bachelor's degree in psychology with a certificate in African American studies from the University of Maryland and his master's degree in counseling with a specialization in college student personnel from Shippensburg University of Pennsylvania. He earned his PhD from the College Student Personnel Administration Program at the University of Maryland. His concentration was teaching and social justice in higher education. His dissertation explored the relationship between sociocultural issues discussions and social change behaviors among undergraduate students.

Jeremiah Shinn serves as the associate vice president for student affairs at Boise State University, where he provides leadership and support for a collection of campus units dedicated to fostering a vibrant learning environment. Additionally, he serves as an adjunct faculty member in the College of Innovation and Design and in the graduate program in athletics leadership. Prior to his time in Boise, Shinn served in various college student development roles at Indiana University and Eastern Michigan University. As a frequent facilitator and consultant, he has collaborated with more than 30 college campuses and nonprofit organizations on projects related to leadership, change management, and organizational development. As an active volunteer, Shinn has served on a number of professional association and nonprofit boards and was named to *Idaho Business Review*'s "Accomplished Under 40" list in 2015.

Tori Svoboda is an assistant professor at the University of Wisconsin–La Crosse. Svoboda teaches master's and doctoral students in the Student Affairs Administration program. Svoboda worked in a variety of student affairs administrator roles at University of Wisconsin–Madison and the University of St. Thomas (Minnesota) for nearly 20 years before changing lanes to become a full-time faculty member.

Roxanne Villaluz is a queer writer, baker, experienced cook, and worker-owner at a bakery and pizzeria. In addition to her production work at the bakery, she convenes the finance committee of the cooperative, whose mission is managing all financial aspects of the business. She is a certified social justice mediator and trained facilitator for critical dialogues across differences. Nine years of her career in higher education was spent at Fresno State working in the Learning Center, and her last three years in higher education were spent at University of California (UC) Berkeley working with academic support in the residence halls. At Fresno State, she facilitated courses intended to work with students who have had little to no exposure to the cultural expectations of higher education. She also facilitated a dialogue course at UC Berkeley designed to address the topic of class. Villaluz's excitement for learning and growing in a collaborative environment influences what she writes about. She enjoys being able to continue learning and broadening her skills, knowledge, and leadership skills. Villaluz seeks ways to stay engaged and keep pushing for equity, accessibility, critical engagement, and self-awareness in her writing. She has a BA in liberal studies and an MA in linguistics.

Brenda Lee Anderson Wadley was born and raised in Toledo, Ohio. She is a first-generation college student and proud alumna of her respective institutions of higher education. During her undergraduate career, Anderson Wadley earned her bachelor's degree in social work from the University of Tennessee at Chattanooga and was involved in many campus and community organizations committed to empowering and enacting change within communities. Anderson Wadley earned her master's of education in student affairs administration at the University of Georgia. Anderson Wadley credits her education and social class upbringing as her way to disrupt systematic and generational trends of poverty within her life. Anderson Wadley is dedicated to justice and centering the voices of those who are marginalized so that they are heard. Anderson Wadley professional interests include case management, advocacy programs, and supporting students who have been impacted by trauma. Anderson Wadley research interests include the impact of racialized trauma on students of color, social class identity development, college access, collegiate experiences, and identity development of former foster youth. Outside of her professional life, Anderson Wadley can be found reading, running, watching movies, and living her best life. Anderson Wadley is involved in grassroots activism and actively works to support organizations that help people of color and women run for government offices.

Téa N. Wimer is an undergraduate at Princeton University studying religion with certificates in ethnographic studies and gender and sexuality studies; she is interested in the intersections of class and/or queerness and church community. Beyond her academics, Wimer is a radio DJ at WPRB, a community-supported independent radio station, and serves as the membership and fund-raising director there. She is the copresident of the Princeton University Letterpress Club, an analog graphic design club, and also does activist work on campus, especially around workers' rights, with the Princeton Young Democratic Socialists. She loves going to DIY music shows, everything to do with graphic novels and comics (she also makes her own!), birds, and being the mom friend in her friend groups.

from religion, 74
scholarship for, 12–13, 37
SCWM in, 29
self-esteem and, 10
from SES, 154–55
sexuality in, 100–101
social capital in, 27–28
social class and, 1–4, 30–31, 45–46,
    55, 61–62, 155–57, 172–78
social justice for, 82–83
from stereotypes, 137
from stories, 54–55
for students, 23–25, 33–37, 39–40,
    115–16
success from, 55–56
from television, 69
after upward mobility, 102, 113,
    134–35
vulnerability and, 172–73
immigration
    for children, 63–64
    culture of, 138–39, 172
    external educators from, 155–60
    in narratives, 32–37, 95–100,
        140–44
    politics of, 48
    privilege in, 156
    This Fine Place So Far From Homie
        (Dews/Law), 129–30
impostor syndrome, 76, 107–8, 121,
    127, 167–69
inclusivity, 179–86
intersectionality, 98–99, 172, 174–78

James, LeBron, 117–18
Johnson, Patricia, 68
Johnson, Timothy M. ("Tim"), 63,
    68–72, 77–78
Juarez, Briza K., 146–51, 160–61

knowledge. *See* learning

language
    in classism, 168–69, 182–83
    from education, 61

in higher education, 157
in learning, 24, 180
psychology of, 11
social capital from, 143
lateral classism, 4
Law, Carolyn Leste, 129–30
learning
    classism in, 51–52
    about community, 185
    data and, 172–73
    identity and, 8–9, 21–22, 60,
        174–75
    language in, 24, 180
    from narratives, 162–63
    politics of, 121, 136–37
    psychology of, 105–6
    social class and, 45, 109–10,
        122–23
    from stories, 170, 172–73
loans, 76, 90, 103
low-income. *See* poverty

Macmillan, Armina Khwaja, 63–67,
    77–78
Marcos, Ferdinand, 156–57
marginalization, 138, 173–74
Martin (TV show), 69
media, 69, 84, 96, 185–86
Medley, Christopher L., 70–71
mental health, 40, 101
mentors, 70–71, 136–37, 139–42,
    144–45
methodology, 12–20
microaggressions
    from classism, 23–24, 42, 124
    in higher education, 108–9
    psychology of, 51
    social justice for, 25
    upward mobility as, 27
middle class, 79, 89–94, 105,
    110–11
motivation, 51–52, 71, 136–37,
    141–42, 153–54, 161
multidimensional identity models,
    176–78

to increase learning capacity in and out of the classroom." —*Joseph L. White, Ph.D., Professor Emeritus of Psychology and Psychiatry, School of Social Sciences, University of California, Irvine*

Sty/us

22883 Quicksilver Drive
Sterling, VA 20166-2019

Subscribe to our e-mail alerts: www.Styluspub.com

pseudonym] and how postsecondary educators can do better to support the education, resilience practices, and life chances for trans* collegians."
—*Dafina-Lazarus Stewart, Ph.D., Higher Education and Student Affairs , Bowling Green State University*

"Nicolazzo's book draws much needed attention to trans* oppression in higher education, how we are all implicated, and calls for us to re-think our approach to practices that shape our campus environments." — *Chase Catalano, Assistant Professor, College Student Personnel, Western Illinois University*

"For every higher education administrator and change agent, this book offers a clarion call to consider how the collegiate environment continues to be shaped without trans* students in mind." — *Sumun L. Pendakur, Associate Dean for Institutional Diversity, Harvey Mudd College*

The Strategic Guide to Shaping Your Student Affairs Career

Sonja Ardoin

Foreword by Marcia B. Baxter Magolda

"From the point of view of someone in his first year in Student Affairs, Sonja's book provides honest guidance about what it means to be a new professional. Sonja presents theory and practical insight on how you can create and take advantages of opportunities that will enhance your career, and addresses many of the challenging experiences you will face when starting out. Reading this while I transitioned into a full-time position was extremely fortuitous." — *Thomas Harwell, Resident Director at Boston College*

"*The Strategic Guide to Shaping Your Student Affairs Career* is a one of a kind resource for student affairs administrators in any stage of their career. The book is well organized around five key elements of career strategy that helpfully prompt readers to not only focus and reflect on critical stages in their career development and advancement, but also on their personal motivations and goals. This is enhanced by the inclusion of voices of current

(Continues on preceding page)

administrators who share their stories and insights to illustrate the book's message." — **Ashley Tull**, *Director of Assessment and Strategic Initiatives, Division of Student Affairs, Southern Methodist University*

Social Class on Campus

Theories and Manifestations

Will Barratt

"Author Will Barratt successfully breaks class down in a way that allows the reader to observe it through a variety of lenses (education, capital, prestige, etc.) and helps us to understand it in terms beyond just level of income... the information is also organized in a way that allows the reader to single out specific chapters. Questions designed for discussion and reflection are also placed at the close of each chapter. These features make it useful as both a college text and as a challenge to professionals to think more critically. This design gives it a multi-functionality that many texts do not have." — *NACADA Journal (National Academic Advising Association)*

"Barratt's research is unique, providing his audience with an opportunity to obtain a broader sense of how social class influences their personal lives." — *Indiana State University Newsroom*

Bandwidth Recovery

Helping Students Reclaim Cognitive Resources Lost to Poverty, Racism, and Social Marginalization

Cia Verschelden M.S.W., Ed.D.

Foreword by Lynn Pasquerella

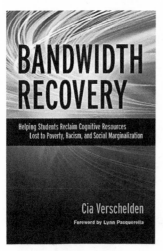

"*Bandwidth Recovery* is a well-written, insightful must-read book that offers educators and counselors who work with socially marginalized youth to develop functional strategies for promoting a growth mindset and self-efficacy

(Continues on preceding page)

Also available from Stylus

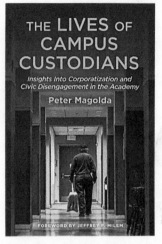

The Lives of Campus Custodians

Insights into Corporatization and Civic Disengagement in the Academy

Peter M. Magolda

Foreword by Jeffrey F. Milem

"The greatest contribution this book makes is that it sensitizes readers to a subculture that remains disregarded, but one that contributes to student learning. Although higher education administrators at best view campus custodians as the 'cleaning people,' or at worst, barely human, custodians view themselves as educators and valuable contributors to the communities they serve."— *The Review of Higher Education*

"Through the use of casual conversation, storytelling and case studies Magolda's writing is compelling, honest and personal. His research stands as witness that the academy espouses inclusivity but does not enact it. This book is a must read, a moral imperative, rooted in social justice."— *Patty Perillo, PhD*, *Vice President for Student Affairs and Assistant Professor of Higher Education , Virginia Tech*

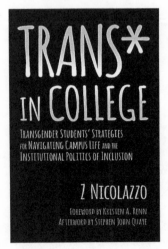

Trans* in College

Transgender Students' Strategies for Navigating Campus Life and the Institutional Politics of Inclusion

Z Nicolazzo

Foreword by Kristen A. Renn

Afterword by Stephen John Quaye

"*Trans* in College* is a beautifully written, rigorous, and masterful insight into the lives of nine trans* collegians at City University [a

(Continues on preceding page)